# THE UNEX[...]
# TRUTH ABOUT ANIMALS

'A riot of facts . . . Cooke scores a series
of goals with style and panache.'
## THE TIMES

'Beautifully written, meticulously researched, with the science
often couched in outrageous asides, this is a splendid read. In fact,
I cannot remember when I last enjoyed a non-fiction work so much.'
## DAILY EXPRESS

'Lucy Cooke's modern bestiary is as well-informed as you'd
expect from an Oxford zoologist. It's also downright funny.'
## RICHARD DAWKINS

'The eclectic stories come thick and fast, with an equally varied
human cast dedicated to uncovering the truth, scientifically or
otherwise. Cooke illuminates and mickey-takes in equal measure,
and the truth as she tells it is not only unexpected but often
bizarre, bawdy and very, very funny.'
## BBC WILDLIFE

'Fantastic. The new *Origin of Species*. A proper page turner.'
## VIC REEVES

'This twenty-first century bestiary is as surprising as it is diverse.
Consummate natural history writing: illuminating,
remarkable – and very, very funny.'
## PROFESSOR ALICE ROBERTS

www.penguin.co.uk

'Lucy Cooke unravels myths that will make you laugh out loud. Her knowledge of all things furry, slimy and scaly is jaw-dropping.'

**SUN**

'Fascinating facts combined with hilarious ridiculousness.'

**TONY ROBINSON**

'Lucy Cooke's *The Unexpected Truth About Animals* was a joy from beginning to end. Who could resist a writer who argues that penguins have been pulling the wool over our eyes for years, and that, far from being cute and gregarious, they are actually pathologically unpleasant necrophiliacs?'

**JOHN CRACE, *GUARDIAN***

'Best of the year's natural history. Best for fun facts. Fascinating.'

**MAIL ON SUNDAY**

'Beautifully written, funny and jam-packed with astonishing information.'

**JOHN LLOYD**

'Best science pick. A deeply researched, sassily written history of "the biggest misconceptions, mistakes and myths we've concocted about the animal kingdom" . . . Dismantles anthropocentric clichés with scientific, global evidence.'

**NATURE**

**LUCY COOKE** is an award-winning broadcaster and filmmaker with a Masters in zoology from Oxford University (where she was tutored by Richard Dawkins). She began her career working behind the scenes in television comedy but is now an increasingly familiar face on natural history TV, having presented prime time series for BBC, ITV and National Geographic. She writes for the *Telegraph* and the *Huffington Post*. Her only previous book (a picture book about sloths – *A Little Book of Sloth*) was a *New York Times* bestseller.

# THE
# UNEXPECTED
# TRUTH
# ABOUT ANIMALS

## STONED SLOTHS, LOVELORN HIPPOS
## AND OTHER WILD TALES

# LUCY COOKE

**BLACK SWAN**

TRANSWORLD PUBLISHERS
61–63 Uxbridge Road, London W5 5SA
www.penguin.co.uk

Transworld is part of the Penguin Random House group of companies
whose addresses can be found at global.penguinrandomhouse.com

Penguin
Random House
UK

First published in Great Britain in 2016 by Doubleday
an imprint of Transworld Publishers
Black Swan edition published 2018

A CIP catalogue record for this book is available from the British Library.

Chapter decorations by Jo Ormiston

ISBN 9781784161903

Typeset in 11.25/15.25 pt Caslon 540 LT Std by Jouve (UK), Milton Keynes
Printed and bound in Great Britain by Clays Ltd, Bungay, Suffolk

Penguin Random House is committed to a sustainable
future for our business, our readers and our planet. This book
is made from Forest Stewardship Council® certified paper.

3 5 7 9 10 8 6 4

# CONTENTS

To the memory of my dad,
who opened my eyes to the wonders
of the natural world.

# INTRODUCTION

'How can sloths exist when they're such losers?'

As a zoologist and founder of the Sloth Appreciation Society I get asked this question *a lot*. Sometimes 'losers' is further defined – 'lazy', 'stupid' and 'slow' being perennial favourites. And sometimes the query is paired with the rider – 'I thought evolution was all about "survival of the *fittest*"' – delivered with an air of bemusement or, worse, a whiff of superior species smugness.

Each time it happens, I take a deep breath and, with as much poise as I can muster, explain that sloths are by no means losers. They are, in fact, one of natural selection's quirkiest creations, and fabulously successful to boot. Skulking about the treetops barely quicker than a snail, and being covered in algae, infested with insects and defecating just once a week might not be your idea of aspirational living, but then you're not trying to survive in the highly competitive jungles of Central and South America – something the sloth is very good at.

When seeking to understand animals, context is key.

The secret to sloths' extraordinary endurance is their

*I love sloths. What's not to like about an animal born with a fixed grin on its face and the desire to hug.*

lethargic nature. They are paragons of low-energy living, with a suite of ingenious, energy-saving adaptations honed over many millennia and worthy of the most eccentric and gifted inventor. I won't launch into the full list now – you can read all about the sloth's innovative, upside-down life in chapter 3. Suffice to say, I'm a sucker for an underdog.

The reputation of the sloth was sufficiently besmirched that I felt compelled to found the Sloth Appreciation Society. (Our motto: 'Being fast is overrated.') I toured a talk on the unexpected truth about this much-maligned creature to festivals and schools. It traced sloth-based slander back to a clique of sixteenth-century explorers who took it upon themselves to brand this quiet vegetarian pacifist 'the stu-pidest animal that can be found in the world'. This book grew out of those talks and the need to set the record straight – not just for the sloth, but for other animals as well.

We have a habit of viewing the animal kingdom through the prism of our own, rather narrow, existence. The sloth's arboreal lifestyle is sufficiently extraterrestrial to make it one of the world's most misunderstood creatures, but it is by no means alone in this category. Life takes a glorious myriad of alien forms, and even the simplest require com-plex understanding.

Evolution has played some splendid practical jokes by fashioning implausible creatures with an absence of logic and precious few clues to explain itself. Mammals like the bat that want to be birds. Birds like the penguin that want to be fish. And fish like the eel whose enigmatic lifecycle sparked a two-thousand-year search for its missing gonads, driving man to the absolute edge of endeavour – a preci-pice eel scientists still teeter upon today. Animals do not give up their secrets easily.

Consider the ostrich. In February 1681, the brilliant British polymath Sir Thomas Browne wrote a letter to his son Edward, a physician at the royal court, requesting a rather unusual favour. Edward had come into possession of an ostrich, one of a flock donated to King Charles II by the King of Morocco. Sir Thomas, a keen naturalist, was fascinated by this big foreign bird and eager that his son send him news of its habits. Is it vigilant like a goose? Does it delight in sorrel yet recoil from bay leaves? And does it eat iron? This final query, he suggested helpfully to his son, might be best uncovered by wrapping the metal first in pastry – like some sort of ferrous sausage roll – since 'perhaps it will not take it up alone.'

This zoological recipe swap had a decidedly scientific purpose. Browne wanted to test an ancient myth that ostriches were capable of digesting absolutely anything, even iron. According to one medieval German scholar, the ostrich's taste for the strong stuff was such that the bird's dinner 'consists of a church-door key and a horse shoe'. As ostriches were bestowed on the courts of Europe by the emirs and explorers of Africa, generations of enthusiastic natural philosophers encouraged the foreign fowl to consume scissors, nails and a glut of other ironmongery.

On the surface this experimentation appears to be lunacy, yet dig a little deeper and there is a (scientific) method to the madness. Ostriches can't digest iron, but they have been observed swallowing large, sharp stones. Why? The world's biggest bird has evolved into a rather unusual grazing animal, whose usual diet of grasses and shrubs is tough to digest. And unlike their fellow plant-munchers from the African plains, the giraffe and antelope, ostriches lack a ruminating stomach. They don't even have teeth. Instead, they must tear the fibrous grasses from the ground with their beak and swallow them whole.

They employ the quarry of jagged rocks in their muscular gizzard to do the job of grinding down this stringy dinner into more digestible pieces. They can clunk around the savannah with up to a kilogram of stones in their stomach. (Scientists fancy this up and call them *gastroliths*.)

Again, understanding the ostrich is about context. But so too we must understand the context of the scientists that have been prodding and poking for the truth about animals for centuries. As such, Browne is just one of a great cast of idiosyncratic obsessives you'll meet in the pages of this book. There's the seventeenth-century physician who tried to spontaneously generate toads by placing a duck on a dung heap (an old recipe for creating life). There's also an Italian Catholic priest with a name befitting a Bond bad guy and the moves to match: Lazzaro Spallanzani wielded a mean pair of scissors in the name of science, whether tailoring tiny, bespoke underpants for his animal subjects or removing their ears.

Although both of these men were products of the earliest days of the Enlightenment, scientists in more recent times have also chosen to pursue bizarre, and often misguided, methods in their search for truth – like the twentieth-century American psycho-pharmacologist whose curiosity compelled him to get a herd of elephants very drunk indeed, with suitably demented results. Every century has its eccentric animal experimenters, and there will no doubt be many more to come. We humans may have split the atom, conquered the Moon and tracked down the Higgs boson, but when it comes to understanding animals we still have a long way to go.

I'm fascinated by the mistakes we've made along the way and the myths we've created to fill in the gaps in our understanding. They reveal much about the mechanics of discovery and the people doing the discovering. When Pliny the Elder described a hippopotamus secreting crimson liquor from its skin, he reached for the explanations familiar to him – those of Roman medicine – and imagined an animal bleeding itself to stay healthy. Of course he did; he was a man of his time. He was wrong, but the genuine explanation for the hippo's scarlet ooze is just as extraordinary as the old myth – and it is actually related to self-medication.

I've found that taking a dissecting knife to our greatest animal myths often exposes a charming logic, transporting us to times of wondrous naivety, when little was known and anything was possible. Why on earth wouldn't birds migrate to the Moon, hyenas switch sex with the season and eels spontaneously generate out of mud? Especially when the truth, as we will discover, is no less incredible.

The most nonsensical animal myths sprang to life after the fall of the Roman Empire when, in the Middle Ages, the nascent science of natural history was hijacked by Christianity. This was the heyday of the bestiary. These early compendiums of the animal kingdom were full of gilded illustrations and earnest descriptions of exotic beasts, from sparrow-camels (ostriches) to camel-leopards (giraffes) to sea bishops (half

*It was a common belief in the Middle Ages that every land animal had a counterpart in the sea: horses and sea horses, lions and sea lions, bishops and . . . sea bishops. This fishy minister, described in Konrad von Gesner's* Historiae animalium *(1558), was allegedly sighted off the coast of Poland (but looks as if he's just wandered off the set of* Dr Who*).*

fish, half clergyman and whole fantasy). But the bestiaries were not the result of some deep commitment to researching the lives of animals. Instead, they all embellished upon one single source, a fourth-century manuscript called the *Physiologus*, which blended folklore with a sprinkling of fact and a heavy dose of religious allegory. The *Physiologus* became the medieval equivalent of a massive bestseller (only exceeded at the time by the Bible) and was translated into dozens of languages, spreading absurd animal legends from Ethiopia to Iceland.

These bestiaries are a fabulously bawdy read with much talk of sex and sin, which must have delighted the monks that transcribed and illustrated them for the Church's libraries. They spoke of extraordinary creatures: the weasel which conceives through its mouth but gives birth through its ear; the bison (or 'bonnacon', as it was then known) which avoids a hunter by emitting a fart 'so foul that its attackers are forced to retire in confusion' (we've all been there); and the stag whose penis has a habit of dropping off following bouts of carnal overindulgence. There were more than a few lessons to be gathered and conveyed to flocks of parishioners in such tales. After all, God had created all the animals, and only one – mankind – had lost its innocence. The function of the animal kingdom, in the eyes of the scribes, was to serve as an example for humans. So instead of questioning whether there was any truth to the descriptions in the *Physiologus*, they looked for the human characteristics of animals and the moral values God had hidden in their behaviour.

This renders some animals in the bestiaries almost unrecognizable. Elephants, for example, were praised for being the most virtuous and wise of beasts, so 'gentle and meek' they were even credited with having their own religion. They were said to have a 'great hatred' of mice but a love of country so deep that just thinking about their homeland could reduce them to tears. When it came to fornication, they were 'the most chaste', staying with their mates for life – and it was a very long life, lasting three hundred years. They were so averse to adultery that they would punish those they caught in the act. All of which would come as something of a surprise to your average elephant, which enjoys a decidedly polygynous sex life.

The urge to look for our reflection in animals and impose moral judgements upon them continued well into more enlightened times. Perhaps the greatest sinner in this department, and the biggest star of this book, is the celebrated French naturalist Georges-Louis Leclerc, Comte de Buffon. The grandiose Comte was a leading figure of the scientific revolution who strove, somewhat paradoxically, to move natural history out from under the shadow of the Church. His epic, forty-four-volume encyclopaedia is, however, a hilariously sanctimonious tome, thanks to a delightfully purple prose which, in the style of most science writing of the period, reads more like a romantic novel than scientific analysis. His withering put-downs of animals whose lives he doesn't approve of, like our friend the sloth (aka 'the lowest form of existence', according to the French aristocrat) are almost as amusingly inaccurate as his overblown adoration of the creatures he exalts. One of his pet beasts was the beaver, whose hard work, you will discover, he positively lost his mind over, turning the great Buffon into something of a buffoon, once you know the truth.

Such anthropomorphic impulses persist even today. Pandas are so powerfully cute, they trigger an innate urge to nurture that smothers our judgement. We want to believe they are bumbling, sex-shy bears that cannot survive without our intervention, rather than veteran survivors with a ferocious bite and a taste for rough-and-tumble group sex.

I studied zoology in the early 1990s under the great evolutionary biologist Dr Richard Dawkins and was taught a method of thinking about the world based upon the genetic relationships between species – how their degree of relatedness influences their behaviour. Some of what I was taught has already been surpassed by recent advancements, which show that the *way* in which a genome is read at a cellular level can be at least as important as its content (which is how we can share 70 per cent of our DNA with an acorn worm and yet be so much more fun at a dinner party). I mention this to make the point that each generation – mine included – think we know more about animals than our predecessors, yet we're still often wrong. Much of zoology is little more than educated guesswork.

With modern technology we are getting better at our guessing. As a producer and presenter of natural history documentaries, I've travelled the world and gained privileged access to some of the most dedicated scientists mining for truth at the coalface of discovery. I've met an animal IQ tester in the Maasai Mara, a peddler of panda porn in China, the English inventor behind a sloth 'bum-o-meter' (it has a scientific purpose) and the Scottish author of the world's first chimpanzee dictionary. I have chased after drunk moose, nibbled beaver 'testicles', savoured amphibian aphrodisiacs, jumped off a cliff to fly with vultures and attempted to speak a few words of hippo (though not all at once). These experiences have opened my eyes to many surprising truths about animals and the state of animal science. This book is my effort to share these truths with you, to gather together the biggest misconceptions, mistakes and myths we've concocted about the animal kingdom, whether the purveyor was the great philosopher Aristotle or the Hollywood descendants of Walt Disney, and create my very own menagerie of the misunderstood.

So, open your mind to these incredible tales. Just don't expect them all to be true.

## CHAPTER I

## EEL

Genus *Anguilla*

*There is no animal concerning whose origin and existence there is such a number of false beliefs and ridiculous fables.*

Leopold Jacoby, 'The Eel Question', 1879

ARISTOTLE WAS TROUBLED BY eels.

No matter how many the great Greek thinker sliced open, he could find no trace of their sex. Every other fish he'd examined on his island laboratory of Lesvos had easily detectable (and often quite delectable) eggs and conspicuous, albeit internal, testicles. But the eel appeared to be entirely sex-less. So, when Aristotle came to writing about them in his pioneering animal almanac in the fourth century BC, this most methodical of natural philosophers was forced to conclude that the eel 'proceeds neither from pair, nor from an egg' but was instead born of the 'earth's guts', spontaneously emerging from mud; he thought the worm casts we see in wet sand were embryonic eels boiling out of the ground.

Aristotle was the first true scientist and the father of zoology. He made acute scientific observations about hundreds of creatures, but I am not surprised he was outfoxed by eels. These slippery characters keep their secrets especially well hidden. The idea that they emerge from the earth is fantastic, but no more so than the truth, since the so-called common freshwater eel, *Anguilla anguilla*, starts its life as an egg suspended in the depths of an underwater forest in the Sargasso Sea, the deepest, saltiest slice of the Atlantic. As a wisp of life no bigger than a grain of rice, it embarks on an odyssey lasting up to three years, to the rivers of Europe, during which it undergoes a transformation as radical as a mouse turning into a moose. It spends decades living in the mud and fattening itself up only so it can repeat the gruelling 6,000-kilometre journey back to its obscure oceanic womb, where it spawns in the shadowy recesses of the continental shelf and dies.

The fact that the eel only becomes sexually mature after its fourth, and final, metamorphosis at the very tail end of this particularly peculiar life has helped to obscure its origins and bestowed it with a mythical status. Over the centuries, unravelling the mystery has pitted nations against each other, driven man to the remotest reaches of the seas and tormented some of the finest minds in the history of zoology, as everyone seemed to compete with one another to concoct the craziest theory to explain the eel's genesis. No matter how outlandish, they couldn't match the true story of the common freshwater eel, which is anything but ordinary: a remarkable tale of eel-starving Nazis, obsessive gonad hunters, gun-toting fishermen, the world's most famous psychoanalyst – and me.

As a child, I, too, was rather obsessed with eels. When I was about seven my father sank an old Victorian bath in the garden, and converting this sterile tub for human ablution into the perfect pond ecosystem quickly became my principal pastime. I was a geeky child and I took this mission extremely seriously. Every Sunday my dad would accompany me to the ditches of Romney Marsh where I would spend happy hours trawling for any form of life with an improvised underwater animal trap he'd fashioned for me out of a pair of old net curtains. At the end of the day we'd return triumphant, heady with the zeal of Victorian explorers, our underwater booty sloshing around in the back of his aged mini pickup, ready to be identified and introduced to my watery kingdom. The animals came two by two: marsh frogs, smooth newts, sticklebacks, whirligig beetles and pond skaters all joined the party in my bath. Alas no eels. My trusty net collected them, but attempting to transfer their slimy bodies into the bucket was like trying to hold onto water. Every time I grabbed one they'd escape, slithering off to safety overland – more like a snake than a fish out of water. They were elusive creatures and catching them became my Holy Grail.

What I didn't know was that, if I *had* succeeded in my mission, the eels would have brought an end to my pleasant pond party by eating all the other guests. Eels spend the freshwater phase of their life like extreme prizefighters bulking themselves up for a championship bout in preparation for the long swim back to the Sargasso to breed. To achieve this they will eat anything that moves – including each other. Their rapacious appetite was exposed in a gruesome experiment conducted by a pair of French scientists in Paris in the late 1930s. The researchers placed a thousand elvers – young eels, about 8 centimetres long – in a tank of water. The fish were fed daily, but even so, a year later there were only seventy-one eels left, now three times as long. Three months later, after what a local journalist reported as 'daily scenes of cannibalism', one champion was left: a female measuring one-third of a metre in length. She lived a further four years all on her own, until she was accidentally bumped off by the Nazis, who inadvertently cut off her supply of worms during their occupation of Paris.

This horror story would have shocked the past generations of naturalists who believed the eel to be a benign vegetarian with a particular weakness for peas – so much so they were said to leave their watery world and seek out their favourite juicy legumes on land. Such accounts came courtesy of the thirteenth-century Dominican monk Albert Magnus, who, in his book *De Animalibus*, noted: 'The eel also comes out of the water in the night time where he can find pease, beans, and lentils.' The eel's hippie diet was still in currency in 1893, when *A History of Scandinavian Fishes* embellished the monk's 'observations' with delicious sound effects. The Countess Hamilton's estate was invaded by eels that gobbled up her legumes with 'a smacking sound, like that made by sucking-pigs when they are eating'. Though perhaps lacking the requisite manners, the dowager's eels were a suitably discerning school that 'only consumed the soft and juicy skin' and discarded the rest. Whilst it's true that eels can survive for a remarkable forty-eight hours out of water, thanks to their slimy, breathable skin – an adaptation that allows them to pond-hop in search of water in times of drought – reports of their lip-smacking, pea-stealing antics were quite delusional.

The eel's greedy freshwater years lead to an impressive increase in size, though maybe not as great as the ancient naturalist would have us believe. Fish engender themselves to tall tales of 'the one that got away'. Still, the great Roman naturalist Pliny the Elder's assertion, made in his epic tome, *Naturalis Historia*, that eels from the river Ganges grew to be 'thirty feet long' – 10 metres – was a cocky overstatement even in this well-worn genre of lies. Izaak Walton, author of a seventeenth-century fishing bible, *The Compleat Angler*, showed a bit more restraint when describing an eel caught in the Peterborough river that he claimed 'was a yard and three quarters long', or roughly 160 centimetres. Walton was keen to fend off any doubters by adding, perhaps a little too quickly: 'If you will not believe me, then go and see it at one of the coffee-houses in King street Westminster' (where it was no doubt happily sipping cappuccinos and regaling customers with stories of its youthful adventures at sea). More measured measurements come from Dr Jorgen Nielsen of the Zoological Museum in Copenhagen, who examined the corpse of an eel from a rural pond in Denmark. He told Tom Fort, author of *The Book of Eels*, that the prizewinning specimen punched in at 125 cm. Unfortunately, the slippery monster had met an untimely death when the pond's owner caught it menacing his beloved ornamental waterfowl and came at it with his shovel.

The eels I caught were quite a bit smaller, not much more than the length and thickness of a pencil. They were no doubt nearer the start of their freshwater life, which can last anything from six to thirty years. Some eels have been

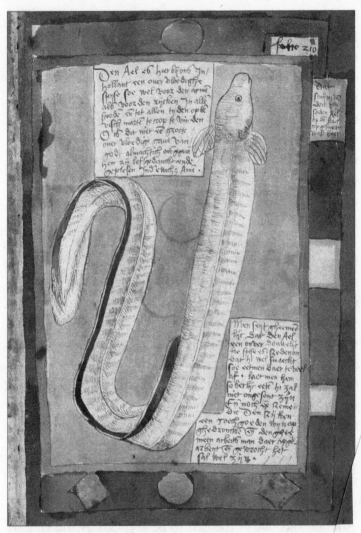

*The eel in Adriaen Coenen's almanac of fish (1577) is a veritable monster that measures a whopping '40 feet' long (having grown a further 10 feet since being described by the Roman naturalist Pliny the Elder).*

known to live much longer. A Swedish specimen nicknamed Putte, caught as an elver near Helsingborg in 1863 and kept in a local aquarium, passed away aged eighty-eight. Her death was mourned with extensive media coverage, her record-breaking age having afforded her the kind of celebrity status not normally available to a long, slimy fish.

Such aged eels have invariably been denied their urge to migrate back to the sea by being kept captive, often as pets. An eel may seem an unconventional choice for an animal companion – not a lot of fun to be had in the snuggling department – but the Roman orator Quintus Hortensius was said to weep at the death of his, 'which he kept long, and loved exceedingly'. All of which makes me somewhat relieved that I never succeeded in catching myself an eel, which I could still be wedded to today.

The eel's freshwater existence may be long and gluttonous, but it is just one of the fish's many lives (albeit the only one obvious to me and countless other naturalists over the centuries). It gives no clues about the rest of its lifecycle – its birth, reproduction and death – which are shrouded by the sea, and come in such unlikely alternative guises that they spawned an intense international quest, lasting some two thousand years, to locate the eel's mysterious gonads.

Aristotle was one of the first to be stymied by the genesis of this apparently sexless fish. He folded the origins of the eel into his theory of spontaneous generation, which he applied liberally to an eclectic collection of critters – from flies to frogs – whose proliferation seemed inexplicable. Several hundred years later, Pliny the Elder took a break from plagiarizing his Greek forebears to trial his own imaginative ideas about eel propagation; he proposed that they reproduced by rubbing themselves against rocks, 'the scrapings come to life'. Hoping to have the last word on the matter, the Roman naturalist concluded with an authoritative flourish: 'This is the only way they breed.' But Pliny's asexual friction was nothing but fiction.

Fantastic rumours of the eel's reproduction bred like rabbits over the ensuing centuries. Eels were said to emerge from the gills of other fishes, from sweet morning dew (but only during certain months) and from enigmatic 'electrical disturbances'. One 'reverend bishop' told the Royal Society he had seen young eels that had been born on the thatching of a roof. The eggs, he claimed, had been stuck to the thatching reeds and incubated by the heat of the sun. Not all ecclesiastical naturalists were so open-minded about such fishy tales. In his *History of the Worthies*, Thomas Fuller poured scorn on the belief widely held in the fenlands of Cambridgeshire that the illicit wives and bastard children of priests were saved from damnation by taking the form of an eel. This, he said, was clearly 'a lie'. To underscore the seriousness of the matter, he added judgementally: 'No doubt the first founder of so damnable an untruth hath long since received his reward.' Perhaps by living out the rest of his life as a slug.

The scientific geniuses of the Enlightenment swept aside such fanciful fables with significantly less silly – but no more accurate – theories of their own. In 1692, Antonie van Leeuwenhoek, the Dutch pioneer of microscopic worlds who discovered both bacteria and blood cells, erred towards credibility with his hypothesis that eels, like mammals, were *viviparous*, that is, their eggs were fertilized internally, with the females giving birth to live young. Van Leeuwenhoek at least embraced contemporary scientific method by basing his supposition on actual observations. He had stared down his magnifying lens and watched what appeared to be baby eels in what he assumed was the fish's uterus. Unfortunately, these alleged newborns were actually parasitic worms squatting in the eel's bladder, and had in fact been observed and dismissed as such by Aristotle nearly two thousand years before.

The eighteenth-century Swedish botanist and zoologist Carl Linnaeus also said that eels were viviparous, claiming to have seen what he believed to be baby eels inside an adult female. Surely no one would argue with the great father of taxonomy – a man so pedantic he even Latinized his own name. But they had little choice once it emerged that the classification connoisseur had got his species in a twist. The awkward truth was that Linnaeus hadn't actually dissected an eel but an eel imposter, a similar-looking beast now known as the eelpout – an unusually viviparous yet altogether unrelated species of fish. Which is not to say his critics had their facts any more straight. One authority who reviewed Linnaeus's work took him to task for a case of mistaken identity – but, influenced by Aristotle, proclaimed the young eels discovered by the Swede to be parasitic worms, sending the live-birth doctrine into a vortex of inaccuracy and confusion.

Into this lofty academic fray stepped a plucky outsider. In 1862, a Scotsman by the name of David Cairncross announced to the world that he, a humble factory engineer from Dundee, had finally solved the riddle of the eel, which had plagued generations of philosophers and naturalists. 'The reader may at once be informed that ... the progenitor of the silver eel is a small beetle,' he stated with the bravado of the truly ignorant. His enthusiastic, if scientifically baffling, theory – the product of sixty years of ongoing experiments by his own reckoning – took the form of a short book, *The Origin of the Silver Eel*.

Cairncross began his treatise with an apology for his lack of any interest in learning the rules and norms of contemporary science. 'I could not be expected to be acquainted with the names and terms used by naturalists in their classifications of the different animals, my knowledge of such books being limited,' he noted somewhat defensively. His unconventional but highly convenient solution was to 'employ names and terms of my own'. This involved a reimagining of animal classification into three nonsensical classes that would have made the great Linnaeus turn in his grave, and succeeded only in creating

23

further challenges to anyone trying to decipher the Scot's already bewildering theory.

Cairncross's journey of discovery begins at the tender age of ten, when he observed a number of 'hair eels' (his term) in an open drain. 'Where can they come from?' he wondered. A friend related to him a common folk belief that young eels 'fall from the tails of the horses while drinking; and the water brings them to life.' The young Cairncross scoffed at this highly improbable explanation, before conjuring up his own, equally implausible idea inspired by a number of dead beetles languishing in the bottom of the same drain. Maybe the two animals were connected? This bewitching scene stayed with the Scot for two decades, 'often did my mind revert to the mystery', he recalled.

Then one summer, the adult Cairncross spotted a familiar-looking beetle in his garden in Dundee. He watched it intently, attempting to read its thoughts as it walked with determination towards a puddle and plunged in. The beetle, he reported, then 'looks about a bit' before exiting its bath 'in a very troubled state'. How Cairncross arrived at his diagnosis of the beetle's mental state is not known. But the book's only illustration provides the reader with valuable assistance in comprehending the insect's next extraordinary move: entitled 'the beetle in the act of parturition', it showed Cairncross's unlikely hero lying on its back with what appears to be a pair of lassoes emanating from its backside. The beetle, according to the Scotsman, was giving birth to two fish.

This was the Eureka moment for Cairncross. He now dedicated himself to furthering his investigation by cutting open beetles, removing 'hair eels' and keeping them alive for various, albeit rather limited, periods of time. He freely admitted that his theory 'may seem strange' but reassured himself by looking at the behaviour of 'members of the vegetable kingdom'. If one species of tree can be grafted onto another, 'Could not therefore the Great Creating Gardener graft a foreign nature on that of an insect?' he mused.

All manner of Frankenstein animals have been conceived in modern labs: human ears have been grafted onto

*a* The Beetle in the act of Parturition.    *b* The Eel fully developed.

*Just in case you had any problems visualizing how a beetle might give birth to a pair of eels,* The Origin of the Silver Eel *includes this charming illustration in an attempt to authenticate the author's wild claims. Nice try, Cairncross, but I'm still not convinced.*

mice and glow-in-the-dark fish have been created with a judicious sprinkling of jellyfish genes. But the 'Great Creating Gardener' had no hand in planting them.

Had Cairncross posed his question to the scholarly community, they would have declared that his 'hair eels' were yet another case of pesky parasitic worms and not the fish in an early stage of development. But the factory engineer knew not of peer review. He presented his exceptional findings not to the Royal Society for serious scrutiny, but instead to a pair of farmers he bumped into one day, who were perplexed by the quantities of silver eel in a ditch on their land. So he explained his theory that this profusion of eels had emerged from a beetle's bum and was delighted by their response. 'They believed me', he announced with pride, 'and rejoiced in the solution of the mystery.'

Despite the enthusiasm of these local farmers, Cairncross's theory failed to alter the broader trajectory of eel research. Beavering away in intellectual isolation for sixty-odd years, he was unaware of the radical progress being made in the hunt for the fish's gonads. Far from Dundee, Europe's scientific intelligentsia were gripped by 'the eel question', and they were about to reach a climax – of sorts.

Leading the charge were the Italians, who embraced the quest to locate the eel's missing sex organs as an unlikely source of civic pride for their troubled nation.

The Italians had cultivated a longstanding relationship

with eels that mostly involved eating them in vast quantities. Eel is an unusually fatty fish – an evolutionary
adaptation to fuel its onerous 6,000-kilometre odyssey back
to its mating grounds deep in the Sargasso Sea. Unfortunately for the eel, this high lipid content also makes it
especially tasty, a quality which did not go unnoticed. The
Roman epicure Marcus Gavius Apicius, author of what is
arguably the world's first cookbook, wrote that six thousand eels were served at feasts celebrating the victory of
Julius Caesar. He recommended that the 'eel will be made
more palatable' by serving it with a sauce containing 'dry
mint, rue berries, hard yolks, pepper, lovage, mead, vinegar
broth and oil'. This doesn't sound wildly appetizing, but
in England we still like to eat them simply boiled and
jellied, surely one of the greatest crimes against gastron-
omy the British have committed in a long and illustrious
history of murdering food. Yet, despite such crude recipes,
eels were long associated with great feasts and gluttony.
Leonardo da Vinci painted the disciples enjoying eels at
the Last Supper, and a surfeit of the slippery fish was
blamed for the death of the infamous gourmand Pope
Martin IV.

The finest tasting eels were said to come from Comacchio and the surrounding vast grey wetlands of the mighty
river Po delta. They were home to Europe's greatest eel
fisheries, hauling in three hundred tons of eel a night at
the height of the season, and the source of some of the
greatest pronouncements and controversies surrounding

the eel's sex. These began in 1707, when a local surgeon noticed an unusually plump eel amongst the many thousands being caught. When the doctor sliced it open, he saw what looked to him like an ovary stuffed with ripe eggs. The pregnant fish was dispatched to his friend, the esteemed naturalist Antonio Vallisneri, who hastily proclaimed the centuries-long search for the eel's private parts was finally over. The learned professor had already lent his name to the formal classification of a water plant known colloquially as the eelgrass, but the genitals of the female eel would not be a further namesake. Upon closer scrutiny, the discovery was written off as little more than a diseased and distended swim bladder.

Vallisneri's flirtation with victory inspired the Italian scientific mafia, who now considered it 'a matter of extreme importance to find the true ovaries of the eel'. These were turbulent times for the inchoate nation, as the peninsula was occupied by foreign powers. And whilst many Italians hung their nationalistic hopes on revolution, this small band of intellectuals dreamed instead of empowering their countrymen by laying claim to the delectable eel's elusive gonads.

The professors devised a plan. Thousands of eels were captured daily around Comacchio; all they need do was offer an enticing reward to the first fisherman who could provide them with a specimen complete with roe. In Germany, a competing plan backfired when the naturalist who had hatched it received so much eel offal in the post that he was moved to 'cry and beg for mercy'. The Italian scheme, however, quickly yielded positive results – or so it seemed. The celebrations were cut short when it was discovered the wily fisherman had simply filled his eel with the eggs of another fish.

This humiliating blow dampened the Italian professors' zeal for eels for some fifty years. Then in 1777, a fresh, fat, slimy suspect flopped up on the shores of Comacchio. It was immediately examined by the anatomist Carlo Mondini, professor at the nearby University of Bologna, who made an ingenious realization: the frilled ribbons inside the eel's abdomen were not fringes of fatty tissue, as had been previously supposed, but the female eel's evasive ovaries.

Italy's scientists rejoiced, perhaps again a little prematurely. After all, the eel's testicles were still missing, along with any clear notion of how this enigmatic fish reproduced. Thus, the mission to complete the eel's genital jigsaw puzzle fell to a rather unlikely candidate: an ambitious young medical student who would later find fame locating the seat of desire, in humans if not in eels. The student's name: Sigmund Freud.

As a nineteen-year-old student at the University of Vienna, the founding father of psychoanalysis took up his very first research job, arriving in 1876 at a zoological field station in Trieste, on Italy's Adriatic coast, with a mandate to find the testicles of the eel.

The only way to determine gender was to slice the fish open, 'seeing that eels keep no diaries', Freud opined sardonically in a letter to a friend. For weeks he did just that, every day, from eight in the morning until five in the afternoon, in a hot, smelly laboratory. He had been tasked with investigating the claim of a Polish professor named Szymon Syrski, who had said he had discovered the eel's testes. 'But since he apparently doesn't know what a microscope is', grumbled Freud in his letter, 'he failed to provide an accurate description of them.'

Four weeks and four hundred disembowelled eels later, Freud gave up. 'I have been tormenting myself and the eels, but in vain, all the eels which I cut open are of the fairer sex,' he lamented in a letter littered with doodles of eels wearing thin mocking smiles. Freud's resulting paper, 'Observations on the Form and the Fine Structure of Looped Organs of the Eel, Organs Considered as Testes', was his first published work. Although he suspected Syrski was right, he could neither confirm nor deny the Pole's claims.

It's anyone's guess how much those long days spent slicing open phallocentric fish in a fruitless search for their sex influenced Freud's later theories surrounding the phallic-envy stage of human psychosexual development. In any case, he went on to probe less slippery subjects, like the human psyche, with significantly more success.

Two decades later, a lone male eel finally exposed his private parts. The fortuitous young biologist to make the eel's acquaintance was another Italian, Giovanni Grassi, who

*Sigmund Freud's doodles in a letter to a friend are a window into his mind during his futile hunt for the testicles of the eel. Here are the enigmatic eels that tortured him so, along with squiggles representing their elusive sperm and eggs (which a psychoanalyst might say look suspiciously like a pair of breasts).*

apprehended the fish – his sex organs swollen with sperm – swimming off the coast of Sicily. Grassi had already produced some seminal, if not particularly scintillating, work on the anatomy of termites, and had named a new species of spider after his wife (there's love for you). But he was on something of a roll when it came to eels. Not only had he won the international eel testicle tournament for Italy, but the year before he had made an equally pivotal discovery by identifying a key stage in the eel's inscrutable lifecycle.

Since the 1850s, tiny, transparent fish the shape and thickness of a willow leaf with bulbous black eyes and terrifying buck teeth had been documented washing up in great numbers on the shores of Italy. These minuscule monsters were classified as *Leptocephalus brevirostris* – a perfunctory piece of Linnaean nomenclature that translates to 'thin-head short-nosed' – and quickly dismissed as just another of the all too numerous, utterly nondescript marine creatures that inhabit the murky depths. Grassi was fascinated by these slivers of life. Suspecting they might be larval, as opposed to adult fish, he pulled a rather cunning trick. He counted up their embryonic vertebrae – which averaged 115 – and looked for a match in another species. He found it in the European freshwater eel. It was a truly momentous revelation, the identification of the missing link in the eel's mysterious lifecycle.

Several learned minds had already proposed that the freshwater eel must breed far out at sea. It was an unconventional idea – the reverse direction of all other long-distance migrating fish, like salmon, which spread their lives across fresh- and saltwater habitats. But why else would eels swim downriver every autumn in such great numbers and with such determination, with minia-ture versions of themselves making the reverse journey upriver every spring? Still, there was no evidence support-ing this logical hypothesis. No baby eels had ever been found at sea. Now Grassi had not only located the missing larval stage; he had also fingered the eel as a world-class shape-shifter.

Grassi set himself up with an aquarium to observe the miraculous metamorphosis with his own eyes. He was clever to do so, as no one would probably have believed him otherwise. Over the course of several weeks, the leaf-like wisp began to thicken at each end, forming an indisputably eel-shaped creature. Its body length shrank by almost a third, its jagged teeth dissolved and, for obscure alimentary reasons, its anus migrated. After a few days a perfectly transparent, bug-eyed noodle known as a glass eel was swimming around the tank. Giddy with discovery, Grassi proclaimed the Strait of Messina, off the coast of Sic-ily, to be the breeding ground of all European eels, thereby claiming the lip-smacking fish and its extraordinary lifecy-cle as the property of the newly united Kingdom of Italy.

But as is the habit of the eel, such hastily grabbed glory quickly slipped out of the Italian's grasp. Grassi had con-veniently ignored the fact that the thin-heads he'd captured were all around 7 centimetres long. So unless they were born from an unfeasibly large egg, these larvae were already quite mature by the time they reached the strait. Could they really have been born so close to Italy's coast?

One man didn't think the riddle of the eel was quite so easily solved.

Like many before him, the oceanographer Johannes Schmidt displayed an almost monomaniacal determination to pin down the obscure breeding ground of the freshwater eel. For nearly two decades the 'pathalogically ambitions' Dane combed the vast expanses of the Atlantic Ocean in search of freshly hatched fry the size of pine needles. His expedition was so immense and so technically demanding – and led to such an unexpected end – that it would snatch the glory of the eel's slippery story from Italy's grasp and deliver it to Denmark.

His mission began in 1903, when the young Schmidt got a job as a fisheries biologist aboard the *Thor*, a Danish research vessel, studying the breeding habits of food fishes such as cod and herring. One day in the summer of that year, as they were sailing west of the Faroe Islands in the Atlantic, a puny fish larva showed up in one of the boat's massive, fine-mesh trawls. Schmidt identified the insignificant larva as that of the European eel – the first of its kind to be found outside of the Mediterranean. It was 'a chance of luck' that suggested to Schmidt that the birthplace of the eel was not off the coast of Italy but approximately 4,000 kilometres to the north, unless this thin-head had got very lost indeed.

The Dane became obsessed with locating the eel's true origins, surpassing even the other eel fanatics – Aristotle, Cairncross, Freud, Mondini or Grassi – who had been seized before him. Fortunately for the tenacious scientist, the year before he had made an auspicious betrothal to the heiress to the Carlsberg Brewery, probably the best lager company in the world for an aspiring thin-head hunter to hitch his wagon to, since the company was known to donate generously to marine research. Whether his bride was as pleased with the deal, which involved losing her new husband to a two-decades-long, seafaring fixation with teeny tiny fish, is anyone's guess.

Suffused with youthful enthusiasm, Schmidt embarked on an almighty quest to locate the smallest possible thin-heads, which would, he thought, logically lead him to the place of their birth. 'I had little idea at the time of the extraordinary difficulty which the task was to present,' he later wrote. 'The task was found to grow in extent year by year, to a degree we never dreamed of.' He trawled fine nets 'from America to Egypt, from Iceland to the Canary Islands', wearing out four large ships, one of which ran aground near the Virgin Islands and sank, nearly taking his precious thin-head specimens with it. Then came the First World War. Many of the boats he co-opted to assist in his mission were shot by German submarines.

Whilst battling the oceans, Schmidt was also forced to lay siege to an academic establishment that was infuriatingly reluctant to recognize his painstaking efforts. In 1912 he had published his first findings: that the further from the European coast he travelled, the smaller the eel larvae became, which indicated that the birthplace of the eel must indeed be in the Atlantic. The Royal Society demurred, however, stating that Grassi's work 'was considered sufficient' on the subject, thereby forcing Schmidt back onto a boat and back out to sea.

A breakthrough came on 12 April 1921, in the southern Sargasso Sea, when Schmidt captured his most Lilliputian larvae: thin-heads just 5 millimetres long, which he presumed were no more than a day or two old. After almost two decades of searching, the Dane's quest was finally reaching its end. He could at last feel confident in claiming, 'Here lie the breeding grounds of the eel.'

It was an astonishing result; even Schmidt was blown away by the import of his discovery. 'No other instance is known among fishes of a species requiring a quarter of the circumference of the globe to complete its life history,' he wrote in 1923, 'and larval migrations of such extent and duration as those of the eel are altogether unique in the animal kingdom.' Grassi and the Italians had been vanquished, and the mantle of eel demystification would for ever be worn by a satisfied Schmidt and his Danish homeland.

But one should never say 'for ever' – in science or in life.

Almost one hundred years later our understanding of the eel's lifecycle is still little more than expensive guesswork. Despite billions of dollars and the best of modern technology, no adult *Anguilla anguilla* has ever been tracked all the way on its journey from the rivers of Europe to the Sargasso Sea. Nor has one been observed mating in the wild. And no eggs have ever been found.

I asked Kim Aarestrup, a senior researcher at the Technical University of Denmark and one of the world's leading eel scientists, whether we could be absolutely certain that the European freshwater eel really is born in the Sargasso. His answer: a sheepish 'no'.

It's not for want of trying. Modern expeditions have been mounted attempting to track adult eels with sonar. Researchers have followed their shadowy deep-sea spectres across the Atlantic but have no way of knowing if they are in fact chasing the right fish – just something that has the look of it. So still more researchers have fitted hundreds of eels with state-of-the-art satellite tags. Alas, many of these expensive tags have wound up inside the stomachs of sharks and whales, their signal relentlessly delivering data to increasingly baffled scientists as the predators journeyed around the ocean, far and away from the eels' usual habitats. One wily researcher attempted to catch an eel *in flagrante delicto* by suspending traps deep in the Sargasso with seductive females, ripened with artificial hormones so they were practically bursting with the desire to mate. Not even these swollen temptresses could lure adult males into revealing themselves, however. The slippery sirens' cages sank without trace in the sea, as did the hope of catching any horny male eels.

Part of the problem is the strange nature of the Sargasso itself. It's breathtakingly deep, almost 7 kilometres in some spots where submarine chasms have formed in the continental shelf. It's thought that the European eel, an ancient species over 40 million years old, started breeding in this deep-sea trench when the continents of Europe and America were much closer (geographically speaking). As the continents drifted apart, so the eel was forced to migrate further and further to return to the place of its birth. The chances of catching it in the act are hampered not only by these great depths but by dangerous swells – the Sargasso is the only sea that isn't bound by coastline but is instead a 5-million-kilometre-square whorl surrounded by powerful clockwise currents known as the North Atlantic Gyre. Not only does eel spawning season coincide with the annual cyclone season, but, as Aarestrup pointed out to me, the Sargasso 'is slap bang in the middle of the Bermuda Triangle'.

I've still got Barry Manilow warbling 'Bermuda Triangle' stuck in my head from the 1970s. That this infamous, chart-topping disaster zone, where countless ships have been swallowed up, is part of the eel's extraordinary story is enough to promote a superstitious belief that Poseidon himself is conspiring to keep the eel's sex life secret. And provide the seventies crooner with a follow-up hit, perhaps concerning the perilous long-distance romance of courting eels.

The prize for cracking the eel enigma is no longer just glory, but considerable wealth. Eels are big business. The fish that sustained Mesolithic man may have slipped off the menu in most countries, but they can't get enough of it in Japan, where the humble eel represents a $1 billion annual market. Its fatty flesh is a traditional dish, particularly during the hot summer months, as it's widely believed to have a cooling effect and help fight off fatigue. Although the Japanese have been known to eat eel ice cream washed down with eel-flavoured cola, they mostly like their freshwater eel barbecued and served with a sweet sauce and rice. More than a hundred thousand tons of this Japanese *unagi* are eaten every year. That's a lot of eels to catch.

Now global populations of eel are plummeting, in some cases by as much as 99 per cent, due to a combination of overfishing, pollution and other environmental inconveniences – such as massive hydroelectric dams blocking their favourite rivers. The global eel crisis has placed many formerly common freshwater species, including the European eel, on the International Union for Conservation of Nature (IUCN) Red List as a critically endangered species, which makes eating them about as PC as putting panda on your sushi. Although it is hard to drum up sympathy for a slimy, snake-like fish equal to that afforded to a big, fluffy bear, efforts to get the eel to breed in captivity have been just as intense – if less relished by the press. After billions of dollars and decades of research, the Japanese have enjoyed some success with breeding their freshwater specimen, *Anguilla japonica*, which spawns in a deep trench in the middle of the Pacific. They have found a way to force adults to breed using hormones and even managed to keep a few of the finicky thin-heads alive by feeding them a special diet – of powdered shark egg. Feeding one endangered species with another endangered species' eggs in labour-intensive conditions is not exactly a practical solution. Eel expert Kim Aarestrup told me the cost of producing a single glass eel in a Japanese lab is about $1,000 a fish. Which is some prohibitively pricey sushi.

So for now the Japanese must get their eel fix exclusively from dwindling stocks of wild glass eels, caught as they head upriver at the start of their freshwater life and then artificially fattened up in Asian fish farms. Some of these eels hail from Japan or Europe, but most are from America, where few people have shown much interest in eels until quite recently. The American freshwater eel, *Anguilla rostrata*, is a close cousin of the European; it is also bred and born in the Sargasso Sea, but the larvae migrate to the freshwater rivers of the US eastern seaboard. It's believed to be one of the foods that sustained the starving *Mayflower* pilgrims, after the Native peoples generously shared their knowledge of how to catch them. The life-giving legacy of the greasy fish has, however, been gobbled up by the turkey (no celebratory stuffed eels served up at Thanksgiving). A few hundred years later, the freshly inaugurated George W. Bush pioneered a fashion for wearing eelskin cowboy boots adorned with the blue presidential seal. He took to handing out pairs to his friends – minus the seal, but bearing his initials instead (just in case they forgot who they came from). But even this lofty endorsement somehow failed to drum up much of a market for the fish in America.

That's all changed now that a glass-eel fisherman can earn $100,000 a night by dipping a $25 trap in the right river. The $40 million domestic glass-eel industry has spawned a veritable gold rush in Maine, one of the only places in the US where elver fishing is permitted. With it has come some slippery business, including shady eel dealers handing millions in cash over to middlemen in motel car parks and fishermen brandishing AK-47s during armed stand-offs over the best fishing spots. According to the local press reports, Central American gangs are moving in, as much of the windfall has been spent by fishermen on illicit drugs – although one fisher-woman with an especially lucrative haul was quoted as using her eel dollars to splash out on a new pair of breasts.

In an 1879 report about the American eel to the US commission of fish and fisheries, the German marine biologist Leopold Jacoby admitted:

> It is certainly somewhat humiliating to men of science, that a fish which is commoner in many parts of the world than

any other fish . . . which is daily seen at the market and on the table, has been able in spite of the powerful aid of modern science, to shroud the manner of its propagation, its birth, and its death in darkness, which even to the present day has not been dispelled. There has been an eel question ever since the existence of natural science.

Not much has changed in the intervening century and more. But time is now running out to crack the eel enigma.

Some experts worry that the survival of the freshwater eel could be a numbers game. Winning depends on a sizeable population of eels making its way back to the Sargasso every year in order to mate along its idiosyncratic oceanic fronts. If not enough eels show up, they may fail to find each other and simply be swallowed up by this vast whorl of water. If that happens, the eel will have succeeded in keeping its sexy secret all the way to its unfathomable grave.

The eel's deep-sea existence preserved its unknowable nature. Secret lives engender mythology; we have a more sporting chance of understanding animals we can observe with at least some ease. Our next menagerie member, the beaver, may seem easier to track than an eel, but its habits are mostly hidden underwater or inside its impenetrable home, and therefore prone to wild speculation. And like the eel, it was the beaver's clandestine 'cods' that aroused the most ludicrous ancient legends about this large amphibious rodent.

## CHAPTER 2

# BEAVER

## Genus *Castor*

*There is a very gentle animal called the beaver,*
*whose testicles are extremely useful for medicine.*
Physiologus *says that when the beaver knows the*
*hunter is following him, he cuts off his testicles*
*with his teeth, and throws them before the hunter,*
*and thus escapes.*

A Medieval Book of Beasts, twelfth century

M Y RESEARCH FOR THIS book has taken me on some strange adventures. But my passion to find the truth about the beaver has probably raised the most eyebrows. It began early one autumnal morning at a rendezvous in a lay-by with a spindly, six-foot man carrying a loaded rifle, complete with silencer, in the boot of his car. His name was Mikael Kingstad and he was a professional beaver hunter.

Mikael is employed by the city of Stockholm – quite possibly the cleanest and greenest capital I have ever visited. Not far beyond the city's historic, pastel-coloured central district, the forests teem with animals, which occasionally spill out of the woodland to explore urban living. Mikael's job is to make sure these interlopers are kept in check. He's dispatched rabbits (a 'problem'), rats (his greatest nemesis), geese ('they produce a lot of shit') and apparently drunken elk. And, on occasion, he has put overly busy beavers in his sights.

Despite our first-name basis, I'm not in the habit of keeping the company of professional animal assassins. But I needed to meet up with Mikael to ask a bona fide beaver hunter an important question: 'Have you ever known a beaver to chew off its own testicles and throw them at you?'

Mikael laughed. I wasn't joking around, however. The beaver's alleged act of self-castration was the main impetus for my trip. Little did I expect that my investigation would unravel an unholy tale of mistaken testicular identity, misplaced moralism, wandering wombs and the virtual annihilation of the beaver from the rivers of Europe.

Of all the myths about animals, the beaver's perhaps wins the prize for being the most nonsensical. In ancient times this notoriously industrious rodent was famous not, as one might expect, for its tenacious lumberjack skills, nor for its exceptional flair for architecture, but for its testicles, which were treasured by ancient physicians for their medicinal qualities.

The beaver of the bestiaries was, however, a cunning creature. When pursued by huntsmen it was said to bare its enormous yellow teeth and promptly set to work castrating itself, surrendering its family jewels to its attacker (perhaps serving them up with a nifty bat of its paddle-like tail), thereby saving its life. The very definition of a smooth manoeuvre. But in most accounts, the animal's craftiness doesn't end there. The twelfth-century clergyman and chronicler Gerald of Wales is one of many to credit the beaver with further smarts. 'If by chance the dogs should chase an animal which had been previously castrated', wrote Gerald, 'he has the sagacity to run to an elevated spot, and there lifting up his leg, shews the hunter that the object of his pursuit is gone.'

The unlikely nature of this flamboyant act of self-gelding didn't much bother the authors of the medieval bestiaries. A biting religious allegory trumped the truth every time. This ribald tale of rodent wisdom had a pertinent lesson: man must cut off all his vices and surrender them to the Devil if he wants to live a life of peace. This no-nonsense message of austerity delighted Christian moralists. No wonder the beaver's story was repeated and shared across Europe.

It wasn't merely the bestiaries that described the beaver's artful unmanning. The legend featured in almost every description of the animal all the way back to the ancient Greeks. The encyclopaedist Claudius Aelianus embellished the absurdity by crediting the beaver with inventing a neat trick, much loved by drag queens. 'Often', he wrote in his epic animal tome, 'beavers will tuck away their privates.' This allowed the savvy rodents to waltz off into the distance, Aelianius informed us, whilst 'keeping their own treasures'.

Later, Leonardo da Vinci duly recorded the beaver's astonishing awareness of its gonadal worth in his notebooks: 'We read of the beaver that when it is pursued, knowing that it is for the virtue in its medicinal testicles and not being able to escape, it stops; and to be at peace with its pursuers, it bites off its testicles with its sharp

*This woodcut from a German edition of Aesop's fables (1685) is a fine example of beavers self-gelding in order to pay their testicle tax to the hunter.*

teeth, and leaves them to its enemies.' Sadly, there are no accompanying illustrations in the great artist's hand and so we can only imagine Leonardo's beaver boasting a suitably enigmatic Mona Lisa smile.

In 1670, the Scottish cartographer John Ogilby was *still* writing about how beavers 'bite off their Pizzles and throw them to the hunter' in his *America: Being an Accurate Description of the New World*. The story was just too irresistible not to repeat, a perfect mix of delicious bawdiness and righteous morality.

What was needed was a dispassionate mind to tackle the truth about the beaver's tackle and rescue the poor creature from permanently losing its pizzles. Enter the seventeenth-century myth-buster Sir Thomas Browne – who, despite an unhealthy obsession with feeding iron pasties to ostriches, was a lone voice of logic in decidedly muddled times. The Oxford-educated physician and philosopher was the author of *Pseudodoxia Epidemica* (1646), his intellectual assault on what he referred to as 'vulgar errors' – the vast suite of popular misconceptions propagated by the likes of the bestiaries that were busy clogging up the emerging discipline of natural science.

Browne's crusade adhered to an unflinching use of 'the three Determinators of Truth', which he defined as 'Authority, Sense, and Reason' – placing him at the vanguard of the scientific revolution by pioneering the modern scientific process. 'To purchase a clear and warrantable body of truth', he wrote, 'we must forget and part with much we know.' And so he began an unsentimental investigation into an array of entrenched untruths ranging from badgers allegedly having legs shorter on one side of their body than the other – an idea he considered to be 'repugnant unto the course of nature' – to whether dead kingfishers make good weathervanes. (They don't, as Browne discovered after experimenting with a pair of the bird's corpses. He hung them in the air by silk threads and observed that 'they will not regularly conform their breasts', but instead swung uselessly in opposite directions.)

Browne's nose for nonsense detected something

equally fishy about the beaver's testicles. The fallacy of the beaver, said Browne, was 'very ancient; and hath had thereby advantage of propagation'. He deduced it had started in a misreading of Egyptian hieroglyphics, which, for no obvious reason, depicted a beaver gnawing off its gonads to represent the punishment for *human* adultery. This depiction got picked up by Aesop, who publicized the beaver's tale in his popular fables. These in turn were absorbed into the early Greek and Roman scientific literature – and presented as fact.

Browne assumed the endurance of the tale was largely down to the rodent's quirky biology. Unlike in most mammals, beaver's testicles don't bob around outside the body but are instead hidden internally. Whilst these covert 'cods' served to validate the idea that the animal had been castrated in some way, Browne rightly pointed out that this anatomical design also meant a beaver couldn't chew off his own testicles even if he wanted to. The ability to 'eunuchate' was, he said, 'not only a fruitless attempt, but an impossible act' that might even be 'hazardous ... if at all attempted by others'.

The legend's origins were, in part, etymological – an area in which Browne had a surprisingly keen eye and ear, since he himself was something of a wordsmith. His clear-headed, protoscientific logic was woven with a florid stream of colourful, long-winded words, many of which, like 'eunuchate', he invented himself. Browne is credited with adding almost eight hundred new words to the

English language; his coinages of 'hallucination', 'electricity', 'carnivorous' and 'misconception' are all still very much in use. Others, like 'retromingent' – for urinating backwards – failed to catch on in quite the same way.

Browne astutely noted that the beaver's Latin name, *Castor*, is often confused with the word 'castrate'. The archbishop of Seville is one of many scribes to get his *Castors* in a twist. 'The beaver (*Castor*) is so named from being castrated,' he stated erroneously in *Etymologiæ*, his seventh-century encyclopedia. The Latin *Castor* is not derived from castration but instead connected to the Sanskrit word *kasturi*, meaning 'musk' – which brings us to the very nub of the centuries-old fluster over the beaver's cluster. Beavers were hunted for an oily brown liquid called castoreum that, it turned out, wasn't produced by their testicles, as the legend suggested, but in a pair of doppelgänger organs lurking suspiciously close by.

This case of mistaken testicular identity had first been busted a few years before Browne by a French physician and general bon viveur called Guillaume Rondelet. Sometime before his death in 1566 from an overdose of figs, this master of dissection took his knife to a couple of beavers and discovered that both the male and the female produced precious castoreum, which they stored in a pair of pear-shaped sacs situated near the animal's anus and connected to its urinary tract. Most mammals have a pair of anal scent glands, which produce a musky substance used to attract mates and mark territory. Rondelet was the first to discover that the beaver is uniquely endowed with a second pair, roughly the size of goose eggs and doing an excellent impersonation of beaver testes.

The similarity of these so-called castor sacs to gonads was so great that other, less keen anatomists had often mistaken female beavers for hermaphrodites, and reported mutant males that bore a freaky set of four jewels. But as Browne reminded readers with his characteristic wit, appearances can be deceiving. 'Testicles are defined by their office, and not determined by place or situation; they having one office in all, but different seats in many.' He diagnosed 'the resemblance and situation of these tumours' to be 'the ground of this mistake', and thereby, as far as he was concerned, debunked the beaver myth.

Castoreum was a revered medicine in the ancient world on account of its unusually pungent nature. This was a time when smells were considered to be particularly potent as treatments – and the more overpowering, the better the chances of being healed. Faeces, for this reason, were a firm favourite with doctors, if not their patients. A trip to the doctor might involve inhaling a heady cocktail of up to thirty different medicinal turds (such as mouse and even human). Which could only have made the sick feel even sicker. Sniffing beaver 'testicles' would have been a bed of roses in comparison.

The seventeenth-century British clergyman and naturalist

Edward Topsell dedicated several pages of his celebrated bestiary, *The History of Four-Footed Beasts*, to
castoreum's pungent powers. 'These stones', he wrote, 'are
of a strong and stinking savour.' The secretions cured
everything from toothache (simply pour warmed castoreum in the relevant ear) to flatulence (don't ask). Their
chief use, however, was in the treatment of women's
gynaecological afflictions. This was hardly a surprise.
Ancient and medieval pharmacopoeia positively bulged
with phallic ingredients; gourds, horns and squirting
cucumbers were regularly prescribed for sexual complaints
(the tenet presumably being that all a sick woman needs
is a penis, so prescribing a suggestively shaped vegetable
should just do the trick). Beaver 'stones' nestled in quite
naturally with this phallocentric approach to women's
health.

Castoreum was said to overwhelm a woman's reproductive organs. The Romans burnt the oily brown secretions in
lamps to induce abortions, and Topsell noted that 'a perfume made with Castoreum, Asses dung, and Swines grease,
openeth a closed womb.' In fact such was the purported
abortive power of the beaver's imposturous balls that it was
widely believed that simply stepping over the animal,
whether alive or dead, would cause a pregnant woman to
lose her baby.

But by far the most popular prescription for castoreum
was as a tonic for hysteria, a fictitious feminine disorder
with a list of symptoms so long it would cater to any

*The beaver from Edward Topsell's* History of Four-Footed Beasts *(1607) looks rather taken aback. Perhaps because it is a female, shaved to expose not only her teats but also her 'stones', which Topsell tells were much sought after as a cure for everything from toothache to flatulence.*

hypochondriac, emotional outbursts, anxiety and general irritability being just a few. Hysteria – from the Greek word for the uterus – supposedly arose when a toxic womb wandered about the body, wreaking havoc on a woman's other organs. The nebulous nature of the 'sickness' made it a common, catch-all diagnosis for out-of-sorts ladies from Egyptian times onwards. In the seventeenth century, English physician Thomas Sydenham estimated that hysteria was the most common disease after fever, accounting for a sixth of all human maladies. Amongst women, he wrote, 'there is rarely one who is wholly free from it.'

Over the centuries numerous cures for hysteria were

suggested. Pelvic massage sounds almost pleasant; exorcism somewhat less so. Inhaling deeply on 'beaver balls' was the staple well into the nineteenth century, however. In 1847, the American physician John Eberle was still pushing the aquatic rodent's anal secretions as the ultimate antidote for hysterical ladies, in particular those with 'delicate and irritable habits'.

Waist deep in this book and feeling a tad hysterical myself, I decided to try and get my hands on the beaver's phoney gonads and take a sniff for myself. I wrote a series of surreal emails to hunters I found by searching online, politely introducing myself and then asking them to post me their beaver gland booty. None of them replied. So next I enlisted the help of a friend who knew her way around the 'dark web' and we spent a rainy Saturday afternoon cruising for castoreum. We failed to locate any. In the end I found a pair hanging out on eBay – a snip, quite literally, at $54.99. Beaver castor sacs, it transpired, are still in demand, not as a cure for hysteria, but as something even more bizarre.

For over eighty years the beaver's oily brown anal secretions have been used to add vanilla flavour to a variety of desserts, from fairy cakes to ice cream (ironically, just the sorts of food I typically use to self-medicate against feelings of hysteria). How this fact was first discovered boggles the mind, but castoreum is today listed by the US Food and Drug Administration as a GRAS – 'generally recognized as safe' – food additive. Fortunately for the beavers, it's not used that often. When it is, the manufacturers need only list it as 'natural vanilla flavour' since it is a 'natural' product, 'naturally' produced by the beaver's nether regions. Which may be enough to squash even the most ardent ice cream habit.

Castoreum also pops up as an essential ingredient in a number of classic perfumes, including Givenchy III and Shalimar. This is less shocking, as the perfume industry has had a longstanding love affair with exotic animal essences. Whale vomit (ambergris) and the genital gland secretions of civet cat and musk deer may sound unappealing but apparently they are the quintessence of allure.

'The idea of wearing perfumes is to send out a big open-for-business message,' scent expert Katie Puckrik explained. 'That's what smelling subtly like a critter's hindquarters does for you.' By this reasoning the scent reminds us of our oh-so-sexy, unwashed past. Animal secretions are also valuable for more technical purposes, acting as fixatives for the more volatile ingredients. 'They add a sexy "grrr" to the blend,' Katie told me, using the trade's jargon. ' "Skank" (as we fumeheads call it) provides the bridge between flowers and human skin. Without animalic notes in a perfume, you might as well be wearing air freshener.'

My beaver skank arrived a week later. As soon as I opened the Jiffy bag, it was immediately obvious how the legend of the self-castrating beaver had come to pass: out tumbled what looked like a pair of wizened brown testicles. Their smell was seriously intoxicating. Everything that came into contact with them was infused with a strange, woody, leathery odour – not unlike the intense smell of incense that overpowers your average crystal-waving New Age emporium. Edward Topsell claimed that you could spot fake castoreum by the strength of its smell; the genuine article when inhaled should 'draw blood out of his nose', he said. The odour emanating from mine was overpowering, but, thankfully, not nose-bleedingly so. It was not at all unpleasant – certainly not what I had expected from a set of glands loitering in such close proximity to an animal's refuse chute. But then, castor sacs' unusually fragrant nature can be traced to their even more unusual botanical contents.

There is an evolutionary arms race going on in the natural world, pitting the plants against the animals that like to eat them. To defend themselves, plants have grown into masters of chemical warfare with the ability to produce a wide spectrum of compounds that range from simply bitter-tasting to the downright deadly. Herbivores breach these defences by evolving ways to break down, detoxify or recycle these potentially harmful chemicals. In turn, plants up the ante by synthesizing yet more poisons. And so the battle goes on.

Beavers come from a long and successful line of aquatic rodents that have been chewing down trees for construction and feasting on their bark, roots and shoots for at least

23 million years. In that time, they've evolved an arsenal of tricks to deal with arboreal chemical weapons, the most inventive being to sequester the toxins and recycle them as their very own defence system. Castoreum contains a multitude of plant compounds: alkaloids, phenolics, terpenes, alcohols and acids, all of which the beaver appropriates from the plants it eats and uses to concoct its very own olfactory ID card. Beavers can recognize neighbours and family from the smell of this chemical fingerprint. They use their castoreum to warn off strangers by marking their territory with the very same chemical message they stole from the plants: bugger off!

Many of these chemicals are also quite useful to us humans. Castoreum's vanilla essence is down to the presence of catechol, an alcohol derived from common cottonwood that is used as a pesticide as well as a food flavouring – a rather unnerving combination of uses, but then many of the forty-five compounds decoded in castoreum have surprising qualities. Phenol from Scots pine has anaesthetic properties, benzoic acid from black cherry is used to treat fungal skin diseases and, most crucially, salicylic acid, from the beaver's favourite willow, is the active ingredient in aspirin.

So were ancient doctors correct in prescribing beaver 'pizzles' as medicine? Probably not. As far as we know, popping an aspirin is no help at all with combating 'the evils', or indeed any of the other illnesses, real or imaginary, that castoreum was alleged to cure. Even if castoreum was a wonder drug, the quantities given to patients were too small to really be effective. I emailed a beaver anal gland expert to ask how much I would need to consume to stifle a simple headache and his answer was 'A LOT'.

In the spirit of Thomas Browne, I decided to give it a go regardless. I waited for a suitably feverish moment and took a shy nibble of one of the sacs that had arrived in the post. It had a distinctly bitter taste that stuck in my mouth for some time, refusing to be dislodged by any amount of toothpaste and scrubbing. About an hour later I started to belch out potent leathery emissions. The smell seemed to spread to every pore of my skin and lingered far longer than I was comfortable with. I wound up in the surreal situation of having to meet Dame Shirley Bassey at a BBC recording that evening, overly conscious that I smelled like a beaver's bum.

I should have known better. An eighteenth-century Edinburgh surgeon called William Alexander had a similar experience (minus the Dame) during a self-administered trial of castoreum's efficacy. He started with a small nibble similar to mine and gradually increased the dosage until he reached 8 grams (seriously impressive). Over the week he observed no physiological effect other than 'a few disagreeable eructations' (just a few?). He concluded that the stinky panacea was 'ill deserving of a place in the current catalogue of medicines'.

There is one thing that a beaver's phoney gonads are good for, and that's catching other beavers. According to my

Swedish hunter Mikael, beavers are sufficiently territorial that if you smear the castoreum of one beaver on another beaver's muddy scent mound, the resident beaver will be compelled to overmark it with its own scent. All the hunter has to do is sit tight and wait for it. This brings a dark twist to the legendary tale of the beaver's cunning: it seems the beaver's 'pizzles', rather than rescuing them from an attacker, were in fact an intoxicating means of luring it towards the hunter's trap.

This was bad news for the beaver. Centuries of hysterical women had created a huge demand for castoreum. All across Europe beaver populations were being annihilated in order to harvest their smelly elixir. The last beavers in Britain and Italy were killed in the sixteenth century; elsewhere their numbers were in sharp decline. But just as beavers were disappearing from Europe, a whole new continent was discovered, brimming with beavers and heralding a new and even more far-fetched suite of beliefs concerning this amphibious beast.

'Let us hear no more of the half-reasoning elephant; he is but a ninny to the beaver of America,' wrote Frances Thurtle Jamieson in her *Popular Voyages and Travels Throughout the Continents and Islands of Asia, Africa and America*, published in 1820. That this humble rodent's intellect should be exalted to the level of the elephant, an animal whose brain is at least a hundred times heavier, is evidence that the early explorers of America lost their minds over the beaver's mental power. Influenced by the folkloric tales of Native Americans, and overly impressed by the architectural showmanship of the rodent, they sent home fantastic accounts of an animal Einstein that used its smarts to organize a sophisticated society replete with police, laws and a system of government which rivalled that of man.

Probably the first person to romanticize about the beaver in this way was Nicolas Denys, an aristocratic French explorer who sailed to the New World in 1632 and went on to become a prominent landowner and politician. He was also amongst the earliest Americans to detail the natural history of the continent. Of all the animals 'of which the industry has been most vaunted', he wrote, 'without excepting even the Ape with all that one can teach him', they are all just 'beasts' when compared to the beaver. As an aside he noted how surprising this was, since this lowly creature, in his opinion, 'passes for a fish'.

Exactly what kinds of ape or fish Denys had been acquainted with in the Old World are not known. But Denys described, with extraordinary specificity, his interpretation of four hundred New World beavers uniting as one to build a dam at the start of the summer. They were a highly skilled bunch that walked tall, used their teeth as saws and their tails as hods for carrying mortar or as trowels for plastering walls. There were beaver 'masons', beaver 'carpenters', beaver 'diggers' and beaver 'hod-carriers', each doing his duty 'without meddling with anything else'. Directing this army of skilled labour were a fleet of eight to ten beaver 'commanders' who took their instructions from a single overseeing beaver 'architect' whose vision dictated where and how to build the dam.

Such unionized industry sounds admirable, but Denys was also keen to point out that this was no bucolic beaver Arcadia. If any beaver was neglectful then his commander 'chastises them, beats them, throws himself on them, and bites them to keep them at their duty'. The French explorer gave his sincerest assurance of his credibility to those that might find this portrait of a veritable beaver gulag somewhat hard to swallow by adding, 'I would find it hard to believe myself had I not been an eye witness thereof.'

Perhaps Denys was in need of some new glasses, or he was simply limbering up his lying skills for his future role as a politician. Who knows – but he was by no means telling the truth. When I visited a beaver dam in Sweden with Mikael he laughed hard at Denys' description. Beavers aren't bees. They don't do mass cooperation; they are simply too territorial. Each dam is the property of one beaver family. They build it in order to raise the water level so they can construct a lodge with a permanent underwater entrance, which allows them to stay safely submerged during foraging missions while minimizing their exposure to predators. If another beaver family were to rock up and start helping out, the resident beavers would apparently 'go ballistic' (Mikael's words). Even the most impressive dams, which can measure nearly a kilometre long and twice the width of the Hoover Dam, are the work of just one family – at most six beavers at any one time – over the course of generations. And although they have been observed walking on hind legs, and carrying their young or twigs between their forepaws and chin, no one has ever seen a beaver using its tail as a builder's trowel.

Stories of the New World were eagerly gobbled up by the Europeans back home, and Denys' imaginative depiction of the industrious beaver did the seventeenth-century equivalent of going viral. Endlessly repeated by French colonial travel writers, it inspired a series of highly persuasive paintings that accompanied some of the iconic early maps. One shows fifty-two beavers snaking up a hill in an orderly line, carrying sticks in their arms and mud on their tails, to fashion a dam at the foot of Niagara Falls. It's a charming scene of upright industry until you look closely and read the accompanying legend expanding on the individual beavers' roles. These include 'beaver with a disabled tail from having worked too hard' and a menacing 'inspector of the disabled', to sniff out those beavers pulling a fraudulent sickie and force them back to work.

As the stories spread, beaver society became ever more fantastic in its organization. 'Beavers in distant solitudes build like architects and rule like citizens,' announced Oliver Goldsmith in his popular *History of the Earth and Animated Nature* (1774). The French Jesuit priest Pierre de Charlevoix described the beaver as 'a kind of reasonable animal, which had its laws, its government and its particular language'.

Beavers were said to always gather in odd numbers so that one beaver may have the casting vote on matters of beaver democracy. But the whiff of authoritarian discipline was never far away from this rodent republic. 'Justice is everything among beavers,' warned another French explorer named Dièreville. Those citizens that shirked their civic duties – 'the lazy or idle kind' – were 'expelled by the other Beavers . . . just as Wasps are by Bees' to become 'vagabonds'. According to the French Romantic François-René, vicomte de Chateaubriand (he of big, bony steak fame), such exiles were stripped of their fur and forced to live out their days in solitary degradation in a dirt hole in the ground, hence they were known as *terriers*, from the French *terre*, meaning 'earth'.

The beaver had once again found its life fictionalized and served up as moral guidance. But this time, somewhat perversely, the morals were tailored for a brand-new nation founded off the skin of the animal's own back. Beaver fur had become a valuable commodity, used for the broad-brimmed hats then most fashionable back in Europe. Hundreds of thousands of pelts were exported every year; the Hudson's Bay Company sold 54,760 at a single sale held in 1763. The beaver's skin even became an official unit of currency in the New World, exchangeable for a single 'Made Beaver' coin, which could buy you a pair of shoes, a kettle or eight knives at the local market. Beaver

*Nicolas de Fer's map of America (1698–1705) provides an imaginative tableau of beaver industry, complete with a handy legend to identify the rodent's roles in this new utopia. There is, however, nothing to envy about the beaver lying on his back with his legs in the air, identified as 'a beaver incapacitated by overwork'.*

fever drove the expansion of settlement into the western wilds of America. The beaver was effectively the colonialists' ideal alter ego, its life a parable for righteous living. The rodent's propensity for hard graft, its independence yet willingness to cooperate in order to create public works, appealed to the Puritan ethic. Much greatness could be achieved with a beaver chain gang for moral guidance. But woe betide those who abandoned civilized society and struck out alone to make a quick buck (another unit of currency based on animal skin).

In the Old World, naturalists rushed to interpret the Americans' beaver tales. With the near-eradication of its European cousins, beaver architectural wonders and societies were nowhere to be witnessed there. Nor had they apparently ever been. The ancient philosophers had spoken only of the animal's testicles, and thus it was assumed their extraordinary industry must be an exclusively New World trait. The French naturalist Georges-Louis Leclerc, Comte de Buffon, no stranger to outrageous thinking, took this as evidence of something even more profound. Buffon enrolled the beaver as the centrepiece of one of his more extravagant theories, proposing what glory animal societies might achieve if allowed to flourish far away from the corrupting influence of man.

'In proportion as man rises above a state of nature, the other animals sink below that standard: Reduced to slavery, or treated as rebels, and dispersed by force, their societies have vanished, their industry has become barren, their arts have disappeared' began Buffon's epic entry on the beaver from his eighteenth-century encyclopaedia. In Europe, where beavers had been subject to man's oppressions, 'their genius, withered by fear, never again expands,' pronounced the Comte. No wonder 'they lead a timid and a solitary life.' But in the wilds of the New World, where man was a stranger, Buffon believed that beaver society afforded 'perhaps, the only subsisting monument of the ancient intelligence of brutes'.

The Comte crafted his elaborate theory not just from traveller's tales, but from his first-hand experience of a beaver he'd been sent from Canada in 1758. This beaver lived under his watchful eye at the royal gardens in Paris for several years. After their first year of acquaintance, the French aristocrat was far from impressed by his pet. The beaver was prone to 'melancholy', its 'efforts feeble'. Although it spent much time gnawing on 'the gates of its prison' (and who can blame it), it lacked any impetus to start construction. The bitterly disappointed Comte was under the impression that New World beavers were capable of creating elaborate homes, big enough for up to thirty inhabitants and consisting of several floors with windows and even 'a balcony to receive the fresh air, and to bathe'. All his beaver had done was mope around and occasionally bust loose to take a swim in the subterranean vaults of the gardens.

The Comte also became transfixed by the semiaquatic nature of the beaver, which he believed was in the habit of keeping its 'tail and posterior parts' continually in the water. This inspired a bonus bogus theory from Buffon that beavers had 'changed the nature of their flesh' to that of a 'fish', complete with the associated taste, odour and covering of scales. This mishmash of body parts only served to further lower the creature in the Comte's estimations to some kind of 'link between quadrupeds and fishes'. Such a lowly, lumbering beast would have amounted to little more than an anatomical anomaly were it not for the stories of the astonishing power of beaver community, which, in Buffon's eyes, remained untainted by man and offered hope of a Utopia we humans could only dream of:

> In this society, however numerous, a universal peace is maintained. Their union is cemented by common labours; and it is rendered perpetual by mutual convenience, and the abundance of provisions which they amass and consume together. Moderate appetites, a simple taste, an aversion against blood and carnage, deprive them of the idea of rapine and war. They enjoy every possible good, while man only knows how to pant after it.

The rather unromantic truth is that solitary beavers build perfectly well. If Buffon had wanted his beaver to show off its skills all he needed to do was place it near the sound of running water in order to trigger its industry. The urge to stop the flow is so deeply ingrained that even a tape recording of a babbling brook will encourage a beaver to start blindly heaping sticks on top of a loud speaker, despite being nowhere near any actual water.

This astonishing finding was rumbled by the Swedish zoologist Lars Wilsson, who spent most of the 1960s basically playing practical jokes on beavers in the name of science. He raised a number of kits away from their parents in a manmade environment in order to figure out whether their dam-building skills were instinctive or learned. By hiding a speaker behind a wall in their enclosure he discovered the eager beavers needed only the vaguest audio stimulus to build. He didn't even have to play the sound of running water; anything similar did the trick. Even the whir of an electric razor would incite a fury of twig-shoving against the wall by the beavers in a futile attempt to stop the flow.

Such mechanistic behaviour makes Buffon's idea of republic-founding beavers look decidedly foolish. But Wilsson's experiment would have made another French scientist, Frédéric Cuvier – younger brother of the famous zoologist Georges – nod sagely, and perhaps even mutter an imperious, 'I told you so.' In 1804, Cuvier became head keeper of the very same Paris menagerie where Buffon had observed his melancholic beaver a few decades before. Cuvier's observations were, however, very different to the Comte's. His new beavers were full of beans and, despite having no parental guidance, busily built away, urged on, in his opinion, by the blind force of instinct.

Cuvier was a follower of yet another famous French scientist, René Descartes, who in the seventeenth century had argued that animals were nothing more than automatons, and only humans were capable of operating with reason. Such unsentimental thinking was now all the rage, a knee-jerk reaction to the overt anthropomorphism of the bestiaries and their ilk. Cuvier held that intelligence gradually increased from rodents to ruminants, through pachyderms and carnivores, until one ascended to the lofty pinnacle of the animal kingdom to marvel at the brains of primates, and most especially humans like himself. As a result, Cuvier denied his beavers – mere rodents – any glimmer of ingenuity. But a school of tool-wielding octopi, problem-solving pigeons, counting crows and communicative parrots, all revealed in the last decade or so, could have told Cuvier – quite literally in the case of the verbose grey parrot – that his view of animal intelligence wasn't entirely reasonable.

I spoke to Dr Dietland Müller-Schwarze, a world expert on the beaver, to try to get to the bottom of the animal's brainpower. Talking to me on the phone from his New York State home (in a dry German drawl reminiscent of the film director Werner Herzog), the professor explained to me that we still have much to learn.

Müller-Schwarze told me he believed the beaver's extraordinary feats of engineering are mostly achieved instinctively, guided by a set of simple rules, like 'build where you hear running water', which we are only just beginning to decode. He gave me one particularly interesting example to chew on. Beavers are often credited with great foresight when it comes to felling trees to ensure they fall towards the water and without becoming entangled in the rest of the forest. 'But all the beaver has to do is just make a notch in the tree and let it fall randomly,' said Müller-Schwarze. 'The chances are that it will fall in the direction of the open water because the tree grows towards the light, so there will be more branches, and it will be heavier, on that side. It will fall there anyway.'

Instinct isn't perfect. The British tabloid press recently

featured a photo of a rather unfortunate beaver in Norway flattened to the ground by a tree it had just felled, with the caption: 'Wood You Believe It?' This demonstrates not only our species' endless capacity for *schadenfreude*, but also the fact that beavers don't always get it right. On most occasions, however, their mistakes are relatively innocuous and provide a means for learning and adapting their behaviour. They have been observed to do both with great resourcefulness, especially when creating and mending their dams. Their capacity to learn, and the complexity of their life skills, may be why beaver kits spend such a relatively long time – over a year – in the shadow of their parents.

One of the beaver's greatest cognitive champions in recent years was another French scientist, P. B. Richard. When Richard tested the aquatic rodents with a puzzle box – a classic animal intelligence test – he discovered that they had the magic mix of nimble minds and fingers in combination with the required amount of perseverance to master the complicated latches and solve the challenge with ease.

The beaver's powers of learning and innovation have been duly noted by the many humans who have found themselves locked in cerebral combat with these enthusiastic architects when attempting to control their urge to build. One scientist studying beavers in a small pond tried to prevent his subjects from chewing down his pretty ornamental trees by erecting tall walls of chicken wire. He sank the base deep into the ground and tied the top to the branches with confidence. It didn't take long before one of

*Timber! This beaver's bad day at work is an unfortunate reminder that, no matter how smart you are, not all mistakes can be learned from.*

the adult beavers outsmarted his inquisitor by building a ramp out of mud and sticks, sauntering up and over the chicken wire and swiftly severing the tree trunk. Night after night, the other beavers followed in their leader's ingenious footsteps until all the shade in the park was gone.

Storm drains and culverts are a favourite vandalism target for delinquent urban beavers, whose maddening problem-solving skills cost the US authorities billions of dollars every year.

However, the cognitive case for the beaver remains controversial. Intelligence is always tricky to assess, but especially so in an animal that is not only nocturnal but spends most of its life underwater or hidden inside an impenetrable lodge. The beaver's physical attributes are far easier to appreciate. Millions of years of evolution have equipped this aquatic architect with the perfect tools for its job: ever-growing, self-sharpening teeth, transparent eyelids that act as swimming goggles, ears and nostrils that shut automatically underwater, and lips that can close *behind* their front teeth (allowing for the beaver to gnaw wood underwater without drowning and keep out irritating splinters when felling trees). Its brain must be similarly well-tuned; it's just harder to peek inside the cognitive toolbox.

What we know of the beaver's behaviour raises fascinating questions about the boundaries between instinct and learned behaviour and about a rodent's capacity for reason. The beaver may not be prescient enough to chew off its own testicles to save its life or capable of establishing a democratic republic, but even the most conservative ethologist would probably agree with the carefully chosen words of the great animal behaviourist Donald Griffin, who said: 'the beaver thinks consciously in simple terms about its situation, and how its behaviour may produce desired changes in its environment.'

That's a far cry from Descartes's clockwork creatures.

I'd like to end with one final beaver tale, a story that perhaps calls into question the intelligence of our own species.

By the twentieth century humans had managed to virtually eradicate the beaver throughout most of its range. Across Europe and Asia populations had fallen to less than 1,200 individuals, who were holding on in just eight small territorial pockets. American beavers were flown in to bolster their numbers and help save the Eurasian beaver.

These introductions were wildly successful, and the new beavers thrived. But then it emerged that American and European beavers are in fact two separate species. They look identical but the American beaver is more aggressive than its European cousin. The Yankee beaver's bullying behaviour was having the unfortunate effect of driving the Eurasian beaver even closer to extinction, so it was swiftly declared an invasive species that had to be expunged. But how could government officials, environmentalists and hunters tell them apart? The two species were almost impossible to distinguish without counting their chromosomes.

Then in 1999, a pair of scientists from Central Washington University proposed a 'quick and easy' way to identify the two beaver species by colour-coding castoreum, which varies in tone between the two species. They even developed a handy identification legend for use in the field (bearing an uncanny resemblance to a Farrow & Ball colour chart for their most fashionable forest greens and musty yellows house paints).

So in a final twist, the beaver's 'testicles' could save them from the hunter's gun, but only if they were first 'milked' and their contents carefully colour-coded to reveal if they were the right kind of beaver to kill – an ending perhaps even more absurd than the original beaver legend.

And thus from one of the animal kingdom's most respected members, praised high and low for its industrious life, we now turn to the opposite extreme – a creature eternally damned for being lazy. In the next chapter we will meet the sloth, the founding member of my misjudged menagerie, and discover what makes the world's most laid-back mammal such an enduring success.

## CHAPTER 3

# SLOTH

### Suborder Folivora

*The degraded species of sloths are perhaps the only*
*creatures to which nature has been unkind.*

Comte de Buffon, *Histoire Naturelle*, 1749

People say, what's in a name? Well, quite a lot when it is a synonym for a deadly sin.

The poor old sloth was damned from the moment it was branded with one of the world's most wicked transgressions – a pretty damaging public relations blow by anyone's standard. But even before the sloth acquired its infamous tag, its inscrutable nature inspired some of the harshest words ever heaped upon an animal. This was an especially low blow for an animal that is not exactly bothering mankind, but is a quiet vegetarian pacifist – the original tree-hugger, no less – simply trying to live a tranquil life in the forests of Central and South America.

Chief amongst the sloth's earliest antagonists was the Spanish knight Gonzalo Fernández de Oviedo y Valdés, who spent several years exploring the New World and then many more documenting his discoveries in a sprawling, fifty-volume encyclopaedia which he published in 1526. The science of natural history was still at the stage where fact was firmly entwined with religion and myth, but Oviedo's main concerns in his tour of the animal kingdom seem to have been steered by his stomach.

The tapir, he said, was 'good to eat', adding with rather unconvincing gastronomic flourish, 'and the feet delicious when boiled for twenty-four hours'. The sloth found less favour, or perhaps flavour, with him, as he described it as 'the stupidest animal that can be found in the world'. A man not known for mincing his words (or telling the truth, for that matter), he elaborated by exaggerating the sloth's lacka-daisical nature: 'so awkward and slow in movement that it would require a whole day to go fifty paces.' He ominously appended this by noting, 'neither by threat, blow nor prod-ding does he move any faster than he is accustomed without tiring.'

Oviedo's lethargic lie passed like Chinese whispers through numerous travellers' tales. By the time the great buccaneer and wordsmith William Dampier came to write about the sloth in 1676, its pace had slowed to a virtual standstill. 'It takes them up to eight or nine minutes to move three inches forward,' he wrote with imaginative precision. 'Neither stripes make them mend their pace; which I have tried by whipping them; but they seem insensible, and can neither be frighted or provoked to move faster.' Dampier and Oviedo were quite the pair.

I've spent many happy hours watching sloths and can confirm they are mesmerizingly slow, moving as if they are in, or perhaps on, glue. Their average cruising speed is a leisurely 0.3 kilometres per hour, which is unlikely to challenge even a tortoise, but still not nearly as slow as Oviedo or Dampier suggested. I've seen a sloth book it up a tree at a surprising lick, given the right motivation. But they are physically incapable of going faster than a top speed of 1.5 kilometres per hour, since their muscles are engineered to be sluggish – up to fifteen times slower than those of an equivalent-sized mammal like a domestic cat.

To see them in the trees is akin to watching *Swan Lake* in slow motion; they pirouette, sway and dangle with the grace and control of a tai chi master. But if you turn the sloth the 'right' way up, gravity removes their dignity. Their limbs sprawl on the ground and they are forced to drag themselves forward by the hooks on their arms, as if mountaineering on a flat surface. This laborious form of locomotion was the main reason why those early natural-ists had such a miserable opinion of the sloth – they were observing the animal the wrong way up.

'They are quadrupeds', Oviedo proclaimed in a rare moment of scientific-sounding prose, 'and on each small foot they have four long claws webbed together like those of a bird.' For the record, there is no such thing as a four-toed sloth, let alone one sporting webbed claws, but let's not have such technicalities deter us from hearing out the bold knight's end. 'But neither the claws nor the feet will support the ani-mal. The legs are so small and the body so heavy, that the animal almost drags its belly on the ground.'

Sloths are indeed quadrupeds – the world's only *inverted* quadrupeds. They have evolved to hook on and

*The Spanish conquistador Oviedo was quick to condemn the sloths he found in South America. I'd like to have a word about his drawing skills. I have seen some dodgy illustrations of sloths in my time, but this effort, scrawled amongst the pages of his sixteenth-century encyclopedia, is, to borrow his own words, 'the stupidest that can be found in the world'.*

hang from trees as the animal incarnate of a hairy hammock. As a result, they have almost dispensed with the need for weight-bearing extensor muscles, like our triceps, which stiffen and protract the limbs. Instead they manage almost exclusively with retractor muscles, like our biceps, that pull them along branches. This unusual arrangement demands about half the muscle mass needed to prop up an upright existence, and means sloths can hang out for long periods whilst expending hardly any energy. It also affords them surprising strength and agility. They can clasp a vertical trunk with only their hind limbs. They can also lean over backwards 90 degrees with freed forelimbs – a trick that, as one sloth researcher pointed out, would, in humans, be 'exceptional enough to be shown in a circus'.

Oviedo probably never saw sloths in the trees. Instead, local indigenous people probably would have collected specimens and brought them to a village for the Spanish knight's inspection. In this completely unnatural situation, the sloths would have been observed crawling pitifully along the ground, like a dying man just short of a watering hole. Which is presumably why Oviedo concluded: 'I have never seen such an ugly animal or one that is more useless.'

These were pretty savage words, but at least at this stage in the sloth's story, the creature had less cursed, if rather more sarcastic, names. The Spanish liked to refer to it mockingly as *perico ligero*, meaning 'swift so-and-so'. Others, like British cleric Edward Topsell in his seventeenth-century animal guide, referred to 'this very deformed beast' as the 'Ape Bear'.

The Christian church had already begun peddling the concept of 'seven deadly sins' – a set of spiritually fatal vices designed to keep the community in check – but sloth, or spiritual and physical laziness, had yet to hit the charts. Then finally, in the seventeenth century, after years of arguing, the holy powers-that-be decided on its definitive seven. Sloth snuggled in at number four, providing Catholic explorers with the inspiration for a catchy new alias for this alien creature. And once they began associating the sloth with sin, all bets were off in terms of a sympathetic understanding of the animal's eccentric biology.

The ensuing tidal wave of abuse reached its grandiloquent peak with none other than the French aristocrat Georges-Louis Leclerc, Comte de Buffon. He pulled no punches when providing the first scientific description of the sloth in his encyclopaedia, *Histoire Naturelle*. 'As Nature is lively, active, and exalted in the ape species, she is slow, constrained, and cramped in the sloths,' he sneered. 'Slowness, stupidity, and even habitual pain, result from its uncouth conformation.' The sloth, in the Comte's opinion, was the lowest form of animal existence: 'One more defect and they could not have existed.'

Buffon was writing a hundred years before Darwin's *On the Origin of Species* rocked the world with its radical idea of natural selection. Nevertheless, the Comte is considered to be a forerunner of Darwin, and credited by many, including the eminent evolutionary biologist Ernst Mayr, with ushering the concept of evolution into scientific thinking. The abominable sloth, Buffon presumed, had somehow escaped the positive forces that had shaped all other animals towards their singular form of perfection: 'All these circumstances announce their wretchedness, and call to our mind those imperfect sketches of Nature, which, having scarcely the power to exist, only remained a short time in the world, and then were effaced from the list of beings.'

Buffon was the most respected naturalist of his time,

and his encyclopaedia an international bestseller. The die had been cast. The sloth's destiny as an aberration of evolution was set.

It is no secret that I have a soft spot for sloths. I find their freaky lifestyle utterly fascinating. But as founder of the Sloth Appreciation Society I am frequently asked to explain how such an apparently flawed creature could have survived the rigours of natural selection, which ruthlessly weeds out the weak. This is when I gather my poise and explain that sloths are not a defective remnant; they are a group of animals in reasonable vigour, with six living species in two genera, albeit with deeply disparaging names: *Choloepus* (meaning 'crippled') sloths and *Bradypus* ('slow-footed') sloths.

The cripples and the slow-foots are actually as genetically different as cats and dogs, having diverged from each other on separate branches of the evolutionary tree some 30 to 40 million years ago. Yet they continue to share the same topsy-turvy, slow-motion life. Such an adaptation must have its benefits if it was worth evolving *twice*.

The *Choloepus* are more commonly known as the two-toed sloths. Which is something of a misnomer, since they actually have three toes, but only two fingers. They look like a cross between a Wookiee and a pig, turned upside down and with hooks for hands. Their long, shaggy fur ranges from blonde to brunette but, whatever their

SLOTH

colour and despite their cuddly appearance, they are surprisingly bad-tempered. Solitary by nature, they object to
being petted, and if approached by something unfamiliar,
like a hand, they will hiss with mouth open to expose a
pair of quite terrifying-looking teeth. Along with their
hooked hands, their dirty great fangs could inflict a nasty
wound – if their slow-mo swipes weren't so easy to dodge.

The various *Bradypus*, or three-toed, sloths have both
three fingers and three toes. They sport medieval haircuts
and immovable smiles (even when enraged). They are
slightly smaller than their two-fingered cousin – about the
size of a domestic cat under their shaggy, mottled grey and
brown fur – and less cranky but significantly more cryptic.
Of the four species, the largest of the bunch is the marvel-
lously maned *Bradypus torquatus*, which looks uncannily
like a coconut with a mullet. The smallest, and perhaps
most peculiar, are the pint-sized pygmy sloths, *Bradypus
pygmaeus*; they are less than half the size of other *Bradypus*
and only found in the mangrove swamps of a single island
off the coast of Panama. These dwarf sloths have few natural predators and thus the fabulous luxury of spending
their time grazing on leaves that are believed to contain
alkaloids with a property similar to Valium. So they don't
just look stoned, they are stoned – making them something of an evolutionary cul-de-sac if ever there was one.

All sloths are members of the Xenarthra – an ancient
superorder of mammals that sound like they're straight out
of *Star Trek*, and have the sci-fi looks to match. This

wonderfully eclectic group includes some of the planet's most otherworldly-looking oddballs: the armadillos, anteaters and, of course, the sloths. On the surface, this kooky band of modern-day misfits appear to have little in common. But closer inspection reveals they all share tiny brains, a distinct lack of teeth and no external testicles. Fortunately, in this instance, they were named not after these rather unflattering features, but after their other unifying feature – an unusually flexible spine (*Xenarthra* means 'strange joints').

This strange superorder owe their oddness to the fact they evolved in isolation from a common relative back when South America was still an island, just after it had torn itself off Africa, some 80 million years ago. Over millennia early sloths flourished in this primeval, forested land, diversifying into over one hundred species, each filling a unique niche. There were giant aquatic sloths that lounged around on beaches (much like a very different form of modern sloth – the human tourist) and grazed on sea algae (not quite so human-like); giant burrowing sloths that excavated underground tunnels some 2 metres wide; and the most successful of the bunch, the giant ground sloths – the largest of which, *Megatherium*, was the size of an elephant.

Around ten thousand years ago these jumbo sloths all disappeared, leaving behind only the handful of diminutive arboreal cousins that we know today. What wiped out these giant vegetarians has long puzzled palaeontologists, who have rifled through caves full of bones and fossilized sloth dung in search of clues.

For a while, the consensus was that the last ice age had finished them off. But no; the awkward answer is that we probably ate them. After South America finally collided with North America some 3 million years ago and the land bridge was formed between the two continents, some ground sloths ambled north to colonize these inviting new lands. Surging south and carrying spears were scores of hungry humans, smacking their lips at the size of these lumbering lumps of meat. Having survived for many millennia with no natural predators, these defenceless giants ended up on the barbecue.

The other possibility is that they succumbed to our diseases once the land masses converged. Either way, we are likely to blame. And it makes sense that the only sloths to survive did so by being small enough to hide in the tops of the trees.

For those, like me, who mourn the loss of these majestic beasts there is a chink of hope. Amazon tribal folklore tells of a monstrous creature known as *mapinguari* – taller than a man, with thick matted fur and a fetid odour, it stalks the deepest corners of the jungle.

Could this legend betray a lost clique of giant ground sloths roaming the remotest corners of the Amazon? I like to think so.

As a group the sloths have haunted the planet in one shape or another for around 64 million years, managing to outlive both the sabre tooth tiger and the woolly mammoth with their stratagem of stealthy living. Of the half dozen species alive today, only the pygmy and maned sloths are considered endangered. That's pretty good going for a lazy loser, and significantly better than other, flashier mammals of comparable size, like the ocelot and the spider monkey. In fact, one scientific survey from the 1970s found that sloths 'are the most numerically abundant large mammal', accounting for almost a quarter of the mammalian biomass – which is a sophisticated biological way of saying you can take your patronizing looks and direct them at some other animal.

'They are survivors,' British sloth scientist Becky Cliffe asserted to me. And the very secret to their survival is their slothful nature.

I met Becky whilst making a documentary about a sloth sanctuary in Costa Rica at which she was working. Sloths may be survivors but they don't get on very well with the roads and power lines that now crisscross their jungle home. Injured adults and orphaned babies are brought to this sanctuary, where they are cared for by self-styled sloth whisperer Judy Avey-Arroyo, who had some rather unorthodox ideas on how to care for wild animals. These included dressing sick babies in bespoke pyjamas crafted out of sports socks and keeping a pet sloth called Buttercup (which she referred to as her 'daughter') in a wicker hanging chair. It was Becky's job to add some scientific research to all the worthy sentimentality.

*The inverted existence of sloths has no need for protractor muscles to hold their limbs erect, so when they are turned the other way up, gravity removes their dignity. Which is why this sloth crossing the road in Costa Rica looks as if it has already been flattened by a car.*

'It's almost as if people don't want to know the truth about sloths. There's something charming about thinking of them as lazy and stupid,' Becky said. 'As scientists, it's a bit frustrating that's how the sloth has always been portrayed, because we know it's not true.'

Becky is determined to debunk the many myths that surround the sloth with sound science and experimental observation. She believes the key to understanding the sloth's slothfulness is to start with its stomach.

The conquistador Oviedo may have thought that sloths 'live off air', but the truth is they dine almost exclusively on leaves, many of which have evolved to be tough and often quite toxic in order to avoid being eaten. In the battle between folivore and foliage, the sloth's secret weapon is its massive Buddha-like belly, a multi-chambered monster much like the one found in cows. But sloths are not ruminants and do not chew the cud (regurgitating food whilst hanging upside-down from a tree would be challenging, to say the least). Chewing is also not a sloth speciality, as three-toed sloths lack front teeth and the ones in the back of their mouth are little more than pegs. Thus sloth stomachs receive barely masticated leaves, which can only be broken down with the help of friendly gut bacteria – a process that needs rather a lot of time.

The precise length of this digesting marathon was investigated by an American scientist by the name of Gene Montgomery in the 1970s. Montgomery took it upon himself to feed a sloth something it could never digest, namely glass beads, and timed the length of their passage through the alimentary canal until they once again saw daylight. Montgomery waited. And waited. And waited. Just as he thought he had truly lost his marbles, the glass poops arrived, a full fifty days after their journey began.

When Becky repeated Montgomery's study she chose to use red food dye rather than glass beads. She feared the beads may have skewed the results by becoming lodged in the sloth's system, thereby 'lengthening the retention time' (no shit!). Nevertheless, she basically replicated Montgomery's results, finding that sloths have amongst the slowest digestion rate of any mammal.

'For the majority of mammals, digestion rate scales with body size, so larger animals should take longer to digest their food. Sloths appear to break this rule quite spectacularly,' Becky explained to me. She thinks it takes the sloth stomach, on average, over two weeks to slowly break down the cellulose and toxins of a leaf. If it happened any faster, their liver might not cope, and the sloths would be in danger of poisoning themselves. The leaves that make up the bulk of their diet deliver little calorific value – about 160 calories – the equivalent of a packet of crisps a day. So the sloth has evolved to spend as little energy as possible. They are nature's couch potatoes, hanging out in the trees, slowly digesting leaves and assiduously avoiding unnecessary exertion.

Sloth bodies have an assortment of nifty modifications to enable their energy-saving, inverted existence. Their blood vessels and throat are uniquely adjusted to swallow food and circulate blood against the force of gravity. Their fur grows in the opposite direction to the norm, with a parting down the middle of their tummy so that rain can run off easily; after a tropical drenching they simply hang out and drip dry. Becky recently discovered that they even have sticky bits on their ribs to keep their stomach, which can be tasked with holding up to a third of a sloth's body weight in slowly digesting leaves, from crushing their lungs.

Sloths also maintain a freakishly low metabolism, around half that expected for a mammal their size, and a low core temperature of just 28 to 35 degrees Celsius, whereas most mammals rely on a constantly toasty 36-degree internal environment. Rather than keeping themselves warm by stoking their internal combustion engine with calories, sloths wear a thick coat, worthy of an Arctic animal, whilst inhabiting the warm tropics. Energy from the sun is free, unlike energy from toxic leaves, and sloths take advantage of it by hanging out at the treetops, basking like lizards to soak it up. And like cold-blooded animals, they are able to withstand fluctuations in their body temperature of several degrees throughout the day. 'They are very economical animals and they make the most of every single thing they have available to them,' Becky said. 'If they have to and they are pushed to the extremes, then they are more than capable of pushing through and using alternative ways. Like their metabolic rate – it looks like they can raise their metabolic rate and heat themselves . . . if they absolutely have to. But most of the time they don't need to.'

It has long been asserted that sloths completely lack the ability to control their body temperature, which helped contribute to the idea they were somehow less evolved than other warm-blooded mammals. But then, the sloth is subject to more scientific rumour than almost any other animal, much of it based on crude studies and hearsay from the first half of the twentieth century. Becky has refined the research on sloths by incorporating modern techniques and equipment. To study sloth metabolism, for example, she used a custom metabolic chamber and a 'bum-o-meter', which she 'lubed up' and inserted into an accommodating sloth as part of her experiments. (The extraction of a sloth's secrets may not always be dignified.)

'Every time I get a new piece of data it just shows me more and more that sloths are not as incapable of surviving as we think they are,' she said righteously. 'I mean, they've been around for 64 million years ... If they were completely incapable of raising their own body temperature they'd have died out a long time ago.'

Becky suspects the sloth's low metabolism could be the cause of the ultimate sloth survival superpower: its seeming ability to cheat death, another longstanding rumour about the sloth, but one which might have a bit of truth to it.

The sloth's ability to cling to life has been the subject of much speculation over the centuries. Back in 1828, a British naturalist called Charles Waterton noted the trait. 'Of all animals, this poor ill-formed creature is most tenacious to life,' he wrote. 'It exists long after it has received wounds which would have destroyed any other animal.' There have been reports of sloths falling 30 metres to the forest floor without injury, of surviving 40 minutes immersed underwater and of lasting 24 hours in a fridge. One sloth was even said to have lived for 30 hours following decerebration, a genuinely mind-boggling claim.

Das Faulthier oder der Ai.

Tab. C.

G. Edwards ad viv. delin.  J. N. Seligmann excudit.  Joh. Sebastian Leitner sculps.
Cum Priv. S. Rae. Cae. Majestatis.
Ignavus.  N.º 100. VIII.ter Theil.  Le Paresseux.

*The illustrators of the early natural history books churned out some fantastically bad drawings of sloths, which were often quite human-like in appearance. This one from the 1770s by George Edwards and Mark Catesby has more than a touch of hippie about it (apart from the terrifying Freddy Krueger claws).*

Many of these stories were certainly exaggerated, but Becky agreed that sloths are extraordinarily tough. Over the years, the team at the sloth sanctuary in Costa Rica had seen animals make near-miraculous recoveries, whether they'd been zapped by power lines, attacked by dogs or hit by cars.

'Why and how they are capable of bouncing back after horrible injuries is still a bit of a mystery,' she told me. A conversation with Professor Enrique Amaya of the University of Manchester, who specializes in gene expression and limb regeneration in gecko lizards, provided her with a fascinating lead. 'When a gecko needs to regrow its tail, it enters what he calls an "embryonic state" – basically it lowers its metabolic rate in order to put all of its energy into healing.' She suspected that the sloth's low metabolic rate might work in a similar fashion, but so far she hasn't been able to back up her hypothesis with experimental evidence.

Others have speculated that the sloth's slow metabolism might protect it from cancer, or aid evolution by allowing birth defects to persist and develop into beneficial new structures – including features like its unusually long neck, which has more vertebrae than any other mammal's, even the giraffe's. The long neck allows nature's couch potato to turn its head 270 degrees and graze leaves all around it without wasting precious energy moving the rest of its body. It appears to have evolved from extra rib cage bones, which were co-opted into neck vertebrae – the kind of large-scale deformity that's normally wiped out by a mammal's immune system but which survived in the sloth as an adaptation.

The sloth's metabolism is verifiably slow, but that doesn't mean it's sleeping all the time. Although it was long reported that the so-called world's laziest animal spent around twenty hours a day snoozing, a recent study found that sloths in the wild actually sleep less than half that amount, an average of 9.6 hours a day.

'Just because they are not moving doesn't mean they are asleep,' Becky told me with the authority of someone who has spent a lot of time living alongside sloths. '*Brady-pus* in particular don't sleep like other animals do, for nine or ten hours at a time.' The majority of their day (and night) is spent quietly hanging in the trees in a seemingly meditative state, motionless, with their eyes open and staring blankly into space. This wakeful but inactive state is crucial for energy conservation, and their ultimate survival.

So far, so Zen. But how does a compulsively napping, virtually immobile bag of fermenting leaves avoid getting itself eaten?

The sloth's main predator is the harpy eagle, an animal so terrifying it is named after the wind spirits of ancient Greek mythology who carried the dead to Hades. The harpy is one of the world's biggest and fastest raptors, with talons the size of grizzly bear claws and a 2-metre wingspan. It can fly at speeds of up to 130 kilometres per hour. It boasts razor-sharp eyesight and a ring of feathers around its face that focus sounds so that it can detect the slightest rustle of a leaf.

The sloth doesn't seem like much of a match for this apex predator. With its poorly developed ears and eyes it lives its life in a muffled blur. These severely blunted senses are unlikely to provide advance warning of a savage, winged assailant. And with its top speed of less than 1.5 kilometres per hour, running from danger is clearly not an option.

Sloths' apparent lack of defence was one of the Comte de Buffon's big beefs with the species. 'Sloths have no weapons either offensive or defensive. They have no cutting teeth, the eyes are obscured with hair,' he wrote, punctuating his assessment with the acerbic observation that the hair itself 'resembles withered herbs'. Perhaps if Buffon had studied living sloths in their jungle home, as opposed to inspecting a set of long-dead skins in a museum, then he might have been more charitable about their coiffure.

The sloth, you see, is a master of illusion, capable of disappearing into the rainforest behind a cloak of invisibility. Its coat is a miniature ecosystem that rivals Edward Lear's old man with a beard. Special grooves in the fur collect water and act as hydroponic gardens for eighty different species of algae and fungi. This gives the sloth a greenish hue. It also supports a wealth of insects. One study found a single sloth playing host to nine species of moth, six species of tick, seven species of mite and four species of beetle – including 980 individuals from just one of those beetle species. (For the nit-picking scientists out there, three of those mite species were, strictly speaking, anus-dwellers, but let's not split hairs.)

Crawling with bugs and looking as if they have been dragged through a hedge backwards isn't going to win the sloth any beauty contests. But it means they look and smell exactly like a tree. And most of the time they are as motionless as one too. When they do move they don't crash about like monkeys; their arboreal ballet is as silent as the gentlest breeze and so slow it is thought to slip under the radar of the monstrous harpy as it swoops above the canopy, scanning for any movement.

The first person to appreciate the sloth's stealthy strategy for survival was the American naturalist William Beebe, an advocate of studying animals in their native habitats who is widely considered to be the father of field ecology. Beebe devoted most of his life to a series of increasingly dangerous expeditions. He circumnavigated the globe to document the world's pheasants – a study which briefly cost him his sanity and more permanently his marriage. He also probed the depths of the ocean more than thirty-five times in a precarious-looking metal eyeball he called the Bathysphere, becoming the first human to dive to depths beyond 5,000 metres. He was still shinning up tropical trees to look at bird's nests well into his eighties.

Beebe spent much of the 1920s observing sloths in the wilds of Guiana, an experience that led him to consider rather than condemn the curiosities of this creature. He ridiculed the Comte de Buffon for his antiquated, narrow-minded views. 'A sloth in Paris', wrote Beebe, 'would doubtless fulfill the prophecy of the French scientist, but on the other hand, Buffon clinging upside down to a branch of a tree in the jungle would expire even sooner.'

Many of Beebe's findings are still quoted today, even if some of his methods were a little, shall we say, *alternative*. He was, for instance, amongst the first to report that sloths can swim, something he discovered after repeatedly chucking one in a river.

'One of the most remarkable phases of the sloth's history', he wrote, 'is the readiness with which they take to water'. Especially if being hurled in by a human hand. But Beebe was right, sloths are great swimmers. Their unique digestive system produces a surfeit of gas, and evolution – God love it – has found a suitably resourceful use for this excess of trapped wind. It acts as a built-in, biological buoy. Sloths can actually bob along three times faster in water than they can move on land, using their long arms to do a half-decent doggy-paddle. According to one scientist, if you flip them over, they can even do a passable backstroke.

When Beebe wasn't throwing sloths into the water, he was shooting at them. 'I have fired a gun close to a slumbering sloth and to one feeding and aroused but little

*Here we see the father of field biology, William Beebe, limbering up to hurl one of his sloth study subjects into the river in order to check out its backstroke.*

attention.' From which he concluded that sloths are not so much deaf but show a 'general disinterest in the noise'. They didn't even react to the sound of a predator such as a nearby crying hawk: 'neither sight nor sound penetrated the dull aura of mental opacity which invests the senses of these mammals'.

I know this from my own experience. I have experimented not with a gun, but by shouting 'Boo!' at a sloth. The only response, if any (yes, I did it more than once), was a much delayed and distinctly dreamy turn of the head. The fact that it is impossible to startle these masters of mellow could be yet another cunning camouflage tactic. Jumping out of your skin every time you see a harpy eagle is an impractical reflex response for a creature wishing to stay concealed.

Sloths are largely solitary characters, so their apparent deafness may also be down to the fact that they have dispensed with virtually all forms of vocal communication except one: female *Bradypus* will scream for sex. A lusty female sloth will climb to the top of a tree and let out an ear-piercing shriek that travels several kilometres to advertise her window of fertility. We have Beebe to thank for the precise note of this yodel – D-sharp. No other note, not even D-flat, had an effect on the males. 'They are attuned to this sound and only this sound. I gave a C and E, then upper B with no result whatsoever. Again I whistled D-sharp and the reaction was as instantaneous as a sloth can achieve.' This shrill whistle, noted Beebe, perfectly mimics that of a kiskadee flycatcher – another sneaky sloth adaptation for remaining hidden, even when a female is broadcasting her location at the top of her lungs.

Beebe may have heard their love songs, but he never saw sloths mating. Despite their high-pitched courtship yodelling, sloths manage to keep their actual sex life on the down-low, making it prone to much mythologizing. There is a persistent rumour on the internet that sloths are so slow that it takes twenty-four hours for them to have sex. This isn't true. As the first person to film wild sloths mating I can report that sloth sex is a surprisingly swift and athletic affair. The male approaches the female and, after a short display of flamboyant posturing, the deed is done and dusted in a matter of seconds. It appears sex is the only thing sloths do quickly.

This may not sound wildly romantic, but it makes a great deal of sense. The movement of mating exposes the surreptitious sloths' position to predators, so it's a good idea to get it over and done with, *tout de suite*. Prolonging the act would also waste precious energy. That said, the sloths I observed were at it repeatedly over the course of an afternoon, mating every half-hour or so, with the male retreating to snack on a cecropia leaf and take an intense snooze between each bout.

The biggest controversy in sloth biology is perhaps even more intimate: it concerns the sloth's curious defecation customs. The ordinarily idle folivore has a rather perplexing habit of descending all the way to the ground in order to relieve itself. It's a lengthy and highly ritualized affair, with the sloth hugging the base of the tree and wiggling its bottom on the ground to neatly dig a hole with its stumpy little tail in which it can do its business. Afterwards, the sloth generally has a good sniff and then neatly covers its work with leaves, before making the long commute home. Five to eight days later, it goes through the whole routine again.

This extravagant ritual is such a key part of sloth behaviour that the sanctuary in Costa Rica potty-trained orphaned baby sloths at designated 'poo poles' stuffed in the ground around the front lawn. The woman in charge of teaching them was a distinctly un-sloth-like character called Clare who'd spent most of her life working with the inmates of a high-security US prison and positively vibrated with nervous energy. She'd found her own sanctuary with the sloths in an early retirement, but she treated her job of teaching the babies the 'poo dance' with the intensity you'd expect from someone accustomed to the stressful conditions of a correctional facility. Clare showed me how you could identify when a sloth was actually on the job by the 'blissed-out' look on its face. That famous sloth smile 'gets a little bit wider and they kind of zone out,' she told me (a feeling that perhaps we can all relate to).

Sloths' bathroom rituals may be satisfying, but they come at a cost: the laborious expedition to the forest floor is energetically expensive and can be quite perilous. Forsaking the cover of the canopy strips them of their invisibility cloak, exposing them to the sharp eyes of ground-based predators such as the jaguar. More than half of sloth deaths are estimated to occur whilst they are doing their business. For these animals that spend their life trying not to be seen, and which are so perfectly adapted to a life hanging in the trees that they are born there, mate there and even die there, it is strange they don't also simply defecate there, as monkeys do.

This pooping problem is a source of vigorous debate amongst sloth researchers, who have split between various, entrenched camps. Staff at the sloth sanctuary told me sloths come to the forest floor to fertilize their favourite tree. That's a lovely, hippie ideal, but sloth dung, having taken around a month to digest, returns to the forest as highly compacted cellulose bricks that make for poor compost. Others have argued sloths come to the ground to eat dirt in order to absorb minerals missing from their leafy diet, a hangover from their days as giant ground sloths. This theory has thus far failed to get much traction.

In 2014, American ecologists made a big splash when they claimed to have solved the scatological mystery once and for all. The answer, they said, was hidden in the furtive relationship between the sloth and a moth that lives exclusively in the sloth's fur. Wild sloths are hopping with these drab little insects, which creepily crawl over their faces and rise in fluttering plumes of silvery-grey wings when disturbed. The moth's lifecycle appears to be intricately tied to the sloth's bizarre bathroom behaviour. The larvae are *coprophagous*, or, put more bluntly, dung-munchers. So the adult moths lay their eggs in the sloth's excrement, and once the larvae metamorphose, they fly up into the trees and hitch a ride on another sloth on its way to the loo. And thus the lifecycle continues endlessly.

The singularly unenviable lifestyle of the sloth moth had been known for many years. The novel aspect that the US ecologists proposed was a bit more convoluted, so bear with me. The scientists charitably described these moths as 'little more than "flying genitals" ', since their brief adult life is all about sex; as soon as they mate they die. As a result sloth fur is chock-full of both living moths and decomposing ones, the latter of which the ecologists believed serve as fertilizer for the algae growing in the fur. This could very well be true, but their theory did not end there.

The Americans pumped the stomachs of two- and three-toed sloths and found they contained algae. From this evidence they concluded that sloths must be grazing off their own fur to supplement their low-calorie, mineral-deficient diet. This led to an imaginative leap that the sloths must therefore be risking their lives in order to perpetuate the lifecycle of the moth because it fertilizes their 'algae gardens'. Which would make sloths the most committed farmers in the entire animal kingdom, risking death for the health of their crops. The fact that no one had ever seen a sloth licking or eating its fur did not deter the ecologists' enthusiasm. They simply presumed the sloths were doing it at night, or in secret.

When the ecologists' paper was published it generated a lot of attention in the media: sloths and eccentric pooping habits are *made* for a slow news day. The scientific community were a touch more sceptical about the sloth's alleged surreptitious midnight feasts. 'It's a very unfortunate conclusion,' said Becky Cliffe. 'Anyone who has observed sloths in the wild for any amount of time knows this is not the case. It paints a picture that they hadn't spent much time in the field observing wild sloths themselves. The fact that sloths have this algae in their stomachs simply says to me that the algae must exist in nature, that they ingest it some other way.'

Becky had other issues with the ecologists' theory. If the sloths were simply providing the moths with a place to reproduce, why would they need to return to the base of the same few trees? 'Wild sloths always poop in the same places. In fact, multiple poo piles can be found at the bases of certain trees,' she said. She'd even set up surreptitious poo-cams to catch their habits. 'I have camera traps set on some of these places and we frequently see the sloths coming and going. (Admittedly, the sloths' slowness occasionally struggles to trigger the camera traps!) Why wouldn't the sloth just climb down any old tree? Why travel to these specific spots?'

Becky has her own theory as to why the sloths make these risky loo runs: she thinks it's all about sex.

The penny dropped for her whilst she was conducting her red-dye digestion study. She was collecting the faeces of several subjects at the sloth sanctuary – just your typical day as a field scientist. The glamour of the scientist's life didn't stop at harvesting sloth dung, however; it also involved storing it in her bedroom, since her makeshift jungle lab was also the hut where she lived. A visit to Becky generally required picking your way across a floor strewn with dozens of dung piles, each heaped on a piece of A4 paper with enigmatic scribbles on them, like 'Brenda, Day 4'.

One night, whilst sleeping amongst her dung heaps, Becky was woken by a 'tap, tap, tap' at the window. She drew back the curtain and was shocked to see a male sloth staring back at her, apparently trying to break into her bedroom. When she went to leave her hut in the morning, he was still there. The next night he came again, making a slow dash for the inside of her hut when she opened the door. After several days of being stalked by this persistent sloth, Becky realized what he was after: Brenda's poo.

Brenda had been screaming for days at the time of her faecal collection. This led Becky to conclude that sloth dung must contain pheromones and their latrines must act as message boards, as they do for many other mammal species. Depositing a humongous dump of fibrous dung is therefore the sloth equivalent of leaving a personal ad. Females come down to the ground to advertise their location, readiness for sex and a host of other personal details, as well as to check out the competition – and so do males. Which I suppose makes a trip to the toilet the sloth equivalent of speed dating (without the speed).

'It makes sense – a big risk like coming down from the trees requires a big pay-off, and the biggest pay-off of all is reproduction,' Becky said.

If Becky's right, this clandestine communication system is yet another way the sloth blends in with its rainforest home to keep its existence secret – the motivating drive of their lives that has made them so successful in their native habitat and so hard for us humans to understand. As busy bipedal apes, intent on moving faster than nature intended, we have for centuries rushed past the genius of the sloth's stealthy success story. If we just slowed down a little, I can't help thinking the sloth, with its energy-saving survival skills, has much to teach us.

The same goes for the next member of my menagerie, the hyena – an animal similarly condemned for its lifestyle 'choices' that has some latter-day lessons to share. As we'll discover, the hyena also happens to be a fabulously effective freak, but with a startlingly feminist spin on the animal kingdom's typical phallocentric dominance.

## CHAPTER 4

# HYENA

Species *Crocuta crocuta*

*The hyena, hermaphroditic self-eating devourer of the dead, trailer of calving cows, ham-stringer, potential biter-off of your face at night while you slept, sad yowler, camp-follower, stinking, foul, with jaws that crack the bones that the lion leaves, belly dragging, loping away on the brown plain, looking back, mongrel dog-smart in the face.*

Ernest Hemingway, *Green Hills of Africa*, 1935

THE HYENA HAS BEEN censured by more scandalous untruths than even the sloth. They are considered nature's thugs – condemned throughout history and across cultures and continents as dim-witted cowards, skulking in the back alley of the animal kingdom waiting to mug more noble beasts for their dinner.

There are four species, with quite different lifestyles, but the most widespread and most misconstrued of the pack is the spotted hyena, *Crocuta crocuta*. With its scrappy fur, hunched back and wide drooling grin, I'll admit this so-called laughing hyena may not be the prettiest of animals. But our disdain goes more than skin-deep; it's personal. Picking it apart exposes an ancient rivalry between mankind and a sisterhood of super-smart, badass predators with a rather astonishing anatomical secret weapon against male domination.

Hyenas specialize in bewildering biology. Here is an animal that looks and hunts like a dog but is in fact a souped-up member of the mongoose family and therefore more closely related to a cat. The hyena cackles in the face of the human compulsion to impose order on the animals, causing no end of vexation amongst the taxonomy tribe, whose chief, the great Carl Linnaeus, was forced to hedge his bets when it came to *Crocuta*. Over the course of several editions of his tome *Systema Naturæ*, the outrageously organized Swede classified the hyena first as a cat, then later as a dog. He never got it right.

Others labelled the hyena as some kind of hybrid – a serious denunciation since, according to Sir Walter Raleigh's

*Topsell's encyclopaedia was very confused about the hyena. It was perhaps a bear, or a dog, but its short tail reminded the cleric of an ape and it had the feet of a woman. He also claimed that hyenas continually hold up their short tails in order to flash their backside – flaunting their hermaphrodite nature.*

analysis, it made them unfit to travel on Noah's Ark. In his seventeenth-century classic *Historie of the World*, Raleigh had wrestled at great and earnest length with the issue of how to fit the entire animal kingdom, Noah's family *and* enough food for all onto the Lord's lifeboat. It would, he hypothesized, be quite some squeeze. His 'rational', space-saving solution was to leave hyenas (the unholy off-spring of foxes and wolves) to drown: 'For those Beasts which are of mixt natures', he intoned, 'it was not needful to preserve them; seeing that they might be generated again by others.'

But even more baffling than what kind of animal the hyena is, was the basic question of its gender. 'It is the vul-gar notion, that the hyæna possesses in itself both sexes, being a male during one year, and a female the next,' wrote Pliny the Elder in his animal encyclopaedia.

The Roman naturalist wasn't the first – or the last – to suggest the hyena was an hermaphrodite, capable of swing-ing its sex according to the seasons. The rumour was rife in African folklore and debated by Aristotle. And hermaphro-dites aren't unknown in nature. Many species of worm, slug and snail are both male and female; there's even a whole class of bony fish that can switch between the two sexes willy-nilly. Indeed, modern science has estimated over 65,000 known cross-sexual species. The hyena is not one of them.

The stimulus for Pliny's sexual mythologizing may have been the female spotted hyena's wildly unconventional genitalia, which are a near-perfect facsimile of the male's. A *Crocuta*'s clitoris extends an impressive 20 centimetres and is shaped and positioned exactly like a penis (hence known in polite biological circles as a 'pseudo-penis'). The original chicks with dicks can even get erections. To complete this trans trickery, the female spotted hyena also appears to sport her very own pair of testicles: her labia have fused to form a false scrotum and are filled with fatty-tissue swellings, which are quite understandably mistaken for male gonads. No wonder she's having such a laugh.

The authors of a scientific paper on sexual mimicry in the spotted hyena declared the appearance of males and females 'so close that sex could only be determined with certainty by palpation of the scrotum'. Rather them than me. Copping a feel of a spotted hyena's soft bits would seem a rather foolhardy pastime for anyone wishing to hang on to their hands. But it certainly helps to explain Pliny's slip-up: he was a prolific plagiarist and highly unlikely to have ever clapped eyes on a spotted hyena's genitals, let alone fondled them. It wasn't until the late nineteenth century that the British anatomist Morrison Watson got his hands on a hyena's nether regions and the hermaphrodite rumour was finally crushed. Fortunately for Watson, he survived his intimate encounter.

Today, the female spotted hyena is the only known mammal with no external vaginal opening. Instead she must urinate, copulate *and* give birth through her strange, multitasking pseudo-penis. This last eye-watering feat is like squeezing a cantaloupe out of a hosepipe, and one in ten first-time hyena mothers die in the process. The fate of their cubs is even more precarious, since the umbilical cord is too short to navigate a birth canal that's not only twice the length of a similar-sized mammal's but includes a cheeky hairpin turn halfway down. Up to 60 per cent of cubs suffocate on their way out.

It is easy to see how the sight of a 'male' hyena giving birth through his penis led to the hermaphrodite myth (as well as a few lingering nightmares). Yet with so many fatalities during reproduction, it's less easy to see why the hyena's pudendum took such a peculiar evolutionary path in the first place.

The female's gender-bending doesn't end with her fake phallus. Spotted hyenas are unlike all other mammals in that the females are significantly bigger than the males and much more aggressive.

'You do not want to be a male spotted hyena,' Kay Holekamp told me – and she should know. A professor of evolutionary biology and behaviour at Michigan State University, she's spent over thirty years studying *Crocuta* in the wild, painting a fresh portrait of these miscast creatures and earning a reputation as the Jane Goodall of hyenas.

Every hyena clan is a matriarchy ruled by an alpha female. In the clan's strict power structure, dominance passes down the alpha female's line to her cubs. Adult males rank last in the hierarchy, reduced to submissive outcasts begging for acceptance, food and sex. At a communal carcass, where thirty or so hyenas might be vying for their pound of flesh, adult males eat last – if there's anything left – or risk violent retribution from the sisterhood.

Holekamp believes the driver of the female spotted hyena's aggression and dominance is this intense competition over carcasses. A frenzied scrum of hyenas can turn a 250-kilogram adult zebra into a bloody stain on the grass in under thirty minutes. An adult can gobble up to a third of its body weight per feeding – between 15 and 20 kilograms of meat. It's a frantic, frenzied and, at times, quite frightening scene. A female that is bigger and meaner has a better shot of ensuring her surviving cubs get a place at the table and don't get hurt in the process.

Dominant females have another trick for giving their cubs an aggressive advantage. A recent study has shown that the more powerful the female, the more testosterone her foetuses are exposed to during the final stage of pregnancy. These androgens are produced by the mother's ovaries, which is unusual enough. But it is Holekamp's belief that female cubs are more sensitive to their effects than males are. Spotted hyenas have an unusually long gestation period, and marinating in this prenatal androgen bath affects the development of the cub's nervous system so that they are wired to fight from the moment they are born. And they already have the necessary weapons: unlike most mammals, hyena cubs emerge with eyes open, muscles coordinated and teeth already pierced through their gums and eager to bite. These belligerent newborns frequently fight to the death over dinner, and siblicide is commonplace.

Scientists presumed that this excess of prenatal testosterone also caused the runaway growth of the female hyena's clitoris. But when the same researchers gave captive pregnant spotted hyenas a diet packed with anti-androgens (which blocked the male sex hormone), female cubs still surprised them by popping out of the birth canal sporting 'a large pendulous phallus' and a 'normal pseudo-scrotum'.

According to Holekamp, the spotted hyena's extraordinary sexual equipment remains 'one of the most interesting mysteries in biology'. Some scientists have suggested the hyena evolved her pseudo-penis in order that it could be licked by subordinates, which is how female spotted hyenas tend to greet each other (and assess dominance). But as appealing as this theory may be, Holekamp can't see how this would be a strong enough evolutionary driving force to create a structure as reproductively damaging as the pseudo-penis. 'I am convinced we can rule out all the hypotheses that have been forwarded in the literature to date: it is definitely not merely a "side-effect" of female androgen exposure, and it is not there to permit greeting behaviours.'

Holekamp's educated guess – and it is still a guess – is that the female's gender-bending is a result of the age-old war between the sexes. Unlike most animals, where the males duke it out and the winner gets the girl, in spotted hyena clans the females dictate the who, where and when of copulation. Sex is an undignified affair that sees the male forced to squat at the female's rear, stabbing away blindly in an attempt to insert his erect actual penis into her floppy, half-foot pseudo-penis. It's a bit like the male's trying to have sex with a sock – a pretty tricky exercise that's completely impossible without the female's full cooperation. Brute force alone simply won't work, as it does for the males of other mammal species like dolphins, amongst which non-consensual sex is surprisingly commonplace. So the female hyena's pseudo-penis may be acting as an 'anti-rape' device, allowing her to exercise choice over who she mates with.

This is pretty handy because – in addition to the dangers lurking in her precarious birth canal – a spotted hyena suffers a few other reproductive challenges. Her ovaries have comparatively little follicular tissue and produce relatively few eggs, and so it pays for her to be picky. Although you'd never imagine this was the strategy from observing her behaviour, since female spotted hyenas are highly promiscuous. Holekamp reckons the pseudo-penis allows the female to choose not just who she mates with but, more impressively, who actually fertilizes her precious eggs, by acting as a form of built-in birth control. That strangely elongated reproductive tract, with its various twists and turns, slows down sperm as they swim towards

*Sex for a male spotted hyena is no laughing matter. Inserting his erect penis into the female's flaccid pseudo-penis is a challenge akin to one of those fairground games that you can never win. No wonder this brave male has attracted a spectator, keen to see how it's done.*

their goal. If the hyena changes her mind about a male after mating, she simply flushes out his semen by urinating. Go sister!

'I can imagine an evolutionary arms race in which males can't use force any longer to secure paternities, and in which females want to be sure to allow only the best (or best-matched) sperm to fertilize their few ova,' Holekamp explained. 'This arms race may have led to the enlargement and more anterior positioning of the female's clitoris. I suspect this was only one part of a very weird, long, convoluted reproductive tract that evolved in unison in females, one full of blind alleys and dead ends for most sperm.'

I wonder whether this new image of the spotted hyena as a pioneering feminist, strutting around the savannah with a counterfeit cock, beating up on submissive males and taking control of her sexual destiny, would have been any less sacrilegious to the male bestiary authors than the original hermaphrodite myth. In the hands of these religious scribes, the animal's suspicious sexuality rendered it 'a dirty brute', and hyenas were frequently used to warn against the evils of homosexuality.

This set the stage for a resolutely damning portrait of the hyena that often included grisly tales of grave robbing. This ghoulish habit of the hyena was first put forward by Aristotle, but the bestiary authors were emboldened to embellish such tales to service their moralistic needs. The hyena was said 'to live in the sepulchres of the dead and devour their bodies'. It was a terrible fiend 'without pity for the living and ominous to the dead'.

The myth of grave robbing persisted all the way into the nineteenth century. The Victorian naturalist Philip Henry Gosse was inspired by the hyena to pen particularly purple prose that owes more to Mary Shelley and the fashion for Victorian Gothic horror than it does to the truth. 'In the Place of Tombs, gleam two fiery eyes,' he wrote, in his massively popular *Romance of Natural History*, 'with bristling mane and grinning teeth, the obscene monster glares at you, and warns you to secure a timely retreat.' Other naturalists of the era showed a tad more restraint, but they still described the hyena as 'a most mysterious and awful animal', 'rank and coarse' with 'revolting habits'. This creature, they decided, was 'adapted to gorge on the grossest animal substances, dead or alive, fresh or corrupted', and as such was 'cordially detested by the natives in all countries'.

Kay Holekamp told me that spotted hyenas in East Africa have indeed been known to dig up human corpses. The Nuer of Sudan have a saying that the only way to heaven is through the gut of a hyena. And some tribes actively try to encourage hyenas to consume their dead by covering corpses in fat and leaving them outside where they can be easily found – a tradition Western missionaries worked hard to curtail. But Holekamp insists hyenas only exhibit such behaviour when 'times are tough'. The perpetuation of this gruesome legend is more a mark of our disgust for any animal scavenger.

Western society tends to admire animals that are perceived to do a hard day's graft, like beavers, and who earn their living by hunting or gathering. But scavenging, as we shall explore in more detail through the life of the vulture, is an honourable profession, one that recycles energy and prevents the spread of disease.

And the hyena is *very* good at its job. It is the garbage

tatione fustentant : DE ỵ E N A · Hiena

ut aliquando masculus sit aliquando femina ·

*Most medieval bestiaries featured a graphic illumination of a hyena, back arched and teeth bared as it busted into a tomb to savage a corpse – a striking image that ensured their negative branding.*

truck of the African plains, using its powerful jaws and stomach acids to digest what most animals can't. The fact that it fails to get sick even after gorging on a putrid carcass riddled with anthrax may explain why many cultures believe the hyena possesses magical powers.

In terms of tonnage of meat consumed, hyenas are the most significant terrestrial carnivore on the planet. However, only the brown hyena and the striped hyena are primarily scavengers. Spotted hyenas are highly efficient predators, killing 95 per cent of the food that they consume. Hunting parties are capable of bringing down dangerous animals, like water buffalo, several times their size. But even lone hyenas have been known to catch impressively large prey – one bold strategy being to lock onto the animal's testicles and hang on, dodging a battery of defensive hooves, until the victim bleeds out.

Such tactics are not for the faint-hearted, yet somehow hyenas have an enduring reputation for being a bunch of wimps. 'All writers agree that the hyaena lacks courage,' wrote one naturalist in 1886. This rumour can also be traced all the way back to Aristotle, who developed an arcane theory about how bravery could be predicted by the size of an animal's heart. In his formulation, courage was viewed as proportional to the heat of the blood, which was in turn related to the size of the organ pumping it around the body, 'when the heart is of large size the animal is timorous, while it is more courageous if the organ be smaller and of moderate bulk.' Or so the grandfather of zoology said in his magisterial work *De Partibus Animalium* ('On the Parts of Animals'). He lumped the hyena, somewhat incongruously, in with 'the hare, the deer, the mouse', along with 'all other animals that are either manifestly timorous, or that betray their cowardice by their spitefulness' for having a disproportionately large heart. The persuasive details of Aristotle's theory may have been lost to time, but the idea that hyenas are cowards has persisted well into the modern age. Even the twentieth-century biologist's bible, E. P. Walker's *Mammals of the World*, published in the 1960s, stated authoritatively that spotted hyenas 'are cowardly and will not fight if their prospective victim defends itself'.

On safari one misty morning near Lake Nakuru, Kenya, I caught up with a pack of spotted hyenas hunting a zebra, their favourite prey. I'll admit it was a tough watch. When I arrived on the scene the hyenas had already ripped the hide from the right flank of the zebra, as the skin trailed behind the animal like a piece of semi-discarded clothing, exposing the beast's innards in the manner of a living, breathing Gunther von Hagens anatomical sculpture. The hyenas were doing little but follow this semi-eviscerated beast, waiting for its inevitable collapse. It was hard not to anthropomorphize the actors before me: the zebra seemingly dignified in the face of death, the hyenas cruel and cowardly. But survival is an unsentimental sport, and the hyena's hunting strategy is based on endurance. It often involves 'testing' prey to see how much fight they have left, which could be interpreted as timidity but is better understood as a key part of their winning long game. There's no point risking fatal injury from a kick or a claw when all you need is patience.

So the idea that hyenas spend their time sneaking about and stealing the spoils from more 'noble' animals like the lion is another misconception. Field studies have found that lions actually steal more kills from spotted hyenas than vice versa. The animosity between the animals is, however, very real: these two species are arch-enemies, locked in battle over territory and food. Whilst lions may have the size advantage, the hyena makes up for this with intelligence. 'Lions are not the sharpest tools in the shed,' as Kay Holekamp put it. Don't tell Disney, which portrayed the hyena as a pathetic fool in *The Lion King*, but these feminist freaks are the brains of the savannah – and smarter than your average carnivore.

A few years ago, I got to spend a couple of days watching spotted hyenas in the Maasai Mara with Dr Sarah Benson-Amram, an expert in hyena intelligence. 'I think their reputation for being stupid has a lot to do with their gait,' she told me. 'They have this sort of lope which is very beneficial in terms of being super efficient runners, energy-wise; they can run really long distances. But it gives them this sort of awkward, dopey appearance.'

To find the truth, Sarah invented the world's first carnivore IQ test – a metal puzzle box with a meaty treat trapped inside that can only be released by using brains, not brawn. She has plonked her puzzle box before various predators from polar bears to panthers in order to gauge their problem-solving skills. She discovered that the animals which performed well tended to share a rich social life. Sarah believes sociability could be the evolutionary force responsible for the hyena's superior intellect.

Spotted hyenas gather in social groups bigger than any

other carnivore. Their packs can number up to 130 individuals and they have been observed defending territories of up to 1,000 square kilometres. You might say hyenas are more tribal than football fans. They live by the clan, and everything they do is tied up with the female dominance hierarchy that underpins it. But they don't remain together all the time. Instead, they spend much of their time in smaller splinter groups that coalesce in order to fight, hunt or feed. This arrangement is known as a *fission–fusion society*, and maintaining it demands sophisticated communication skills.

The great Georges-Louis Leclerc, Comte de Buffon, may have dismissed the hyena's calls as simply sounding like 'the sobs or reachings of a man in a violent fit of vomiting', but spotted hyenas have one of the richest vocal repertoires of any terrestrial mammal, including primates. They make a wide range of sounds including that famous giggle (actually a sign of submission), but the whoop – a quintessential sound of the savannah – is their signature call. It is a ghostly echo that can carry on the wind for up to 5 kilometres, transporting with it a wealth of information about the caller including its identity, sex and age.

Hyenas' big brains have evolved to memorize the identity and rank of each of their clanmates. And they appear to be able to recall each member's voice and status throughout their lives – no mean cognitive feat, and one that ensures they have the political savvy to both recognize friend from foe in a single call and negotiate their strict social hierarchy, without endless conflict.

Sarah demonstrated this to me near a communal den where half a dozen females and their cubs were whiling away the heat of the day. The adults were mostly dozing in the shade of an acacia tree whilst their cubs tumbled about looking surprisingly cute. Sarah pressed play on her iPhone and the whoop of a stranger hyena, not from this clan, rang out from a portable speaker. Even though the recorded call was slightly distorted, it still gave me goosebumps, stirring some atavistic fear locked deep inside my limbic brain. A pack of hyenas would make mincemeat of us in minutes. Impersonating a rival gang member was asking for trouble.

Sarah wasn't taking any chances; we conducted our research from the secure confines of a large Land Rover, positioned about a hundred metres from the resting clan.

Sure enough, as soon as they heard Sarah's recording, the hyenas' ears pricked up and they looked over in our direction, instantly on alert. They stood up and sniffed into the breeze seeking more information. Their sense of smell is strong, a thousand times stronger than ours, with each clan throwing off a distinctive scent, a fragrant flag they wave in the wind. One particularly well-built hyena started to gallop towards us and whoop. My heart rate quickened. But the hyena loped straight past our vehicle as if it didn't even see us. It was searching for something that looked and smelled like a hyena, and my sweaty head popping out of the top of a safari vehicle did not fit the bill.

Sarah has shown that hyenas respond differently depending on whether they hear the whoops of one, two or three individuals. This means the spotted hyena sister-hood can, in some sense, count – a useful tool when trying to gauge whether to fight a rival gang. She has also shown that rival hyena clans will use their numeracy and communication skills to band together and fight off a common enemy, such as the lion.

Despite being wired for aggression, spotted hyenas use their intelligence to keep the peace and collaborate. 'Hyenas are very cooperative with their clan members and close relatives,' she explained. 'You see these sisters and they spend a lot of time together, eating, hunting and resting together, and they have long-term, very close relationships. While they can be very competitive, in many respects they are also very cooperative.'

Ultimately, the hyena's extraordinary success at bringing down large prey, intimidating lions and raising their cubs in a hostile environment depends on their capacity for teamwork. Recent fieldwork suggests that the social structures of the spotted hyena are every bit as complex as those of baboons, and CT scans have confirmed that hyena brains have evolved in a similar frontal direction to primates', with the region involved in complex decision-making enlarged. They have even outperformed chimpanzees on certain cooperative problem-solving tests. This supports the idea that living in a complex fission–fusion society – as both chimps and hyenas, along with dolphins, other apes and, of course, humans, do – is key to the evolution of big brains. This may even help explain why our species evolved a brain that is seven times bigger than would be predicted for an animal our size.

This shared portion of the evolutionary path may also provide the ultimate clue to our unswerving contempt for these calculating creatures. Humans and hyenas are longstanding enemies. The Australian anthropologist Marcus Baynes-Rock, who has spent several years living in Ethiopia studying the relationship between our two species, has some insights as to why.

Both humans and hyenas are highly intelligent social predators with origins on the African savannah, he explained to me. But the hyenas were there first, so when our distant hominin relatives came down from the trees, they were muscling in on the spotted hyena's patch. 'There must have been a huge amount of antagonism,' Baynes-Rock said. 'Just looking at the way that hyenas and lions get along today – they absolutely hate each other – we can just imagine humans and hyenas at the beginning were the same – hating each others' guts.' The early hominins were also at risk of being eaten by hyenas. 'This is a slow, fatty, very edible primate, and the only way they have to protect themselves is forming large groups. Hyenas would definitely have taken the opportunity to eat a *Homo habilis* if it strayed too far from the group.'

Baynes-Rock thinks the hyena's bone-crunching bite could even be the reason for the sparse evidence of early human evolution. 'Most hominin remains are just teeth and jawbones. When you are finding teeth it's almost a guarantee that the dead person has been through the digestive tract of a hyena, because that's all that comes out.'

Our early ancestors had only very basic stone tools, and were probably scavenging more than they were hunting. They would not have been able to fight off a pack of hungry hyenas to protect their prize meal. A theory borne out by bones from the period which show cut marks from early stone tools mixed with tooth marks of hyenas, suggesting that hyenas were laughing at us *and* stealing our dinner for as much as 2.5 million years. No wonder we don't like them.

Hyenas aren't the only scavengers with a reputation that needs rescuing. In the next chapter we'll meet another, the vulture, whose association with death has led to centuries of human suspicion, resulting at varying times in accusations that they are clairvoyants, sleuths and even – quite recently – international spies.

## CHAPTER 5

# VULTURE

## Order Accipitriformes

*The eagle attacks his enemies or his victims one on one . . . Vultures, on the other hand, join together in troops, like cowardly assassins, and would rather be robbers than warriors, birds of carnage rather than birds of prey . . . The eagle, on the other hand, has the courage, the nobility, the magnanimity and the munificence of the lion.*

Comte de Buffon, *Histoire Naturelle*, 1793

THE GRANDIOSE NATURALIST GEORGES-LOUIS Leclerc, Comte de Buffon, was especially bombastic when it came to describing the vulture. 'They are voracious, cowardly, disgusting, odious and, as with wolves, just as noxious during their lives as they are useless after their death,' he said, throwing his thesaurus at the vulture in a frenzy of unflattering adjectives. Clearly, the Comte was not a fan. Few people are. Scavengers in general have a tough enough job commanding respect from mankind, but looking like the grim reaper *and* dining on the dead has done little to promote an unbiased understanding of these magnificent raptors, whose reputation has long been haunted by a queasy combination of disgust and mistrust.

Our uneasy relationship with death, with which these birds seem to be so at one, rubbed off on their hunched shoulders. Early Christian taboos against touching corpses put vultures in a singular category of grotesquery. The Old Testament stigmatized them as unclean, 'an abomination among the birds'. They were seen as otherworldly creatures in possession of mystical powers. 'Vultures are

accustomed to foretell the death of men by certain signs,'
one twelfth-century bestiary warned. 'Whenever two lines
of battle are drawn against each other in lamentable war . . .
the birds follow in a long column [and] show by the length
of this column how many soldiers are to die in the struggle.' These clairvoyant powers were, according to the
chronicler, self-serving: 'They show in fact how many men
are destined to be the booty of the vultures themselves.'

Vultures are unsentimental about what – or who – they eat.
Medieval European battlegrounds, dotted with dozens of felled
humans and horses, would have been the equivalent of an all-
you-can-eat buffet. Battles often waged for weeks, frequently
during the summer months – conveniently coinciding with
the vultures' nesting season on the continent. Birds must
have set up camp in Hitchcockian numbers, dispassionately
picking over the dead to feed themselves and their chicks. An
observer some distance away might thus be able to predict
something about conditions on the battlefield by counting
the vultures circling above. But despite popular mythology,
vultures do not stalk their prey whilst it's still living, and they
are not able to predict mortality.

How vultures know where to congregate is indeed
mysterious. Their eerie ability to arrive apparently out of
nowhere, and in great numbers, at the scene of death has
engendered a longstanding belief that their senses must
be of supernatural strength. But precisely which senses are
being used has been the subject of one of the longest and
bitterest arguments in ornithology.

Audubon's illustration of turkey vultures in his famous avian encyclo-pedia, Birds of America *(1827–38)*, *is exceedingly true-to-life. Which makes it all the more unfortunate that the great ornithologist got the species muddled up with black vultures, a mistake that sparked one of the biggest controversies in ornithology.*

The defining feature of the vulture's dinner is that it stinks to high heaven. So it was long held that this bird's sense of smell must be the source of its mystical power of tracking down the dead. As the Franciscan monk Bartholomew the Englishman wrote in his influential thirteenth-century bestiary, 'In this bird the wit of smelling is best. And therefore by smelling he savoureth carrions that be far from him, that is beyond the sea, and ayenward.'

The scavenger's admirable olfactory ability was widely accepted and reported in later natural history books. Oliver Goldsmith, for example, in 1816 grudgingly conceded in his *History of the Earth* that although the vulture's nature may be 'cruel, unclean and indolent', their 'sense of smelling, however, is amazingly great.' He even qualified this alleged talent with physiological evidence: 'Nature, for this purpose, has given them two large apertures or nostrils without, and an extensive olfactory membrane within.'

Just a decade later, the vulture was spectacularly robbed of its sense of smell by an ambitious American naturalist named John James Audubon. Today, Audubon is one of the most recognized names in ornithology, famous for his exquisite lifelike drawings of birds. But back in the 1820s, he was a wandering go-getter, hawking his paintings around Europe and hungry for a bit of fame. He got what he wanted by courting controversy at a gathering of the hallowed Edinburgh Natural History Society in 1826. The rambling yet provocative title of his subsequent paper betrays Audubon's desire to make a big splash with the stuffy science crowd of the day: 'An Account of the Habits of the Turkey Buzzard (*Vultur aura*) Particularly with the View of Exploding the Opinion Generally Entertained of Its Extraordinary Power of Smelling'.

In his audacious paper, Audubon explained how, as a child growing up in France in the late 1700s, he had been taught that vultures scavenged using their sense of smell. This didn't make any sense to the budding ornithologist, who laboured under the spartan belief that 'nature, although wonderfully bountiful, had not granted more to one individual than was necessary and that no one was possessed of any two of the senses in any very high state of perfection; that if it had a good scent, it need not the acuteness of sight.' Years later, whilst living in America, Audubon had begun testing his theory by casually creeping up on wild turkey buzzards (also commonly known as turkey vultures), but they seemed only to be spooked by his sudden appearance, not his body odour. He decided to take the matter further and 'assiduously engaged in a series of experiments to prove, to myself at least, how far this acuteness of smell existed, or if it existed at all'.

Audubon's grand experiments basically amounted to a very smelly game of hide-and-seek involving some dead animals and a committee of wild vultures. First, he roughly stuffed a deer skin with straw and left it in a meadow with its feet in the air. His taxidermy skills were not the finest, but the misshapen beast still quickly attracted a vulture, which launched a futile attack on the dummy's clay eyes, then 'voided itself freely' and unpicked some stitches from the dead deer's rear end, releasing 'much fodder and hay'. The disillusioned bird then flew off and killed a small garter snake as comestible compensation, thereby proving to Audubon's satisfaction that the bird had used vision to hunt.

Next, on a hot July day, Audubon turned his sights to the vulture's sense of smell. He hauled an exceedingly smelly, putrefying pig into some woods, which he then hid in a ravine, obscuring the animal from plain view. Although vultures cruised overhead, none came down to seek out the source of the stench. Audubon's suspicions were once again confirmed: these vultures did not scavenge by smell.

Audubon's results were far from conclusive, but the man was a consummate showman with a reputation on an upwards roll after the phenomenal commercial success of his book *Birds of America*. Many respected members of the ornithological establishment stampeded to support his explosive proposition. There was, however, one very vociferous exception from the herd: an aristocratic adventurer by the name of Charles Waterton, commonly known as 'the Squire'.

To describe Waterton as an eccentric would be to contain him within a crowded category that he alone should own. The Squire's outrageous accounts of his exotic escapades, which allegedly included riding a crocodile and punching a boa constrictor in the face, had earned him a certain infamy. At home in Walton Hall, his actions were no less unconventional. He was said to have a habit of hiding under the table at dinner parties to bite his guests' legs like a dog, and delighted in elaborate, taxidermy-based practical jokes. A particularly inspired prank involved his fashioning an effigy of one of his (many) enemies out of a howler monkey's buttocks.

Despite such antics, Waterton was a talented naturalist – an original thinker whose sideways view of the world afforded him a relatively unprejudiced understanding of

*It did not pay to annoy 'the Squire'. The government jobsworth who dared to tax Charles Waterton on the exotic specimens he collected abroad found his likeness fashioned from a howler monkey's buttocks and labelled 'A Nondescript'. The taxidermist's prank was further immortalized in this copper engraving from his book* Wanderings in South America *(1825).*

nature. He was, for example, one of the first to stand up for the sloth, whose 'extraordinary formation and singular habits' he felt were in fact reason for us 'to admire the wonderful works of the Omnipotence'.

Waterton had written about the turkey vulture's unique talent for smell in his own bestseller, *Wanderings in South America*, and took the cocky American's counterclaims as a personal attack on his admittedly somewhat shaky credibility. This spurred the Squire to wage a lengthy war of withering and occasionally witty words against Audubon. These missives of seething sarcasm were printed in the *Magazine of Natural History* – the nineteenth-century equivalent of a very public Twitter spat.

'I grieve from my heart that the vulture's nose has received such a tremendous blow, because the world at large will sustain a great loss by this sudden and unexpected attack upon it,' wrote Waterton. 'Moreover I have a kind of fellow-feeling, if I may say so, for this noble bird.' As the self-appointed leader of what became known in ornithological circles as 'the Nosarians', the Squire offered to 'carefully gather up the shattered olfactory parts, and do my best to restore them to their original shape and beautiful proportions'.

As part of the bird's nasal defence, Waterton took a surgeon's knife to Audubon's experimental acumen, his reputation and even his scientific prose. 'Its grammar is bad; its composition poor; and its statements are so unsatisfactory,' he complained. 'In my opinion, any person who reads the paper with any moderate share of attention will feel inclined to condemn it to the same kind of fate as that to which the curate and the barber condemned the greater part of Don Quixote's library.' He called Audubon a liar and a charlatan, entirely incapable of having penned a bestselling bird book. 'Mr Audubon's story of a rattlesnake swallowing a large American squirrel, tail foremost, still sticks in my throat, and that positively I cannot gulp any thing else till they manage to ease me of that foreign body.'

Audubon remained aloof throughout, preserving his dignity with silence. Instead, he encouraged his growing band of 'Anti-Nosarians' to answer Waterton's attacks on his behalf. Chief amongst his defenders was a Lutheran pastor, the Revd John Bachman, who attempted to settle the quarrel by repeating Audubon's experiments, augmenting them with a few of his own, in front of a select committee of learned gentlemen in his hometown of Charleston, South Carolina.

The pastor's experiments were brutal and bizarre in equal measure. In one, he commissioned an oil painting of 'a sheep skinned and cut open', which he then placed in his garden, about 3 metres from a hidden pile of decaying offal. The painting was crude – not up to Audubon's fine standards – yet the undiscerning birds still attacked the artwork with great gusto. Bachman said the vultures 'seemed much disappointed and surprised' at their lack of satisfaction, but not once did they move towards the meat festering nearby. He repeated the escapade fifty times, which according to his report on these highly alternative avian happenings, 'proved very amusing' to the learned men in attendance (who perhaps didn't get out that much).

In a bonus experiment, he enlisted some 'medical gentlemen' to blind a vulture in order to test a rumour doing the rounds that the bird could restore its perforated peepers by simply placing its head under one wing. When the sorry bird resolutely failed to restore its own eyesight, Bachman saw his opportunity to probe its remaining senses. He consigned the wounded vulture to an 'out-house' containing a dead hare and watched to see if the poor blind bird could sniff it out. It could not. In an uncharacteristic fit of charity, the reverend conceded that 'the bird might not have been wholly free from the pain inflicted by the operation.' Indeed. But beyond that, Bachman showed no sign of remorse, his only concern being whether his malodorous experiments might 'become offensive to the neighbours'. This weighed on him mightily, so he called an end to the investigation, satisfied that he had settled the score. Before publishing his findings, he took the rather heavy-handed measure of pressing his medical men into signing a contract confirming they'd witnessed definitive proof that vultures scavenge 'through their sense of sight and not of smell' – proving that the pastor's campaigning techniques were as punishing and peculiar as his quest for scientific truth.

Waterton's response to Bachman was suitably scornful. 'Pitiable, indeed, is the lot of the American vulture! His nose is declared useless in procuring food, at the same

time that his eyesight is proved to be lamentably defective,' he grumbled. 'I am now quite prepared to receive
accounts from Charleston of vultures attacking every
shoulder-of-mutton sign in the streets, or attempting to
gobble down the painted sausages over the shop doors, or
tugging with might and main at the dim and faded eyes in
some decaying portrait of the immortal Doctor Franklin.'
This was no scientific endeavour in the Squire's eyes. 'The
absurdity of all this must be evident to every body.'

Over the course of five years, Waterton wrote no less than
nineteen letters to the *Magazine of Natural History* attacking
Audubon and anyone in his orbit. When the journal finally
stopped publishing his letters he reportedly continued to
print and distribute them himself. His efforts were futile.
His impenetrable, rambling diatribes, punctuated with sar-
donic *ad hominems* and obscure Latin phrases, won him few
allies. Audubon's anti-Nosarians branded the Squire 'stark,
staring mad' and refused to alter their opinion of the flashy
American. The louder Waterton shouted, the more he was
ignored. In the end, he was forced to give up.

Which is a shame, because he was right.

It would take science almost 150 years to catch up with
Charles Waterton. Meanwhile, the waves from Audubon's
explosion engulfed an expanding circle of anatomists, naturalists and ornithologists, who went to work performing ever
more incredible experiments on a widening variety of birds.

In one of the more ludicrous, a domesticated turkey was substituted for a turkey vulture, its food hidden in a saucer containing sulphuric acid and potassium cyanide. The turkey did not survive the plumes of poisonous gases long enough to reveal whether it could smell its supper or not.

The vulture's other senses, both real and imaginary, were also drawn into the debate. In the early twentieth century, a chap called P. J. Darlington argued the bird actually used its ears, listening for the distant buzz of hundreds of flies to find its meal. Another theorist, named Herbert Beck, reverted to medieval mystical thinking in a 1920 paper entitled 'The Occult Senses in Birds', which supposed that the vulture was in possession of a mysterious 'food-finding sense' that remains completely inexplicable to humans because we do not possess it.

The turkey vulture's sense of smell was finally restored in 1964, when Kenneth Stager, another maverick American field scientist, presented conclusive evidence based upon his years of careful and clever experimentation, along with a little serendipity. Stager's major revelation came during a random exchange with an employee of Union Oil who let slip that since the 1930s the company had been exploiting the turkey vulture's keen sense of smell by using the birds to locate leaks in their gas pipelines. They had started adding ethyl mercaptan, the rotten-cabbage smell that flavours stink bombs and flatulence, to their natural gas, as it invariably attracted vultures which then homed in on and exposed any leaks before humans could detect them.

Stager realized the same compound is also released by decaying corpses. And sure enough, when he used a mercaptan-dispensing device to fart rotten odours into the Californian sky, the turkey vultures soon came circling.

The decades of confusion over the vulture's sense of smell can be traced to a handful of basic misunderstandings. First, it would seem that the most esteemed American ornithologist wasn't quite as attentive to his birds as one might suppose. Some of the species Audubon described showed an interest in hunting down live animals as well as dead, which suggests they were black vultures (*Coragyps atratus*) and not, as he identified them, the black-plumaged turkey vultures (*Cathartes aura*). Second, it was assumed that all vultures would exhibit similar olfactory abilities. They don't. The twenty-three species of vultures fall into two distinct groups – Old World vultures, which inhabit Africa, Asia and Europe, and New World vultures, which live in the Americas. Though they look and behave in a similar fashion, the two groups are distantly related, not even falling into the same family, let alone genus, of the animal kingdom. It turns out that all vultures hunt by sight but only a handful of the New World vultures, including the turkey vulture, hunt by smell. Crucially, black vultures are amongst those which do not use smell. Third – and despite conventional wisdom – vultures are surprisingly discerning about what they eat. Like us, they prefer to eat dead herbivores rather than carnivores, and they don't like them *too* rotten. Yet another rather eccentric experiment, this one conducted in the 1980s, involved hiding seventy-four chickens in a Panamanian jungle. It revealed the turkey vulture's perfection of putrefaction was a decidedly *al dente* two days after death, neither older nor younger. American turkey vultures may well have turned up their nose at Audubon's perished pig and Bachman's ancient offal simply because the meat was too far gone.

In more recent years, news of the turkey vultures' olfactory detecting talents has attracted the interest of the German State Office of Criminal Investigation, which has pioneered a scheme to train vultures to replace sniffer dogs. Police officer Rainer Herrmann got the idiosyncratic idea after watching a wildlife documentary that bragged of the birds' smelling skills. He hoped the vultures, fitted with GPS trackers and followed by a fleet of land cruisers, would be able to cover more ground, more quickly, than dogs.

A turkey vulture from a local bird park was chosen for the pilot and given the predictable nickname of Sherlock as well as a dedicated personal trainer with the very German name of German Alonso. With such a whimsical cast, the scheme got plenty of media attention, and before too long requests for the vulture's services were flooding in from forty police departments around the country.

Alonso had some reservations about his charge. He thought vultures might struggle with differentiating between dead humans and dead animals, causing a fair few false alarms. But the trainer showed surprisingly little concern about the prospect of the birds eating any evidence

*German Alonso attempts to encourage trainee detective Sherlock in sniffing out some missing persons (but hopefully not attack their eyes or anus).*

they found. 'That will happen and you can't stop it,' he announced to a national newspaper before adding, more helpfully, 'But they won't remove the entire corpse, they can't eat that much. And if they take a nibble, what the hell, the victim will be beyond help anyway' – an attitude unlikely to soothe the nerves of a missing person's mum, or please a forensic scientist in need of pristine clues.

Sherlock, however, was significantly less enthusiastic about his new job than everyone else. He didn't like to fly when searching for his training material – a mortuary cloth previously used to wrap a dead body. Instead, he hopped around the ground nervously investigating a small area on foot. At times he was so anxious he would hide in the woods or bolt when given the command to search. Two younger vultures, named Miss Marple and Columbo, were brought on board to make him feel part of a big vulture detective family. All they did was fight.

Wild turkey vultures may be good at spotting gas leaks, but a handful of captive vultures cannot, despite their pet names, be relied upon to solve crimes by following their nose. It shows that, even in modern times, the vulture's sensory skills are subject to exaggeration. Police officer Herrmann was under the impression the birds would be able to sniff out a dead mouse from more than 1,000 metres. This is unlikely to be true, as recent research has shown that the birds must fly low in order to pick up the scent of the dead. So whilst turkey vultures do scavenge by smell – exactly as Waterton claimed – their olfactory abilities are nowhere near as good as a sniffer dog's, and possibly not that much better than a human's.

The vulture's eyesight has also been elevated to mythological status. In southern Africa, it's believed the bird's ocular abilities are so keen they possess what is called 'clear sight' – the ability to see into the future. A few years ago, I visited the main *muti*, or traditional medicine market, in Johannesburg to investigate. Amongst a sea of stalls selling dismembered animal parts I discovered dozens of people trading in small vials of vulture brains, which I was told were smoked or snorted to attain clairvoyance. Since the arrival of the Lotto, vulture brains had become the biggest seller in the market – something vulture conservationists could never have predicted, no matter how much of the stuff they inhaled.

Marginally more credible is the bird's oft-quoted ability to spot a carcass from 4 kilometres away, a mainstay of most vulture 'fact sites' online. Anatomists dissecting vultures' eyes have been surprised to discover the bird's eyesight may actually only be twice as good as our own. Vultures lack binocular vision and, thanks to a well-developed ocular ridge that protects their eyes from the glare of the sun (and which bestows on the birds their characteristic ferocious stare), they also have significant blind spots.

Vultures' spooky ability to arrive at the scene of death in such great numbers so quickly is down to the assistance of another highly developed organ: their brain. Vultures are canny creatures that watch and learn from each other. In most instances, a vulture won't discover a carcass itself; instead, it spots a column of circling birds, which *are* visible from several kilometres away, and heads in their direction. Young vultures spend a significant amount of time learning scavenging techniques from their parents. And families of birds stay close to each other, with clans of related birds roosting together. Different vulture species also roost together in large numbers. Scientists have proposed that these scavenger social gatherings are a way for the birds to acquire information about the location of their ephemeral food sources.

Whether large groups of vultures really are distributing intelligence about dinner is yet to be proved. But one thing is for certain: the arrival of vultures is rarely welcomed, even in our modern world. When, for example, a kettle of around five hundred turkey vultures, pushed north by global warming, decided to add Staunton, Virginia, to their winter migratory route, the human residents of this picture-postcard historic town were not exactly pleased.

'They're disgusting,' a local woman told the *Washington Post*, describing her new neighbours. The birds had carpeted her neatly manicured driveway with excreta as if it were a giant Jackson Pollock. That's to be expected: turkey vultures are precocious pooping machines. They practise *urohidrosis*, a scientific euphemism for crapping on your legs to keep cool. It's not the most elegant of thermoregulatory solutions, but it is nevertheless a crafty substitute for sweating, which birds cannot do.

The results of urohidrosis aren't just offensive to the eye. 'They smell like ammonia and sewage,' another Virginia resident said. The stench wasn't the only complaint, however. 'They're ugly as \*\*\*\*. I walk around the corner and fifty of them are sitting on gravestones, hissing. It's like living in a horror movie. If it were up to me, I'd kill every one of them.'

Unfortunately for the gun-happy citizens of Staunton, turkey vultures are protected in the US and cannot be killed without incurring serious fines. One frustrated local tried to improvise by shooting at the vultures with paint balls only to discover the birds have a rather unsavoury means of fighting back: 'It vomited on my son,' he told the

*Washington Post*. 'It was like a half pound of ground beef on his shoulder. It was so disgusting. We got it off him. Got his shirt off. And got him to stop screaming.'

Vultures' first-line defence, if full, is to chuck their dinner at you. Given that their supper probably wasn't terribly appealing first time round – the Virginia turkey vultures were likely dining on a menu of road kill and animal excrement – it's easy to see how defensive puking pushed neighbourly relations over the edge in Staunton. The US Department of Agriculture's 'environmental police' were called in to run the avian outlaws out of town. Dead vultures were hung in roosting sites, firecrackers were set off and, in a dramatic final showdown, a number of birds were permanently dispatched from the planet.

As the good people of Virginia discovered, the vulture boasts an arsenal of unappealing habits that have long offended human senses. 'The sloth, filth and the voraciousness of these birds almost exceed credibility,' spat the big-talking Comte de Buffon in another of his tirades against the vulture. But even Charles Darwin, who unlike Buffon was rarely swayed by sentimentality, couldn't stomach the bird's personal habits. In *The Voyage of the Beagle*, he described the turkey vulture as 'a disgusting bird, with its bald scarlet head, formed to wallow in putridity'. Not only was Darwin's description coloured by prejudice, it was also probably wrong. Other avian scavengers – including the giant petrel – do perfectly well getting gory with feathered heads. The vulture's baldness may instead help the bird stay cool, thereby joining urohidrosis as yet another aesthetically challenging adaptation for regulating body temperature.

Looks can be deceiving. Just because these big scavenging birds are wandering around with legs encrusted in their own faeces doesn't mean they are dirty. And scavenging, though wildly unappealing to posh Parisian naturalists, is far from being a degraded means of procuring dinner. Indeed, it's quite the opposite, as I learned when I spent some time with conservationist Kerri Wolter at her vulture sanctuary in South Africa, where she has been working with the birds for more than fourteen years.

Kerri is on a crusade to change the public perception of these much-maligned creatures before it is too late. Globally, vultures are the fastest declining category of bird. Of the nine species found in southern Africa, all but one are threatened with extinction.

It's a short drive from the Johannesburg airport to the sanctuary, nestled somewhat incongruously at the edge of Pretoria's bland, boxy concrete sprawl. Kerri cares for around 130 rescued birds, victims of power-line electrocutions or accidental poisoning, most of them the critically endangered Cape vulture, or *Gyps coprotheres*, an Old World vulture. I arrived just in time for their lunch. Kerri put me to work straight away, helping her wheel a freshly killed cow's carcass into the main enclosure, home to a breeding group of a dozen or so birds.

The first thing that struck me was their size. Weighing in at around 10 kilograms and standing about a metre tall, Cape vultures are the largest Old World vulture in southern Africa and one of the world's bulkiest flying birds. Being big is important for a carnivore that must rely on scattered and infrequent food sources. If you can't go out and kill something when you are hungry, it helps to be able to gorge on food when it's available and live off your fat reserves. Size also helps intimidate fellow scavengers competing for morsels from a communally shared corpse, and these birds certainly intimidated me. I was already feeling a certain amount of trepidation about entering their cage when Kerri advised me to put on some sunglasses, just in case the vultures took a fancy to my eyes.

Bird scavenging, she explained, has developed into highly specialized professions of behaviour, with vulture species divided into various 'guilds' according to the design of their beaks. There are 'tearers', 'peckers' and 'pullers', each type working in an uneasy, belligerent teamwork to get the job done on a shared carcass. I guessed that the pullers were the ones most likely to be interested in my eyes, and I was right.

'In South Africa, the lappet-faced vultures are the knives,' Kerri said. These tearers are able to rip through tough hides using their short necks and powerful narrow beaks, which can exert pressure of 1.4 tonnes per square centimetre. And Cape vultures are indeed pullers, with long muscular necks and sharp beaks ideal for reaching deep inside a carcass to gobble up soft flesh and organs. Yet, despite their imposing size, the Capes cannot tear open the carcass themselves. So if there are no lappet-faced vultures around, the only way for them to get to their meal is through a natural orifice – like the eyes or anus. 'They go for the soft bits,' Kerri explained. I double-checked my sunglasses and backed into the fence.

Kerri was proud of her wards. 'Vultures are the most efficient scavengers. They have special adaptations in which to clean meat off bones by their hooked tongues. Strong feet and legs to stand and hold the carcasses down. Some with long bare necks to dig into the carcass and eat from the inside out,' she enthused. She noted that one species had even evolved to consume the bare bones, once the peckers and pullers have removed all the flesh.

This division of labour explains why you'll sometimes see vultures standing around, looking a bit gormless, near a freshly dead animal – a behaviour that helped contribute to the myth that they prefer putrid flesh to fresh kill. 'There'll be an elephant carcass that's been sitting there for days and the vultures haven't touched it,' Kerri said. 'The simple reason is not because they prefer rotten carcasses, it's that they can't get in so they're waiting for it to become soft so they can rip it open.'

Once the vultures get inside a corpse, the resulting frenzy can be quite the show. Buffon described feeding vultures as 'displaying the bitterness of unprovoked rage'. I thought it was more of a dark comedy, something directed by Quentin Tarantino and starring the original 'angry birds' stuffing their faces with the bilious speed of an American hot dog-eating contest. There was much strutting and hissing, drooling and sneezing, posturing and pecking, as the cow quickly disappeared behind a writhing mass of spaghetti necks and bald heads caked in bloody remains and buzzing with flies.

We have a visceral revulsion to the vulture's eating habits, and with good reason. If we were to feast on rotting flesh we'd likely get very sick very quick from a host of nasties, including some very unforgiving ones, like botulism or anthrax. Vultures survive by obliterating disease-bearing bacteria with some of the strongest stomach acids in the animal kingdom, with a pH similar to that of battery acid. As an added bonus it makes their excreta so caustic they can disinfect their feet after dinner simply by defecating. Kerri told me that vulture excrement is such an effective disinfectant that I could use it to clean my hands before we ate our own lunch. I decided to take her word for it.

Like some form of socially awkward hand sanitizer, this effluvium not only keeps the bird clean but it also helps prevent the spread of disease. By hoovering up pestilence and pooping out purity, vultures are their own highly effective, double-quick forensic clean-up unit. One hundred vultures can strip a carcass in twenty minutes, before contagion has had a chance to set in or spread very far. What little has attached itself to a bird gets washed away in a cleansing stream of ordure.

The speed with which vultures consume their food has been reviled by natural historians as 'a revolting sight of selfish greed'. But Kerri said it should be rebranded as an act of heroic generosity. Recent studies have shown that in areas where there are no vultures, carcasses take up to three to four times longer to decompose, a situation that favours contagion. Scavenging vultures ultimately save us humans huge quantities of cash in medical and litter collection bills.

You can see the costs to humans most vividly in places where vultures have suffered dramatic declines. 'Look at India and Pakistan, where the government has spent over thirty-four billion dollars on human health issues because vultures have been almost eradicated,' Kerri pointed out to me. India's vultures have been virtually destroyed by accidental poisoning after eating the carcasses of cattle treated with an anti-inflammatory drug called diclofenac; it's estimated that up to 99 per cent of the three main species have been killed. Without so many vultures around, there's an excess of carrion. The knock-on effect has been a massive increase in feral dogs and a huge rise in rabies.

'The amount of money that's going in for rhino poaching in comparison to vulture conservation is astronomical,' Kerri said. 'There's only a certain amount of funding for scavengers because people don't like them, which is crazy because if we lose our rhinos, yes, it's going to be sad; I love rhinos – but the world will continue. If we lose our vultures there will be collapses throughout Africa and it's going to affect every single one of us.' She continued. 'That's what people don't understand. People's mindsets need to change. It's almost like a beauty contest. You know you have Miss World and everyone's rooting for the most beautiful woman and yet the most beautiful woman is not going to change the world. It might be the person who's behind the scenes that's changing things.'

It helps that Miss World – and the rhino, for that matter – doesn't vomit on small children or poop down her own legs. But none of this put off Kerri from her mission – or from her belief that the vulture is in fact a beautiful bird. 'I find them charismatic,' she insisted. 'To me they are the epitome of freedom.' And the way to truly appreciate a vulture's beauty, she said, is to watch one fly.

Cape vultures need to be able to cover vast distances, as economically as possible, as they search far and wide for their next meal. Weighing about the same as a human toddler doesn't exactly facilitate energy-saving flight. Simply getting airborne is tricky enough, let alone travelling thousands of kilometres without the need for hours of exhaustive wing-flapping. Vultures have evolved to crack this problem: they can glide at speeds of up to 80 kilometres per hour whilst expending hardly any energy at all.

To understand how vultures achieve this aerodynamic marvel I was encouraged to jump off a mountain. Kerri and her partner, Walter, a keen paraglider, assured me that this experience would bring me closest to the magnificence of these birds, as well as showing a different, more gregarious side to their nature. I thought it sounded like a reasonable idea until I got to our launching point on the crest of the Magaliesberg range; an ancient crust of almost sheer cliffs one hundred times older than Everest and nearly 900 metres high.

The biggest vulture species, like the Cape vultures that nest in the craggy contours of this aged escarpment, must make use of altitude in order to launch themselves into the air with minimal exertion. Their impressive 2.5-metre wingspan then hitches a lift on updraughts or rising thermals, which propel them, like unseen elevators, thousands of feet into the sky. Today, I would be doing something similar, strapped to Walter and flying tandem under his trusty glider.

I peered over the edge of the cliff to a valley shimmering far below and felt decidedly un-bird-like. Walter handed me a plastic helmet which I dutifully strapped to my head whilst thinking how this flimsy pacifier offered even less protection than my cotton shorts had done earlier in the day against a potential backdoor, beak-based burglary.

Paragliding is a counter-intuitive sport. We had to literally run off the cliff into thin air, like they do in cartoons. It was the ultimate leap of faith, followed by a terrifying moment of weightlessness. Then the glider's wings caught the rising air and we started to circle upwards.

Initially, we rode the thermals alone. Then, as if out of nowhere, we were joined, one by one, by spiralling vultures. As Kerri had predicted, the birds were very different in the air, curious and quite playful. And they *were* magnificent. For us, the thermals were like an invisible rollercoaster, bumpy and unpredictable, if not for the constant peeping of Walter's altimeter. We were jolted, tugged and tripped up by capricious currents. Yet the vultures were apparently at one with the wind, their massive wings barely twitching as they effortlessly swooped in close to give us a good eye-balling, before peeling off and shooting high above us, as if flaunting their aero-perfection.

The vulture's wings are so perfectly adapted for soaring flight that they provided Wilbur Wright with a model for stabilizing the wings of his first successful aircraft, which he developed after hours of observing turkey vultures. Unfortunately, today the conceptual descendants of the Wrights' first flight are colliding with their inspiration in our overcrowded skies.

Bird strike, as it's known in the aviation business, is a hazardous affair, one that costs the US government over $900 million a year and has destroyed thirty aircraft since 1985, making birds significantly more lethal than terrorists. This might explain why the American military have some-one testing their latest jet-engine aircraft for bird resistance by firing chickens out of cannons at point-blank range. Dead chickens, one presumes.

In an attempt to better understand the 'enemy' and predict its moves, the Feather Identification Lab of the

Smithsonian Institution in Washington DC takes forensic ornithology quite seriously. There, researchers perform DNA sequencing to ascertain the most common bird threats to planes. Every week the institute receives hundreds of packets of what they call 'snarge', aka the bloody remains of when bird meets plane. Turkey vultures win the prize for being the No.1 most damaging bird to American aircraft, which doesn't do much for their popularity with pilots.

The most puzzling snarge cases could belong to an episode of *The X-Files*. A Smithsonian Scully told *Wired* magazine, 'We've had frogs, turtles, snakes. We had a cat once that was struck at some high altitude.' After a certain amount of head-scratching about how such typically terrestrial creatures could have been caught more than a kilometre up in the air, the researchers realized they must be quarry dropped during flight by loose-taloned birds of prey. Thus, Buffon's magnanimous eagles are equally to blame for bringing down American planes, but for butter-fingered reasons.

Over the years the Smithsonian's snarge detectives have identified about five hundred species of bird and forty species of terrestrial mammal, including a rabbit that hit a flight at 500 metres. But perhaps the most incredible was a collision that forced a commercial craft to make an emergency landing on the Ivory Coast after an impact at 11,000 metres – the highest known flight of a bird ever recorded. The feathered remains were identified, with a fair amount of fanfare, as a Rüppell's griffon vulture. The bird earned its crown (and associated messy end) through the assistance of a specially adapted form of haemoglobin that enables its blood to absorb oxygen at pressures so low most other animals would pass out.

That griffon vulture was probably a high-flying freak. But vultures have been known to cruise at more conservative, but nevertheless head-spinning, heights of around 6,000 metres. By soaring from thermal to thermal they're able to chase the dry season as it creeps across the African continent and lays waste to infirm animals.

One recent study observed a Rüppell's griffon vulture travelling north from its nest in Tanzania, across Kenya, to a region in Sudan and Ethiopia as it searched for food. Such border-hopping has occasionally got these birds, and their human saviours, in political hot water. A longstanding project to reintroduce endangered griffon vultures back to their native Israel has been thwarted by paranoia and politics. Researchers at Tel Aviv University have begun tagging and tracking vultures, but the birds' long-distance lifestyle means they frequently fly over the country's borders and into hot water. Such is the fraught state of international relations in the Middle East that these vultures have been captured and accused of being Mossad spies. In 2011, the Saudi Arabian government arrested a bird they believed was part of a Zionist plot. Three years later, another vulture was detained in Sudan. And in 2016, the UN were forced to intervene and return a vulture apprehended by Lebanese villagers who were suspicious that the bird's GPS tracker was in fact a covert camera.

Ohad Hatzofe, the exasperated conservationist behind the scheme, pointed out that it's not terribly surreptitious, labelling a spy's legs with your email address. His somewhat sarcastic response to a Middle Eastern newspaper which asked him about the project was that if he were indeed recruiting secret agents, he might choose ones 'less interested in dead camels and goats'.

It seems we humans just can't help being mistrustful of vultures, though they've done nothing to deserve our suspicions. And whilst the idea of a vulture serving as a secret agent may seem like another laughable modern tall tale to be added to our pantheon, it's not as though we haven't tried to recruit animals into our war games. Get ready to meet another creature that we love to hate – the bat – which was genuinely conscripted by the American military in the Second World War, with incendiary results.

## CHAPTER 6

# BAT

## Order Chiroptera

*One of the seamen declared that he had seen the Devil, which he described in the following words. '. . . he had horns and wings, yet he crept so slowly through the grass, that if I had not been afeared, I might have touched him'. It appeared afterwards, that this poor fellow had seen a bat, which is almost black, and as large as a partridge; and his own apprehensions had furnished his Devil with horns.*

Captain James Cook, *Voyages of Discovery*, 1770

THE WORLD'S ONLY FLYING mammal has become a rather unlikely YouTube star. Not because of its cute furry face and toothy grin, but for something much darker – its uninvited presence in people's homes. There's an entire subgenre of man-versus-winged-invader videos to be found online, generally featuring an out-of-his-depth dad forced into defender mode in a desperate bid to pacify his frantic family. Hysterical mums cover their hair and crawl along the floor sobbing, whilst babies get locked in bathrooms and everyone screams like doomed teenagers in a slasher flick. In most cases the dads are armed with an ineffective assortment of ill-fitting oven gloves, brooms and blankets. Although in one, a Texan – built like the Incredible Hulk, yet too scared to trap an animal the size of his thumb in a plastic bag – winds up shooting the bat in his kitchen with a rifle at point-blank range as a toddler in a high chair wails, '*No!*'

These are modern-day video nasties. But the terrifying monster in these real-life domestic horrors is little more than a tiny disorientated insectivore.

162

Bats have probably been flying into human homes ever since we've been building them (for that matter, ever since we first sought out shelter in a cosy cave – which strictly speaking makes us the invaders of their home). The bats are simply searching for somewhere to roost, or chasing insects; they aren't interested in us. But for centuries, ancient folklore has associated such unexpected intrusions with the foretelling of death. Which is enough to make anyone scream.

Today, a person with a persistent fear of bats has a bona fide syndrome. It's called chiroptophobia, after *Chiroptera*, Greek for 'winged hand', the defining characteristic of the taxonomic order that encompasses the 1,100 or so known bat species. Online, you can find a raft of counsellors, mostly based in the US, who offer therapy for this irrational fear and loathing in the form of controlled exposure to a room full of bats – a nightmare worthy of one of Hunter S. Thompson's more menacing acid trips.

It's not just a handful of psychologically challenged Americans that are chiroptophobic. A recent survey by a bat conservation group discovered that one in five perfectly sane British people also claim to hate bats. A common perception is that they are flying vermin, or, as the bat-hating comedian Louis C. K. once called them, 'rats with leather wings'. The surveyed Brits believed that bats are blind, malevolent creatures intent on getting stuck in their hair, sucking their blood and giving them rabies – most of which is total rubbish. Bats are actually more closely related to humans than rodents, they can see perfectly well, thank you very much (some fruit bats even have colour vision that's three times as good as our own), and they have an acutely tuned echolocation system that prevents them from flying anywhere near even the most bouffant barnet. Finally, only three species have vampire tendencies, and you are more likely to get rabies from a dog or a raccoon (less than 0.05 per cent of bats carry the disease).

Bats are long overdue a major rebranding. The bedevilled bloodsuckers are in fact more Buddha than Beelzebub, being amongst the most magnanimous neighbours, charitable friends and generous lovers in the animal kingdom. They save us billions of dollars every year by eating insects that cause devastating diseases and destroy our crops. They are also the key pollinators for many tropical flowers, including bananas, avocados and agave. Without bats, there would be no tequila (which may, or may not, be a good thing for humanity). Frankly, they are more man's best friend than the dog.

What an injustice, then, that their story is in fact an eye-popping horror (quite literally) starring a Catholic priest with a sharp pair of scissors, a maverick dentist with a diabolical plan and an unusually big-balled, benevolent, blood-sharing bat as the innocent victim.

Public relations have never run smoothly for the bat. Along with the vulture they are one of the few animals that the

Bible lists as unclean, which is a little harsh for an animal that can spend up to a fifth of its time grooming and is probably significantly cleaner than most of the big book's holy scribes were.

One early Roman author went a step further: 'the nature of the bat is blood-related to that of the devil.' Their physicality is partly to blame. The arrangement of their bodies, limbs and faces, complete with forward-facing eyes and toothy smiles, are unnervingly human but decidedly inhuman at the same time. Once artists started painting images of bat-winged figures to represent the Devil – like those in the famous representation of Dante's *Inferno* – the negative branding was complete.

It didn't help the bat's standing that the natural history books of the medieval period were penned by religious types who viewed the bat's neither-here-nor-there nature with grave suspicion. The British clergyman and naturalist Edward Topsell felt obliged to include these deviant winged creatures in his seventeenth-century book of birds, *The Fowles of Heaven*. The bats' refusal to conform to the model of their angelic avian cousins caused the man of the cloth much consternation. He was particularly bothered by the tiny mammals' distinctly un-birdlike breasts, teeth and love of darkness, which encouraged all manner of satanic comparisons. Topsell illustrated his concerns with sketches of bizarre bosomy beasts wearing wide, wicked grins. In a final, hallucinatory postscript, he accused these errant birds of guzzling the oil out of his church lamps.

*The bats from Topsell's* Fowles of Heaven *(c.1613) have a distinctly diabolical look about them as they vaunt their un-birdlike breasts and gnashers.*

As science headed into the Enlightenment, biologists continued to be bothered by the bat's anomalous anatomy, which defied classification. The imperious Georges-Louis Leclerc, Comte de Buffon, gave the bat a suitably damning write-up in his encyclopaedia. 'An animal, like the bat, which is half a quadruped and half a bird, and which, upon the whole, is neither the one nor the other, must be a monstrous being,' he said. 'It is an imperfect quadruped, and a still more imperfect bird. A quadruped should have four feet, and a bird should have feathers and wings.' Buffon was also offended by the bat's nether regions, which appeared to have been borrowed from another species, perhaps – rather alarmingly – his own. 'The penis, which is pendulous and loose', he announced, 'is a thing peculiar to man, [and] the monkeys.'

Like the Comte, I was quite taken aback the first time I saw a bat's penis. It was about ten years ago, in a remote corner of the Peruvian Amazon where I had joined Dr Adrian Tejedor, a Cuban Chiroptera specialist, mist-netting for bats. This involved setting up what looked like a very large, very fine badminton net in an opening in the rainforest, then waiting, like spiders, for some bats to fly into our trap (the netting being so fine they could not detect it). We sat for several hours in the dark, sticky gloom of the night, our torches off so as not to scare the bats, an exercise in sloth-like boredom control – although I do recall being entertained by a surreal glow-in-the-dark fungus that looked like something you'd stick on your wall as a child.

The first guest to fly into the net was the lesser spear-nosed bat. Adrian was excited; he had not seen this species for nine years. I was excited by the size of its penis, which dangled almost down to the bat's knee and struck me as anything but aerodynamic. Adrian giddily informed me that 'penis length in mammals appears to be correlated with the degree of promiscuity in females.' Lady lesser spear-nosed bats must be absolute strumpets, then, since the males are famous for their especially elongated appendages. The longer their penis, the further they can insert their sperm into the female, giving their seed a head start over that of their romantic rivals.

Since my first chiropteran date had effectively been with the Dirk Diggler of bats, I thought I might have a slightly warped opinion of their wedding tackle. But the work of another bat specialist I know, Dr Kate Jones, Professor of Ecology and Biodiversity at University College London, has revealed that some bats have not only

*Could that grin be any wider? Me and my big penis bat prize, from a night mist-netting in the Peruvian Amazon (the bat looking rather less thrilled with the unwarranted exposure).*

pendulous penises but big, bulging testicles to boot. In the war of the sexes, upping the ante in sperm production can be another useful tactic for males trying to outsmart highly promiscuous females – especially those, like many bats, that have the sneaky ability to store a male's sperm.

Dr Jones knows a thing or two about bat genitalia. She was part of a team that methodically measured the gonads and brains of 344 bat species. As warm-blooded animals that fly for a living, bats exist on an energetic knife-edge, and both these organs are quite expensive, metabolically. Jones's team had a hunch that there was a trade-off between the two organs, and there was: monogamous bat species had tiny testes and big brains, whilst promiscuous ones had quite the reverse. One particular swinger sports a pair of testicles that accounts for a whopping 8.4 per cent of its body weight – the Rafinesque's big-eared bat (artfully named after its *other* enormous organ) flies about hauling the human equivalent of a pair of large pumpkins between its thighs, guided by an inversely proportional, dumbed-down mental capacity.

The degree of male promiscuity is not a driving force in the brains-to-balls trade-off. Instead, it is the *female*'s philandering which influences the evolution of brain and gonad size in the male bat. Whether this has any bearing on human evolution is hard to predict, but, ladies, you have been warned.

Bats' porn-star credentials don't end there. It turns out they are also amongst a select group of mammals known to engage in oral sex. The female short-nosed fruit bat was the first to be observed performing fellatio on her partners; then a few years later the males got in on the action, when cunnilingus was documented in another fruit bat species, the aptly named Indian flying fox. The scientists were surprised. The only other mammals they could find evidence of regularly indulging in this type of sexual behaviour were primates, and they reportedly 'held many meetings to discuss the functions'.

Their eventual conclusion from these fruity brainstorming sessions was that oral sex prolonged intercourse amongst the bats and therefore increased the chance of fertilization. It may also, particularly in the case of the Indian flying fox, be a way for the male to suck out a competitor's sperm prior to launching his own. The resulting academic paper (complete with graphic blow job-by-blow job descriptions of bat sex that would make a vicar blush) concluded that further voyeurism would definitely be required: 'Observation at close-range is needed to find out whether the male's tongue enters the vagina or not.' Well, quite.

Details of the bat's lurid sexuality would probably have proved quite stimulating for the ecclesiastical authors of the medieval bestiaries, who were always on the lookout for bawdy animal behaviour from which they might weave their high-minded judgements. Edward Topsell, for instance, thought the bat was lustful simply because of its naked wings. Oversized genitals and a proclivity for oral sex would have really given the clergyman something to sink his didactic teeth into.

The bat's disturbing physiology aroused almost as much bad press as its diet. Amongst the more ridiculous rumours was the accusation that bats were after your bacon. This widespread medieval myth was described in one of the earliest encyclopaedias of the natural world, *Hortus Sanitatis* ('The Garden of Health'), published in Germany in 1491. The book even included a helpful woodcut illustrating half a dozen bats hovering greedily around a dangling ham (nestled amongst solemn accounts of dragons and the diagnostic virtues of urine). This spurious craving for cured meat was reflected in the name for bat in German: *Speckmaus*, literally 'ham mouse'.

Such was the sticking power of this exceptionally misleading moniker that a pair of German scientists saw the need to put it to the test. In the early nineteenth century, when other researchers were wrestling with big questions like the origin of the species and the ordering of the elements, these earnest gentlemen contributed to the march of scientific progress by attempting to sustain a cage of would-be bacon thieves with a daily ration of rashers. These were resolutely rejected by the incarcerated beasts, which starved to death after a week. The bats' terminal hunger strike did, however, satisfy the Germans that their beloved hams were safe from *Speckmaus* robbery.

La.rv.
Cespertilio. Aresto. Cespriliões
bñt pedes sicut aues: z carēt cau
da qm sunt agrestes. Jparq ale
sunt membianales id est cozio indistincte
z si caudam habuissent. motum alaz pro

*Half a dozen bats earn their 'ham mouse' moniker as they congregate greedily over some cured meat in the early German encyclopaedia* Hortus Sanitatis *(1491), feeding the paranoia that bats were after people's bacon.*

The bats' reputation only got worse when news emerged of species that sustained themselves with something far more sinister than cured meat: other animals' blood. The association of bats with a certain Transylvanian count would prove to be the nail in the coffin for human–bat relations.

The first reports came from the sixteenth-century explorers of the New World who returned to Europe with vivid tales of bloodthirsty beasts. In 1526, Gonzalo Fernández de Oviedo y Valdés, the Spanish writer and historian who persistently slurred our friend the sloth, described bats that 'suck such a great amount of blood from the wound that it is difficult to believe unless one has observed it.' The following year, the Spanish conquistador Francisco Montejo y Álvarez and his troops were said to be victims of 'a great plague of bats which attacked not only the beasts of burden but the men themselves, sucking their blood when they were asleep'.

These early descriptions win prizes for melodrama, if not for plausibility. For a start, vampire bats don't suck blood; they lap it up from an open wound like a cat drinking milk. And whilst they can consume close to their own body weight during a single thirty-minute blood-drinking binge, they are the size of a mouse, which means their liquid diet amounts to little more than a spoonful – an insignificant portion of the several litres of blood swilling around a mammal the size of a human. They also rarely attack people; they are much more likely to feed on domesticated animals like cattle or chickens. The conquerors of the New World were clearly more interested in gold and land-grabbing than they were in accurate zoological sketches. Their macabre tales put these fiendish beasts on the map, but it would be some time before the bats acquired their infamous blood-sucking handle.

The word 'vampir' means 'blood drunkenness' and is of Slavic origin, but the mythology can be found in a number of ancient cultures from Babylon and the Balkans to India and China, suggesting a fear deeply embedded in the human psyche. And though these supernatural ghouls roamed the night draining humans dry of life, and possessed the power of transformation, they never took the form of a bat. The vampire's alter egos were an unlikely bunch that would struggle to get cast in a modern-day horror flick. Horses, dogs and fleas were common, but vampires were also said to take the form of watermelons (not exactly bitey) and household tools (Help! Trowel attack!).

Nevertheless, during the late seventeenth and eighteenth centuries, vampirism became an obsession in much of Eastern Europe. This was a time of mysterious scourges like the Great Plague and smallpox whose deadly effects were often believed to be the work of the 'living dead'. Newspapers reported vampirism as fact; sovereigns sent delegates to investigate 'vampire epidemics' in Hungary, Prussia, Serbia and Russia. It was only a matter of time before the reports of the mythological bloodsuckers and the authentic blood-lovers collided. When they did, it created a bloody mess.

The great taxonomist Carl Linnaeus officially anointed bats with their infamous title in 1758. He described *Vespertilio vampyrus* as the species which 'draws blood from the sleeping at night' in the tenth edition of his classification bible, *Systema Naturæ*. There followed a flurry of similarly named bats from all over the world: *Vampyressa* (1843), *Vampyrops* (1865) and *Vampyrodes* (1889) were all variations on the theme. Johann Baptist von Spix, curator of zoology at the Bavarian university, showed a little more imaginative flair when he named the new species of bat he'd collected in Brazil *Sanguisuga crudelissima* – 'a bloodsucker most cruel' (known colloquially as the 'long-tongued vampire'). Spix claimed he'd seen them 'hover like phantoms in the profound darkness of the night'.

The problem is that not one of these bats had ever tasted so much as a sip of blood. They were all innocent fruit eaters, damned to carry the misleading baggage of a sanguivorous name for scientific eternity.

Whilst it was easy enough to identify the scene of a vampire bat attack – the anticoagulant in the bat's saliva makes the wound bleed sufficiently to leave a big, bloody clue in the morning – laying hands on the culprit during its nocturnal drinking binge was significantly harder. Taxonomists in Europe, trying to identify the true vampire from a line-up of dried specimens and highly unreliable 'eyewitness' evidence of New World explorers, made a fatal mistake: they assumed the largest bats they were sent must be the bloodsuckers (they were, in fact, benign vegetarians). Adding to this bloody mix-up, when a naturalist finally got his hands on an actual vampire bat, no one believed him that it drank blood.

It was the Spanish cartographer and military commander Félix de Azara who succeeded in collecting the creature that would become known as the common vampire bat in Paraguay in 1801. Azara was a talented amateur naturalist who discovered hundreds of new species. He had, however, dared to criticize the great Buffon, calling the Comte out for what he believed to be 'vulgar, false and

THE UNEXPECTED TRUTH ABOUT ANIMALS

mistaken notices' in the aristocratic Frenchman's epic *Histoire Naturelle*. This impudence did not sit well with the snooty European natural history set of which Buffon was self-appointed royalty. When Azara claimed to have finally laid his hands on this infamous and elusive 'biter', the scientific establishment quickly dismissed him. The animal in question was named *Desmodus rotundus* after its fused front teeth. No mention was made of its gory diet.

The creeping fashion for Romantic Gothic horror literature ensured that vampires had penetrated the popular consciousness by the early nineteenth century. The embrace of bat-like wings, bat-like movements and – eventually – actual bats in these stories made for considerably scarier monsters than blood-sucking melons. And breathed new life into old legends. With the huge popularity of Bram Stoker's *Dracula*, bat fact and vampire fiction were for ever entwined, with an innocent fruit bat cast as the evil villain. This led to some disappointing cases of mistaken identity.

In July 1839, the Surrey Zoological Gardens scored a major coup by procuring a 'Vampyre' that they proudly boasted was 'the first living specimen ever seen in England'. The gardens were home to an eclectic menagerie once owned by the impresario Edward Cross, who had relocated his animals from the Strand in London after an elephant with a bad case of toothache had murdered its keeper. He was looking to start afresh after the scandal, and the gardens were hoping to draw a crowd with this display of the infamous bat. The press, however, were somewhat underwhelmed by the behaviour of the legendary beast. 'Although this bat is the Vampyre Bat, to whom so many bloodthirsty traits have been attributed', went one dispatch, 'his appearance is, by no means, ferocious.' The bat was 'docile' and 'appeared fond of being noticed'. The greatest disappointment: it would 'devour cherries' – and nothing else. This Vampyre was a fruit bat, after all.

Deliciously bloodthirsty 'scientific accounts' of vampire bats had promised a 'formidable species' that flew into bedchambers to attack their unwitting inhabitants. 'If they find any part of the body exposed, they invariably fasten upon it, insinuate their aculeated tongue into a vein, with all the art of the most experienced surgeon, and continue to suck the blood till they are satiated,' said one of the more popular animal encyclopaedias of the period. The author then turned his sharp eye to the details of a vampiric episode: 'It frequently occurs that persons, when awaked from their sleep (through loss of blood), have not sufficient strength left to bind up the orifice. The reason why the puncture is not felt is that, whilst the Vampyre is sucking, it continues to fan the air with its wings in such a manner that the refreshing breeze lulls the sufferer into a still deeper sleep.' This is what the public expected – and wanted – to see.

Had the Surrey Zoological Gardens got their hands on a genuine vampire, it would not have subscribed to the encyclopaedia's Gothic fantasy any more than the fraudulent fruit bat. But its authentic behaviour is arguably far creepier.

Vampire bats tend to approach their victim not from the air but by stalking them from the ground. They use their exaggerated winged hands to drag themselves forward whilst bouncing along on a pair of stunted rear legs. Whilst this may sound awkward, they can move surprisingly fast on foot. One inspired scientist, for instance, placed vampire bats on a treadmill – presumably causing some raised eyebrows down the gym – where he clocked them at an impressive top speed of over 2 metres per second (five times faster than a sloth at full tilt). Not only can these diminutive bats bound past our favourite folivore, they can also launch themselves vertically into the air from the ground, like a Harrier Jump Jet, which helps make for a swift getaway.

Then there's the issue of their iconic liquid diet. The bats tend not to feed indiscriminately, but instead use special infrared sensors in their nose to detect the heat of blood that's pumping nice and close to the skin – and therefore easier to access. Favourite hotspots for incision are fur- and feather-free; think of feet (ticklish), ears (annoying) and anuses (good Lord). As if that weren't alarming enough, the bats will return to feed on the same spot several nights in a row, guided by their unique ability to listen out for and memorize a preferred victim's breathing patterns.

Bloodthirsty bum biters that stalk their prey by listening to them breathe may sound more evil than Dracula himself. In actuality, vampire bats are one of the animal kingdom's most magnanimous animals.

Being a flying mammal is an energetically expensive existence for which an exclusively haematophagous diet provides far from the ideal fuel. Blood consists of 80 per cent water and absolutely no fat. Vampire bats have a specially adapted digestive system that allows them to eliminate excess water quickly by urinating as they feed. Not a great look by human standards, but it enables the bat to consume maximum blood protein in one sitting without its stomach exploding (surely an even less attractive outcome). But with no fat, and no opportunity to build up fat reserves, they must feed at least every seventy hours or they die. And it's not as easy as you might imagine to find an exposed foot or anus (consider what hooves and tails were invented for). Up to 30 per cent of bats fly home empty. Two consecutive nights of feeding failure means almost certain starvation.

One of the world's leading experts on bats, Professor Gerald Wilkinson of the University of Maryland, has discovered an adaptation that improves their odds: the bats have evolved a food-sharing system that sees victorious vampires vomit up congealed blood for their hungry neighbours. The thought of *Exorcist*-style projectile puke might turn your stomach, but it's nothing short of a lifesaver to a starving bat. Wilkinson told me that the 'bats appear to be *competing* to give blood.' More curiously, they regurgitate for roost mates that are not even family members, and are more likely to share with previous blood-regurgitating partners than their own relatives. 'Relatedness has got nothing to do with it,' he explained. 'A bigger predictor of sharing behaviour is whether they have been helped by that individual before.' In this caring, sharing, blood-spewing community, bats form strong and meaningful bonds with one another. 'You can think of them almost as friends.'

So in the case of vampire bats, blood is thicker than, *er* . . . blood. The bats' reciprocal altruism flies in the face of conventional models of what biologists call *kin selection*, in which animals are expected to do favours only for those with whom they share genes. Examples of reciprocal altruism are extremely rare in the animal kingdom. Wilkinson pointed out that 'outside of the primates – baboons and chimps – they are very hard to find.' So it's not just that pendulous penis that we have in common with the bats. 'Vampire bats are similar to primates in that they also use grooming to establish social bonds, and that influences who helps whom and the formation of coalitions,' he said.

If you are a vampire bat you can't get an invite to the blood-puking party with just a bit of casual grooming, however. One of Wilkinson's PhD students recently found that the bats' bonds take a considerable time to form. Bats placed in an enclosure and forced to roost with complete strangers don't start sharing food for a good two years. 'They don't just trust anyone,' according to Wilkinson. Vampires have an extraordinarily long lifespan for an animal of their size – thirty years compared to two to three years for a similar-sized mouse. It would seem that they use their time in this life to develop a wide circle of longstanding, charitable friendships, which flies in the face of their wicked antisocial reputation.

One of the reasons that bats slipped so easily into vampire mythology is that they appear to possess somewhat occult powers, at least when viewed from a human's sensory perspective. Their spooky ability to navigate in the dark branded them familiars of witches, which meant it was genuinely scary for a single lady to have bats visiting her home during the Middle Ages. In 1332, Lady Jacaume of Bayonne, in France, was publicly burnt to death after her neighbours spied 'crowds of bats' fluttering in and out of her property.

Various bits of bats were often used in sorcery. Shakespeare's witches in *Macbeth* included 'wool of bat' in their famous incantation, but they weren't following the usual recipe; bats' blood was the perennial favourite of any genuine wannabe sorceress. It was also a key ingredient in 'flying ointment', which was said to help keep a witch from bumping about in the dark on her broom. Despite the popularity of this concoction from the fifteenth to the eighteenth centuries, no woman is likely to have left the ground, let alone whizzed about the night like a bat. Other ingredients in the salve, like belladonna, might have made certain ladies *feel* like they were flying, thanks to their psychotropic effects.

It took science rather a long time to figure out the source of the bat's seemingly supernatural skills. Not all bats echolocate; most of the fruit-eating mega-bats use their eyes to navigate like normal mammals. Those that do form a complex sonic map of their surroundings by listening to the echo of their calls and judging distances by the quality of sound waves reflected back at them. This is mind-bending enough, but the concept was especially hard for scientists to get their head around since bats themselves seem to be silent. They are, in fact, flying along screaming their heads off about twenty decibels louder than the speakers at a Black Sabbath concert (thereby putting the sonic prowess of the band's famous, bat-eating frontman Ozzy Osbourne somewhat to shame). It's simply that bats' high-pitched squeals fall almost exclusively outside the human range of hearing and are therefore inaudible to us.

It wasn't until the 1930s, when a Harvard biologist named Donald Griffin collaborated with an engineer to build a special sonic detector, that we were finally able to eavesdrop on the bats' silent screams and the notion of their having some kind of supernatural 'sixth sense' was finally swept away. This was a great if late-breaking development for bats, as the cryptic chiropterans had suffered well over a hundred years of torture in the efforts to extract their bio-sonar secrets.

Their trials had begun in the eighteenth century, with an Italian Catholic priest in possession of an insatiable curiosity, a sharp pair of scissors and a résumé that reads like the work of a biological sadist. Lazzaro Spallanzani sliced off the heads of seven hundred snails to find out if they would regenerate (he claimed they could) and forced ducks to swallow hollow glass beads to get to grips with the pulverizing action of their gizzards. He was also the first person to resuscitate the strangely indestructible microorganism known as a tardigrade, the only animal to survive freezing, radiation and the vacuum of space (in addition to Spallanzani's inquisitiveness). With such a keen interest in dissecting and resurrecting life, it is perhaps little wonder that he sought the sanctuary of ecclesiastical sponsorship. The Church helped finance his experimental endeavours and also provided him with some degree of absolution.

In 1793, aged sixty-four, Spallanzani turned his outrageously inquiring mind to the bat's knack for navigating in the dark. He had noticed that his pet owl became totally disorientated and crashed into walls if the candle that lit his room was blown out. Why, he wondered, did a bat not do the same? To find out, the padre sharpened up his clippers for a set of excruciating experiments.

It all started relatively innocently. Spallanzani fashioned a selection of tiny hoods for his subjects, choosing different types of cloth and styles designed to obscure the bat's vision to varying degrees. To increase the challenge for the hooded bats, he released them in a room containing a homemade obstacle course of long twigs and silk threads that hung from the ceiling. The hoods left the bats disorientated in flight, a bit like his owl, but Spallanzani wasn't sure if this was because the bats were flying blind or because their hoods were a bit too tight. So he took the next logical step and blinded the bats.

'We can blind a bat in two ways,' he cheerfully announced in one letter of his long and gory correspondence with his Swiss collaborator, Professor Jurine (pronounced with a regrettably silent 'J'). He went on to inventory his medieval torture-house methods: 'burning the cornea with a thin, red-hot wire, or . . . pulling the eyeball out and cutting it off'.

There is never any glimmer of moral dilemma in the priest's graphic letters to Jurine. This could have been a by-product of the bat's pseudo-satanic status – or something else entirely. Spallanzani's actions appear to have been shockingly cruel, but this was a man who, in an effort to understand his own digestive juices, had once taken to swallowing cloth bags of food attached to long strings, which he could hoik back up after a decent period of stewing. What were a few bats' eyes in the quest for knowledge? Especially when the results would prove so thrilling:

> With a pair of scissors I removed completely the eyeballs of a bat . . . [when] thrown into the air . . . the animal flew quickly . . . with the speed and sureness of an uninjured bat . . . my astonishment at this bat, which absolutely could see, although deprived of its eyes, is inexpressible.

The revelation was indeed nothing short of a miracle. Especially given that Spallanzani had filled the sockets of the bat's eyes with hot wax and covered them with tiny leather goggles, just for good measure.

Having deduced that the blinded bat couldn't possibly be navigating by sight, Spallanzani and Professor Jurine proceeded to creatively eliminate the animal's remaining senses, one by one.

First, they tackled the sense of touch. This was deemed a likely candidate for the bat's wondrous sixth-sense skills, since blind humans at the time were rumoured to find their way 'unharmed through the streets of a city' by sensing 'changes through their skin'. Spallanzani used a pot of furniture varnish to 'coat the whole body of a blinded bat, including snout and wings'. Perhaps unsurprisingly, the heavily lacquered animal at first struggled with flight, but it soon 'regained its vigour' and flew without restraint. Leaving nothing to chance, the priest repeated the experiment with yet more lacquer. 'It is to be noted', he wrote to his scientific confidant, 'that a second and third coat of varnish does not hinder the normal flight of the animal.'

The attempt to eliminate the bat's sense of smell led to his first big experimental setback. 'I stopped up the nostrils', Spallanzani informed Jurine, 'but the creature soon fell to the ground, overcome with the difficulty of breathing.' The awkward problem of the bats' needing to breathe forced the Italian to improvise. He next fastened 'small fragments of sponge' soaked in strong-smelling salts in front of the bats' nostrils. They 'flew as freely as ever', he reported.

The results from the test for taste were more perfunctory: 'The removal of the tongue produced no result.'

One thing did make a difference to the bat's flight: obliterating their capacity for hearing. This the Italian achieved through a variety of means worthy of the Spanish Inquisition. He tried cutting or burning off the bat's ears, sewing them shut, filling them with hot wax and piercing them with 'red hot shoe nails'. The last approach finally proved too much for the bat, which 'fell down in a perpendicular direction when thrown into the air'. It died the following morning, raising uncomfortable questions about whether the not inconsiderable discomfort involved in these experiments was in fact the cause for the bat's blundering flight. Spallanzani, never to be defeated, came up with yet another creative solution, crafting custom-made miniature ear trumpets out of brass. These could either be filled with wax (eliminating sound) or left empty (providing a control).

It was the experiments with these tiny ear trumpets that finally gave our intrepid bat-botherers the confidence to declare that bats need to be able to hear in order to see in the dark. The only issue was the apparently silent nature of bats in flight, which troubled the priest no end. 'But how, if God love me, can we explain or even conceive in the hypothesis of hearing?' asked Spallanzani. In the end he supposed that the sound of bats' wings might somehow be reflected by objects 'and that they judge the distances from the quality of this sound'. He was wrong. But how was he to know that bats are actually screaming louder than a fire alarm, at a frequency outside human perception? The study of sound at this time was still very much in its infancy, although significant breakthroughs were only around the corner.

Given the ingenious and fastidious nature of the experiments, not to mention the eye-popping sacrifices made by the bats, it is unfortunate that this work was mostly ignored by the scientific establishment. But it was. For the next 120 years, it was widely asserted that bats navigated not by sound, or even by sight, but by touch.

This conviction can be traced to one man, the esteemed French zoologist and anatomist Georges Cuvier (brother of the beaver-keeping Frédéric we met earlier). For reasons best known to himself, Georges was unconvinced by Spallanzani and Jurine's methodical mutilations. In 1800, without making a single experiment himself, in the first of his epic, five-volume review of comparative anatomy, the Frenchman authoritatively declared: 'To us the organs of touch seem sufficient to explain all the [obstacle avoidance] phenomena which bats exhibit.'

Cuvier's star was very much in the ascendant, and his word final. Amidst the turmoil of post-revolutionary Paris, the ambitious scientist had the ear of Napoleon, who'd charged him with developing a national science programme. Lone voices of dissension, such as British physician Sir Anthony Carlisle – who after his own experiments concluded that bats avoided obstacles 'owing to extreme acuteness of hearing' – went largely unheard. The more typical attitude was expressed by one George Montagu, who in 1809 sarcastically asked, 'Since bats see with their ears, do they hear with their eyes?'

Whilst such academic jeering must have frustrated our dedicated 'bat men', the bats suffered a far worse indignity; generations of the beast were required to undergo a further century of torture and mutilation. Investigators around the world took to replicating the dynamic duo's experiments. Countless more bats were shaved and covered in Vaseline, their eyes glued shut or gouged out, their ears excised or plugged with cement-like substances. Every attempt failed to produce a conclusive result. Ultimately, salvation (for both the bats and the thwarted researchers) arrived from a remarkable source: the sinking of the *Titanic*.

Sir Hiram Stevens Maxim was an American-born, British-naturalized engineer with a particular flair for innovation. His left-field brain apparently was capable of dreaming up gadgets for everyone – the world's first portable automatic machine gun (for the boys), hair-curling irons (for the girls), automatic fire sprinklers (for the conscientious) and self-resetting mousetraps (for the less so). His most elaborate project was a steam-powered flying machine that briefly 'flew' before crashing in 1894. Disasters perhaps weighed heavily on Maxim's mind after that point. For when the *Titanic* had its catastrophic collision with an unseen iceberg in 1912, he was spurred to devise a means to prevent similar tragedies. His inspiration came entirely from bats.

'The wreck of the *Titanic* was a severe and painful shock to us all,' he wrote at the time. 'I asked myself: "Has science reached the end of its tether? Is there no possible means of avoiding such a deplorable loss of life and property?"' The inventor didn't deliberate for too long. 'At the end of four hours it occurred to me that ships could be provided with what might be appropriately called a sixth sense, that would detect large objects in their immediate vicinity without the aid of a searchlight.'

Maxim borrowed the idea of the sixth sense from a close reading of Spallanzani's long-dismissed work. The engineer was struck by the soundness of the proposal that bats must navigate by hearing. He decided they must be listening for the reflected echo of the sound of their wings, and that the reason they seemed to be silent was that the sound they made was outside the frequencies audible to humans. Here, Maxim made a key mistake: he assumed the bats' pitch was *below* our hearing range rather than above it. He also incorrectly assumed the source of the sounds was the bats' wings instead of their mouth and nose. But he was right that the sounds are *outside* our hearing range. This was the crucial missing piece of the puzzle and paved the way for the next wave of thinking. A few years later, the British physiologist Hamilton Hartridge suggested that bats made inaudible high-frequency sounds. Then it was only a matter of time before their secret sonar was sussed out.

Manmade sonar was worked out first, however. Shortly after Maxim went public with his proposal, two inventors filed patents for an acoustic navigation system that – like bats' – detected sound reflected off objects to judge their size and relative distance. In 1914, an iceberg was successfully detected from a distance of 3 kilometres in a field test. If Cuvier hadn't obscured Spallanzani's gruesome research, nautical sonar might have been invented a good decade earlier, perhaps saving the 1,500 people who drowned with the doomed ocean liner. We will never know how the course of history might have been changed.

But the past has taught us one thing: bats are better inspiration for uncovering ways to save lives than to destroy them.

Sir Hiram Maxim wasn't the only maverick inventor to have his imagination fired up by bats. Sorry to say, however, that he may have been the sanest. A hare-brained scheme to blow up Japanese cities during the Second World War using thousands of bats as incendiary devices was significantly less successful.

Dr Lytle S. Adams, a sixty-year-old dentist from Pennsylvania, was driving home from a holiday in New Mexico on 7 December 1941 when news broke that Japan had attacked the US fleet moored at Pearl Harbor. Shocked and outraged, the dentist began to ponder a plan for American retaliation. He recalled the clouds of bats leaving the famous Carlsbad Caverns he'd seen earlier in his vacation. What if tiny bombs were strapped to thousands of bats and released into a Japanese city? The bats would naturally seek refuge in the nooks and crannies of homes, where the bombs would explode, killing unsuspecting Japanese citizens as they slumbered.

What could possibly go wrong?

Well, quite a lot. The technology of the time had yet to contrive a bomb lighter than a can of beans, which would be a struggle for an animal the size of a mouse to lift off the ground, let alone carry in flight over a great distance. Remote detonation was also very much in its infancy. Then there was the awkward problem that bats, unlike other military animal conscripts such as pigeons, porpoises and dogs, cannot be trained to follow commands. These biological ballistic devices would have a will all their own.

But despite these screaming flaws, the dentist's idea was given the green light for funding by the US military. Adams, you see, had friends in some very high places. This dentist who dabbled in invention had persuaded First Lady Eleanor Roosevelt to check out his earlier idea to deliver and pick up mail from a plane without ever having to land, and somehow his demonstration had made a sensible impression. So when Adams detailed his incendiary-bat plan in a letter to Franklin D. Roosevelt, it didn't immediately wind up in the bin where it belonged. Instead, the letter was forwarded to the National Research Defense Committee – the group from which the Manhattan Project was spun off – with a personal note of recommendation. 'This man is not a nut,' the president wrote before concluding, somewhat rashly, 'It sounds like a perfectly wild idea but is worth looking into.'

Adams' 'Proposal for Surprise Attack' had, in fact, more than a whiff of crackpot about it. He promised somewhat maniacally to 'frighten, demoralize, and excite the prejudices of the people of the Japanese Empire', whilst at the same time providing a purpose for the planet's 'despicable' winged mammals. 'The lowest form of animal life is the bat, associated in history with the underworld and regions of darkness and evil. Until now reasons for its creation have remained unexplained,' he wrote. 'As I vision it the millions of bats that have for ages inhabited our belfries, tunnels and caverns were placed there by God to await this hour.' He signed off with appropriate fanaticism: 'As fantastic as you may regard the idea, I am convinced it will work.'

Adams did indulge one tiny, niggling concern in his letter to the White House. It was important to keep in mind that his 'practical, inexpensive' plan to destroy 'the Japanese pest' might easily 'be used against us if the secret is not carefully guarded'. The batty plan was duly stamped 'top secret' and assigned the suitably sci-fi code name 'Project X-Ray'. A crack team was assembled of senior army types, arsenal experts, engineers and biologists, including Donald Griffin, the Harvard scientist who had decoded the bat's echolocation riddle in the 1930s.

Together, they set about vaulting the scheme's more vertiginous hurdles.

The first stage was to capture thousands of Mexican free-tail bats from caves in the southwest US, where they roosted in astonishing numbers – tens of millions. Then a bomb had to be developed that was light enough for the teeny 12-gram bats to transport. And in a quintessentially American twist, parts for the diminutive bomb were manufactured in a factory owned by celebrity crooner Bing Crosby.

Bats from this enormous network of caves had actually been recruited in previous wars. Or rather, their faeces had. Anyone who has ever visited a busy bat cave is painfully aware of the high levels of nitrogen contained in their guano; the intensely acrid smell of ammonia hits your throat as soon as you enter. When the Confederate states ran short of supplies during the American Civil War, the Southerners improvised by extracting this nitrogen to manufacture their explosives. Although it's unlikely that Bing's bombs were also made out of explosive bat poop, it would have been fitting if they had been.

With bats and bombs sorted, it was time to conjoin them. The miniature explosives were to be attached to the bats with simple twine, the idea being that this low-tech solution would be best because the bats would 'fly into hiding in dwellings or other structures, gnaw through the string, and leave the bombs behind'. This was one of many dangerous assumptions about the capacity for tiny, flying insectivores – which don't typically include twine in their diet – to follow military orders. The clever scientists assumed they could control the animals in other ways using their biology. They placed the bats in refrigerators, forcing them into hibernation, for easy handling and transportation, but timing their thaw proved tricky. Several early tests with dummy bombs were a dud when the bats woke either too late (causing them to plummet ingloriously to the ground with their cargo) or too soon (allowing them to escape the base).

Undeterred, a test using real incendiary devices took place in June 1943, less than two years after Adams had hatched his scheme. Things did not go as planned. A report on the experiment by one Captain Carr stated somewhat evasively that 'testing was concluded ... when a fire destroyed a large portion of the test material.' What the

*Developing a bomb small enough to be carried by a 12-gram bat was just one of the many problems in conscripting Chiroptera as airborne incendiary devices during the Second World War; their inability to follow orders being another (with suitably explosive results).*

captain failed to mention was that the barracks, control tower and countless other buildings at the Carlsbad auxiliary field station were spectacularly set on fire by a bunch of escapee bat bombs. The flames were fanned by the need to maintain military secrecy, which prevented civilian firefighters from entering the scene. People were forced to retreat to a safe distance and simply watch as the flames leapt from building to building, destroying most of the base. As a final insult, a couple of winged missiles went AWOL, taking up roost under the general's car and duly exploding.

I like to think of this as the day bats took control of their destiny and exploded Adams' diabolical death dream. The project never really recovered from this ignominious retreat. It limped on for another year, under new guidance from the Marine Corps, but in 1944 it was finally cancelled. Having set up some thirty tests and spent a couple of million dollars, the Americans put their focus on developing a bomb that exploited the power of atoms – which proved to be quite a bit easier to control than bats.

Adams was bitterly disappointed. He insisted that fires set by bat bombers could have been more destructive to Japanese cities than the two atomic bombs. 'Think of thousands of fires breaking out simultaneously over a circle of forty miles in diameter for every bomb dropped,' he later lamented. 'Japan could have been devastated, yet with small loss of life.'

No matter the final death toll for humans, the bats would surely have struggled to survive their ballistic mission if it had gone forward. When Project X-Ray was shuttered, many bats' lives were spared, but so too was their reputation in one of the few places on the planet where the animals were not reviled. Under the influence of Chinese culture, bats were popular in Japan, where they were traditionally considered a sign of good luck. Transforming them into thousands of tiny suicide bombers could only have ignited the prejudices they suffer elsewhere in the world for their sudden intrusions in homes.

Uninvited beasts are often maligned – especially when their arrival is abrupt or threatening. That is certainly the case for the next member of my menagerie, the frog. Naturalists from the age of Aristotle all the way to the Enlightenment were mystified and mortified when frogs appeared in vast numbers, suddenly and apparently out of nowhere, and concocted crazy theories by way of explanation. In more modern times, it's been the frog's mass disappearance that has preoccupied science – a mystery that hides an even crazier truth.

# CHAPTER 7

ROG

## Order Anura

*It is a most singular thing, but, after a life of six months' duration, frogs melt away into slime, though no one ever sees how it is done; after which they come to life again in the water during the spring, just as they were before. This is effected by some occult operation of Nature and happens regularly every year.*

Pliny the Elder, *Naturalis Historia*, AD 77–9

I SPENT MUCH OF the millennium year in search of a mythical underwater monster with an enigmatic name – *Telmatobius culeus*, aka the aquatic scrotum frog.

I first heard about this baggy beast whilst staying with a well-connected conservationist in Uruguay. He told me that back in the 1960s, a friend of his, Ramón 'Kuki' Avellaneda, had been cruising the vast expanses of Lake Titicaca, high up in the Andes on the border of Bolivia and Peru, in a mini-submarine with none other than Jacques Cousteau. They were on a fruitless search for lost Inca gold, but as consolation discovered gigantic aquatic frogs, which the conservationist assured me were the size of small cars.

Frogs are my favourite animal. Having made the evolutionary leap from water to land they are, to me, the original explorers. They have overcome their inherently vulnerable biology to colonize some of the most uninhabitable corners of the Earth through some truly nifty adaptations. The 6,700 or so known species of frog include those that secrete their own sunscreen, others that make their own antifreeze and some which can even fly. The earliest amphibians were genuine giants that dined on baby dinosaurs and measured almost 10 metres long. Perhaps Kuki and Cousteau had discovered a relic beast – an amphibian Nessie at the bottom of the world's highest lake.

I managed to track down Kuki spending his golden years basking amongst the beautiful near the swish seaside resort of Búzios, in Brazil. On account of being deaf as a post from his years underwater, we communicated on the phone via his son, who relayed the somewhat disenchanting information that his father's aquatic scrotum frogs were merely the size of dinner plates, not cars. I struggled to hide my disappointment from them.

*Telmatobius* was actually first discovered way back in 1867. Its laughable Latin name refers to its somewhat saggy scrotal appearance, which won't win any beauty contests but allows the frog to pull off the kind of endurance trick the great Houdini could only dream of.

Lake Titicaca is an unforgiving home. Almost 4 kilometres above sea level, the sun is fierce and the air is thin. This is no place for a delicate-skinned, cold-blooded amphibian. But *Telmatobius* survives by living almost entirely underwater, protected from the harsh UV rays and dramatic fluctuations in temperature by a big wet blanket. It rarely ever surfaces and breathes almost exclusively through its skin, which has evolved into copious folds that drape around its scrawny frame to maximize the surface area. When it's in need of more oxygen, instead of

Telmatobius culeus *fortunately has no idea that he's been named after his saggy scrotal appearance and is quite likely to end his life in a blender as a form of backstreet Viagra.*

surfacing to gulp air like a normal frog might, *Telmatobius* does press-ups on the bottom of the lake to increase the circulation of fresh oxygenated water around its droopy dermal pleats.

When Cousteau explored the lake in his mini-sub in 1969, he reported 'thousands of millions' of these big amphibians, which he said typically measured some 50 centimetres long. Today, local fishermen report that Cousteau's giants have long since vanished, and even their diminutive descendants are becoming harder to locate.

These days, the best place to find an aquatic scrotum frog is inside a blender in downtown Lima. These wrinkly amphibians are the key ingredient for a traditional form of Peruvian backstreet Viagra, popular across the country but especially in the capital. That's how I ended up begging a taxi driver I met at the airport to race me across town, in the two hours between my connecting flights, to take me to his favourite frog juice bar. As we screeched through the city at breakneck speed, I suddenly realized that my insistence on sampling the cabbie's preferred amphibian aphrodisiac might be interpreted as a come-on, so I tried to keep the conversation science-based. This was something of a challenge given my broken Spanish, his lack of English and the frog's somewhat suggestive name.

We got to the juice bar, which was little more than a ramshackle room opening onto a bustling market street and I caught my first glimpse of the legendary beast. This behemoth ball bag of the deep turned out to be a small, speckled, muddy-green frog with sad bulbous eyes staring out of its dirty glass tank.

The taxi driver ordered his regular Friday afternoon pick-me-up and, with the deftness of Tom Cruise in *Cocktail*, the no-nonsense woman behind the bar whipped a forlorn-looking frog out of the tank by its feet, whacked its head on the counter, peeled its skin like a banana and popped it in a Moulinex with some herbs and honey.

With a discernible twinkle in his eye, my guide handed me the resulting frog shake to taste. In the interests of journalism I took a small sip. It tasted sweet and creamy and not at all froggy. It was actually quite pleasant, until I thought about what was in it, but it failed to make me feel remotely fruity. Although numerous amphibians secrete chemicals that are proving to be extremely useful to science, as with so many traditional remedies, *Telmatobius* is unlikely to offer any genuine medicinal value. It's a cultural thing. Amongst the Andean people, these frogs have long been affiliated with fertility, and frog imagery dates back to before the Inca ruled the region.

They are not alone in making such links. In medieval England placing a frog in your mouth wasn't considered an aphrodisiac but rather an excellent form of contraceptive. It's hard to understand how this could have worked, although it would no doubt have deterred a suitor from kissing. In 1950s China, the Communist government's minister of health promoted swallowing a handful of live tadpoles as the preferred method of birth control. This was a distinct improvement on an ancient Chinese prescription that recommended frying the tadpoles in mercury first, which would prevent pregnancy quite effectively by poisoning everyone involved. Still, it needed some refining. The minister proceeded to run serious efficacy tests of the polliwog pregnancy preventers on mice, cats and humans. But 43 per cent of the women tested fell pregnant within four months, and in 1958, live tadpoles were officially declared to have no contraceptive power, presumably much to the relief of women (and tadpoles) all over the country.

Across cultures and continents, from folklore to science, frogs have acquired an association with sex and fertility. This has led to a legacy of misunderstandings that deliver a twisted tale of pregnancy, pestilence and plague.

Frogs have been worshipped as fertility gods for at least five thousand years. The Aztecs had a giant toad called Tlaltecuhtli as an earth-mother goddess who embodied the endless cycle of birth, death and rebirth. Their neighbours in pre-Columbian Meso-America worshipped an even older amphibian deity by the name of Centeotl, the patron of childbirth and fertility, which took the rather disturbing form of a toad sporting a row of massive udders. On the other side of the world, in ancient Egypt, the goddess of fertility and birth, Heqet, was depicted as a frog.

The most probable source of these wide-ranging myths is the frog's habit of breeding explosively – a process no less dramatic than it sounds. Their survival tactic is to overwhelm predators by gathering in immense numbers to collectively produce so many eggs they couldn't possibly all be eaten. These gatherings can be quite a sight – a writhing mass of amorous amphibians clinging to each other in twos, threes and more, for days on end.

Since almost all amphibians must breed in water, these frog orgies frequently coincide with annual rains or flooding events that are also important for human farmers. The ancient Egyptians, for example, relied on the yearly flooding of the Nile to support their agriculture. As the floodwaters receded in the spring, they left behind a rich black soil that nourished crops – and thousands of horny frogs. The fecundity of the frogs, the earth and the population were thus entwined in people's minds.

But the big mystery was where all those frogs came from to begin with.

Their sudden mass appearance puzzled the ancient philosophers, who ventured that this sexy profusion had erupted out of the earth itself, with the frogs somehow produced from the life-giving alchemy of water mixed with mud. This idea that life could be conjured out of inorganic matter was not only confined to frogs – we've already encountered it in the story of the eel. It was liberally applied to a wide range of animals that, similar to frogs and eels, lacked obvious sex organs or underwent an incomprehensible metamorphosis. Such notions had been bumping around China, India, Babylon and Egypt for some time, but it took Aristotle to pull them all together into one seriously considered, but nevertheless ill-conceived, theory of spontaneous generation.

According to Aristotle's *Historia Animalium*, certain lower animals 'are not produced from animals at all, but arise spontaneously: some are produced out of the dew which falls on foliage ... others are produced in putrefying mud and dung, others in wood, green or dry, others in excrement whether voided or still within the living animal.'

Like most of his teachings, Aristotle's theory was received with great reverence. In addition to unravelling the mystery of the frogs, his formulation provided an explanation for how maggots suddenly swarmed in rotting meat and the unnerving appearance of intestinal worms in human excrement. Naturalists who followed in his footsteps, including Pliny the Elder, ran with the idea, adding to Aristotle's list of animals and ascribing the spontaneous generation of insects out of everything from 'old wax' and 'slime of vinegar' to 'damp dust' and 'books'. Specific dead big animals were believed to give rise to specific small animals: horses transmogrified into hornets, crocodiles into scorpions, mules into locusts and bulls into bees. Carcasses were a popular 'generator of life' in every form imaginable.

As ridiculous as it now seems, spontaneous generation was the theory that would not die. Even as late as the sixteenth and seventeenth centuries it reigned supreme. Aristotle's ideas gestated over two thousand years in a womb of inventive thinking – giving birth to an array of surreal instructions for creating life. Every natural philosopher worth his salt was keen to get in on the spontaneous generation game. The German Jesuit Athanasius Kircher recommended a raft of recipes, some as simple as a Pot Noodle, to the readers of his 1665 opus *Mundus Subterraneus*. To create frogs, for example, you simply collected clay from a ditch where frogs had lived, incubated it in a large vessel whilst adding rainwater and – hey, presto – you got a jar of instant amphibians.

Since some species of frog are known to hibernate in mud during times of drought, there is a chance that someone may have once 'created' a frog in this manner. But the same is unlikely to be true of the imaginative instructions laid out by Jan Baptist van Helmont, a seventeenth-century Flemish chemist who ought to win the prize for being the Gordon Ramsay of the spontaneous generation set, even if his results weren't exactly appealing. Amongst his recommended concoctions were poisonous predatory arachnids, which he said could be generated by filling a hole in a brick with a bunch of basil, covering it with a second brick and leaving it in the sun. In a matter of days, 'fumes from the basil, acting as a leavening agent, will have transformed the vegetable matter' filling your home with 'veritable scorpions'. To create mice, you placed some wheat and water in a flask and covered it with the skirt 'of an unclean woman', and twenty-one days later you had a small rodent companion. Recipes for puppies might have proved a little more popular.

The theory of spontaneous generation was so widely accepted that when the great British doubter of ancient myths Sir Thomas Browne dared in 1646 to challenge whether mice could really be formed in this way, he was ridiculed. 'He doubts whether mice can be procreated of putrefectation!' said one irate Aristotelian believer. 'So he may doubt whether in cheese or timber worms are generated; or if butterflies, locusts, grasshoppers, shellfish, snails, eels and such are procreated of putrefied matter ... to doubt this is to question Reason, Sense, Experience.'

The arrival of the microscope in the mid-seventeenth century opened up tiny new worlds for cynics like Browne to explore in search of new truths. A modern band of microscopists and experimental biologists set about to dismiss the archaic, occult thinking as they conducted the first real scientific investigations. Amongst their leaders was the Italian naturalist Francesco Redi, who took it upon himself to challenge Aristotle's longstanding theory in what must be the stinkiest set of experiments ever undertaken (with perhaps the notable exception of Audubon's hide-and-seek antics with his putrefying pig).

Over the course of a sweaty Italian summer, Redi got his hands on as many animal carcasses – from frogs to tigers – as he could source. He then assiduously followed the instructions for spontaneous generation laid out by the various natural philosophers, turning his home into a malodorous kitchen for the creation of life in the process. No matter how bizarre or rank the methods, Redi treated them with solemn sincerity, testing each several times to see if they might hold the secret of genesis. Redi's notes from his strange, smelly summer recorded, for example, how he followed the directions laid out by his fellow countryman, Giambattista della Porta, that 'the toad is generated from a duck putrefying on a dung-heap' – not just once but three times. Sadly, he wrote, the trials 'brought no result'. He was forced to report that Porta, 'otherwise a most interesting and profound writer', had in fact 'been too credulous'.

Whatever fetid flesh he used, the only animals that Redi could generate were maggots and flies. 'I continued similar experiments with the raw and cooked flesh of the ox, the deer, the buffalo, the lion, the tiger, the dog, the lamb, the kid, the rabbit; and sometimes with the flesh of ducks, geese, hens, swallows, etc.,' he said. 'Finally I experimented with different kinds of fish, such as sword-fish, tuna, eel, sole, etc. In every case, one or other of the above-mentioned kinds of flies were hatched.'

This led Redi to take his own leap of imagination, a leap obvious to us but radical back then: that the flies hanging about the meat may in fact be the progenitors of the maggots. 'Having considered these things, I began to believe that all worms found in meat were derived directly from the droppings of flies, and not from the putrefaction of the meat,' he wrote. 'I was still more confirmed in this belief by having observed that, before the meat grew wormy, flies had hovered over it, of the same kind as those that later bred in it.'

At this point Redi began one final experiment to test his suspicions. It must have been an absolute stinker:

> I put a snake, some fish, some eels of the Arno, and a slice of milk-fed veal in four large, wide-mouthed flasks; having well closed and sealed them, I then filled the same number of flasks in the same way, only leaving these open. It was not long before the meat and the fish, in these second vessels, became wormy and flies were seen entering and leaving at will; but in the closed flasks I did not see a worm, though many days had passed since the dead flesh had been put in them.

The simple genius of this experiment – which proved that those carcasses that were protected from resting flies failed to produce maggots, whilst those that were left exposed were soon swarmed – was the beginning of the end of the theory of spontaneous generation.

Alas, out of its ashes a new but equally erroneous dogma emerged. Enter the 'preformists', who had the goal of explaining the generation of *all* animal life. They believed that every living being developed from a miniature version of itself, called the *homunculus*, which was contained within the animal's seed, and that germination merely reflected an increase in the mini-me's dimensions.

The preformists fell into two opposing camps: the ovists, who thought that the homunculus was contained within the female's egg, and the spermists, who believed it resided within the male's semen.

The idea that both sperm and egg were necessary for life was very much in the minority. That finally changed when, in the 1780s, our favourite scissors-wielding biologist, Lazzaro Spallanzani, proved otherwise. We've seen his work with snips and snails and bats' ears. In this series of experiments, he put his

*One for the spermists – a homunculus nestled inside a spermatozoon, as imagined by Nicolaas Hartsoeker in his 'Essay de dioptrique' (1694).*

clippers to more creative use by tailoring tiny taffeta trousers for frogs.

Spallanzani was obsessed with sex – frog sex, in particular. He believed the frog's amorous couplings would betray the secrets of all conception. With frogs, you see, fertilization happens externally, so the act of conception could be more easily observed and, most crucially, controlled.

But back then, even this very basic truth was contentious. The famous taxonomist Carl Linnaeus was on the books as saying, 'in Nature, in no case, in any living body, does fecundation or impregnation of the egg take place outside the body of the mother.' So Spallanzani got out his scissors and started interfering with frog sex to check the Swede's claims. He grabbed solitary females, sliced them open and extracted their unborn eggs. These, he observed, never developed into tadpoles, growing instead into 'an offensive putrid mass'. Eggs released whilst the female was embraced by the male, in contrast, always developed into tadpoles. This was proof that conception must be happening externally and, although the male appeared to be doing little more than holding on tight (frog semen is invisible in water), Spallanzani suspected he must be contributing *something* to the process. He just needed to find it.

To do so, the enterprising padre borrowed an idea from a French scientist, René Antoine Ferchault de Réaumur, who thirty years previously had gone to great lengths to hunt for whatever substance, if any, a male frog emitted during copulation. This he did in the most ingenious fashion – by forcing the frogs to wear homemade amphibian underpants, which served as a form of full-body prophylactic. Fortunately for Spallanzani (and for us), this fastidious French scientist kept meticulous minutes of the various prototypes for these pants.

'On March 21st we put on a pair of pants made of bladder,' Réaumur wrote in his notes, 'very tight pants, that sealed off the hind end.' The animal bladder was a winning suit in that it was nice and stretchy and easily slipped on the amphibians. But once the frogs got in the water it became 'too soft and floppy' and started to disintegrate. He wasn't sure if 'the frog was adequately covered', so these original organic undies were scrapped.

Waxed taffeta, a waterproof material used to make umbrellas, proved a more durable choice. Unfortunately, it lacked the necessary elasticity to ensure a snug fit. With palpable frustration the Frenchman noted: 'having made the pants and put them on, the frogs abandoned them in front of me.' The leg holes he'd made were too big, and much to his dismay, the frogs could remove the pants by pushing their legs up through the holes and jumping clean out of them.

Réaumur was nothing if not resourceful. He resolved the issue by bespoke-tailoring the pants with tiny braces that slipped over the frog's shoulders and held the get-up snugly in place. Reading through Réaumur's notes,

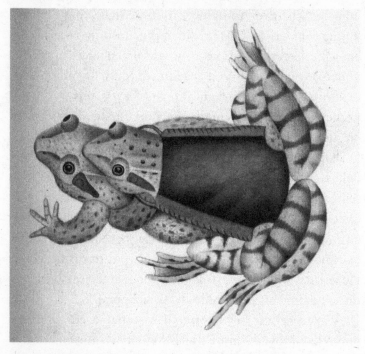

*The French scientist Réaumur was so pleased with his invention of custom-made amphibian underpants that he commissioned an artist, Hélène Dumoustier, to preserve this froggy fashion statement in perpetuity, braces and all. And who can blame him.*

Spallanzani was inspired to fashion similar attire for his own amorous amphibians. 'The idea of breeches, however whimsical and ridiculous it may appear, did not displease me, and I resolved to put it into practice. The males notwithstanding this encumbrance, seek the females with equal eagerness, and perform, as well as they can, the act of generation.'

After the frogs had done the deed, Spallanzani carefully removed their pants and peered inside to inspect his catch. Unlike his French forebear, the Italian priest succeeded in collecting a few precious blobs of semen, which he promptly wiped on a batch of unfertilized eggs. These eggs went on to develop into tadpoles, suggesting that the residue from the frog pants was indeed essential for fertilization. The systematic Spallanzani left nothing to chance, however. He went on to confirm that nothing else could have brought the eggs to life, wiping a series of spawn with blood, vinegar, spirits, wine (various vintages), urine and the juices of lemon and lime. He even tried bringing them to life with electricity. All were fruitless, in reproductive terms.

Spallanzani's sartorial adventures with frogs were a key step in solving the mystery of fertilization. Less than a hundred years later, amphibians were back in the lab, once again being used to divine whether fertilization had taken place – this time not in a frog, but in a human.

It may sound suspiciously like the bogus medieval folk medicine of the bestiaries, but from the 1940s through to the 1960s the world's first reliable pregnancy test was a small, bug-eyed toad. When injected with a pregnant woman's urine the toad didn't turn blue or display stripes, but it would squirt out eggs eight to twelve hours later to confirm a positive result.

There was no such thing as a home-testing toad. The

injecting was done by professional pregnancy testers who whiled away the hours in the basements and adjoining buildings of many a hospital and family-planning clinic alongside tanks of these prognostic toads. I discussed the process with Audrey Peattie, an effervescent eighty-two-year-old former toad tester from Hertfordshire, who told me about her three-year turn with the toads at Watford hospital.

Working in a lab full of urine and amphibians was an unusual occupation for a young woman in the 1950s. Whereas most of Audrey's female friends left school to become secretaries, she headed off to Watford aged seventeen for a career that she told me was a little more 'peculiar' and 'embarrassing to explain', but which she relished nevertheless.

'We did about forty tests a day. The toads were rather slippery but you got hold of them between their legs and injected them under the skin and into their fleshy thighs,' Audrey recalled. 'You then popped them into a numbered jar, left them in a warm place overnight and examined them in the morning to see if they'd laid eggs. If the toad had only laid a few eggs, we repeated the test with another toad. But the toads were practically never at fault.'

According to Audrey, these special sibylline toads were 'not the kind that creep around your garden' but altogether more exotic African clawed toad (*Xenopus laevis*), an ancient species of aquatic frog from sub-Saharan Africa. Armed with long talons, flat bodies and what appears to be Frankenstein stitches down each side of their body, they're not exactly pretty. Their bulbous eyes also lack eyelids, which means they bob around in the water sporting a somewhat ominous stare that follows you around the lab.

The toads' knack for detecting pregnancy was discovered by the British endocrinologist Lancelot Hogben whilst he was stationed at the University of Cape Town in the late 1920s. Hogben had previously used European frogs in his studies of hormones, but in South Africa he began experimenting with the local fauna. He found that *Xenopus*, just like today's chemical pregnancy tests, displayed a dramatic response to the presence of human chorionic gonadotrophin, or hCG, the hormone released after a human egg is fertilized. Hogben recognized the toad's potential as a pregnancy test to be a 'godsend'. He was so enamoured with the amphibian that he later named his house after it.

*Audrey Peattie (right) at work in the 1950s at the family-planning lab in Watford hospital, where she was engaged in the slippery business of encouraging toads to tell her whether women were pregnant or not.*

215

The 'Hogben test', as it became known, quickly replaced the far less reliable 'rabbit test', which involved injecting a rabbit with urine and then dissecting it several hours later to examine its ovaries for any sign of eggs. The previous technique, Audrey explained to me, was far less practical. 'Imagine keeping enough rabbits to do forty tests a day!' The toads had the distinct advantage that they could be reused.

Another plus of the toad test was that the toads were small and could be kept in tanks whilst awaiting their rendezvous with an uncertain woman's hormonal sample. After doing a predictive turn, each toad would get a little holiday from the hormones, Audrey told me, 'about three weeks off'. During this time 'they just swam about' and 'got fed chopped liver'. Then they would get called up for their powers of prophecy.

The African clawed toad single-handedly revolutionized pregnancy testing, de-stigmatizing a process once associated with animal death and making the service practical on a larger scale than ever before. But this doesn't capture the whole of their scientific importance. Hundreds of thousands of toads were exported from Africa to testing labs in Europe and America, where their presence attracted the attention of other scientists, particularly those in the emerging field of developmental biology – the intellectual descendants of Spallanzani – whose attempts to map the growth of embryos required copious quantities of eggs for experimentation. The amphibians they had been using bred seasonally, which severely restricted their work. Here was a frog that could be induced to lay tens of thousands of eggs on command, simply by injecting it with hCG (which is kind of like a very modern recipe for spontaneous generation). As an added bonus, *Xenopus* eggs were unusually large – ten times the size of a human egg – making them ideal for microsurgery and genetic manipulation. The tadpoles were also conveniently transparent, allowing developmental biologists to observe the internal mechanics of metamorphosis into adults. To cap it all, the adults were highly resistant to disease and could live in captivity for up to twenty years. It was a marriage made in scientific heaven.

*Xenopus* would go on to join the ranks of the mouse and the fruit fly as one of the most intensively studied model organisms on the planet, with live colonies in labs in forty-eight countries spread across five continents. By the 1980s, *Xenopus* had become the world's most widely distributed amphibian. It had been decoded, dissected and documented inside and out. It was the first vertebrate to be cloned and had even been to space.

But there was one crucial thing that scientists still didn't know about it – something they didn't discover until, unfortunately, it was too late. It turns out this globe-trotting frog doesn't travel solo.

In the late 1980s, herpetologists started noticing something very odd. Populations of amphibians in Australia and

Central America were disappearing, often quite suddenly, from pristine environments and leaving behind no dead bodies. It was as if they had simply vanished into thin air. Amphibians had been around for 65 million years, and had survived the meteor that exterminated the dinosaurs, a series of ice ages and quite a few dramatic climate fluctuations. What could be killing them off in such massive numbers now?

After years of intense speculation the culprit was eventually identified: a primitive waterborne fungus, *Batrachochytrium dendrobatidis*, aka Bd or amphibian chytrid fungus. Chytrid fungus infects the frogs' skin – an especially sensitive organ that they use to breathe – causing a disease that prevents the absorption of oxygen and essential electrolytes. It eventually results in cardiac arrest.

Over the next thirty years, scientists watched in horror as the chytrid fungus cropped up on every continent on Earth – except Antarctica, where there were no amphibians. Its spread triggered a catastrophic decline in or complete annihilation of at least two hundred species. Even in these extinction-heavy times, this amphibian apocalypse has been described as 'the worst infectious disease ever recorded among vertebrates'.

Where had this frog-killing fungus come from, and how had it spread so far *and* so fast? A few years ago I travelled to Chile, a country hit hard by chytrid, to meet with Dr Claudio Soto-Azat, an up-and-coming scientist determined to find the answer to these big questions and save his country's amphibians. Claudio is one of those people who brims with joy, a great asset to have when dealing with a subject as depressing as the mass extinction of your favourite animal.

Compared with its neighbours, Chile doesn't have a dizzying catalogue of amphibians (a mere fifty species), but the ones that it does have are almost all utterly unique. That's because Chile is essentially a long, thin island isolated by desert to the north, glaciers to the south, ocean to the west and the Andes to the east. So despite being part of a vast frog-filled continent, Chile's amphibians have evolved in a bubble, which makes them especially vulnerable to extinction.

I joined Claudio on an expedition in search of one of the country's most fabulous freaks, the incredibly rare southern Darwin's frog, which was discovered by the big beard himself in 1834 on his epic *Beagle* voyage. What makes this frog so extraordinary is that it has eschewed conventional pond-based metamorphosis for something more sci-fi: after mating the male guards the fertilized eggs until they are close to hatching, then gobbles them up. Six weeks later, like a scene out of *Alien*, he barfs up baby frogs. He is the only male animal other than the seahorse to give birth, albeit through his mouth.

Claudio and I flew to a tinpot airport in Patagonia, little more than a dusty airstrip scratched into the earth and framed by snow-capped peaks. I remember Claudio pointing out the border with Argentina – a wobbly metal gate on a dirt track surrounded by fields and mountains. It really felt like we'd landed in the middle of nowhere. From this isolated spot, we drove a further four hours to reach the forests that the Darwin's frog calls home – a surreal mixture of dense bamboo, giant rhubarb plants with leaves big enough to live under, wild fuchsia bushes popping with hot-pink flowers and lofty trees dripping long, wafting tendrils of pale green moss. A thick mist hung in the air. It was all very *Lord of the Rings*.

The good news was that we quickly found our frog, something of a miracle given that it's only 3 centimetres long and camouflaged to look like a bamboo leaf, complete with a long, thin nose that mimics the stem. The bad news was that the swabs Claudio took from our little green friends came back as positive for the chytrid fungus when tested in the lab.

Contracting chytrid is not an automatic death sentence for a frog. It is a mercurial killer with infuriatingly unpredictable efficacy. Certain amphibians, for whatever reason, appear to have immunity and are able to resist its suffocating grip. We could only hope the southern Darwin's frog, with its largely terrestrial life, would be safe from life-threatening levels of the fungus's waterborne spores. A cousin, the northern Darwin's frog, had not been so lucky, however. Despite a less remote home range, closer to the capital of Santiago, these equally bizarre, mouth-brooding frogs have not been seen or heard from for thirty years. Claudio presumed them to be extinct in the wild and fingered the fungus. And he had a pretty good idea of how it arrived in Chile.

The next stop on our amphibian apocalypse tour was a

small farm in Talagante, a semi-rural area 40 kilometres north of Santiago. Claudio wanted to investigate reports of an alien invader, his suspect No. 1 in the spread of the frog killer.

We arrived in the heat of the day and were greeted by a farmer called Jurgen, an elderly man with watery-blue eyes, a long white beard and a warm smile. He handed us a bag of tadpoles and a bucket of toads and told us his property had been infested with these strange frogs since the late 1970s. With obvious emotion in his voice, he recalled how two years after the toads arrived, he experienced his first 'silent spring', completely absent of the chirrupy sing-song of his beloved native amphibians. He went searching for them in places that were previously inky-black with tadpoles and found nothing. They had completely disappeared.

I peered into the bucket and was greeted by a familiar blank, bug-eyed stare. Well, hello, *Xenopus*, what the hell are you doing here?

Claudio explained that this alien's invasion was thought to be an unlikely addition to the pantheon of crimes committed by Chile's famous dictator, General Pinochet. The story goes that shortly after the military junta took over the Santiago airport in 1973, a consignment of *Xenopus* had come in by plane, destined for lab work in the capital city. Not accustomed with the protocol for greeting a bunch of foreign frogs, the soldiers released them. They and their descendants have been on the run ever since.

The same characteristics that make *Xenopus* an ideal

lab animal also make it the textbook invasive species. It is a highly adaptable, disease-resistant and prolific breeder. Females can reproduce all year round, generating up to eight thousand eggs annually. I asked Claudio how many African clawed toads there are in Chile today, and he put his head in his hand with resignation. 'Millions if not billions. It's impossible to say but it's a huge number. In one small lagoon, for example, they estimate the population is twenty-one thousand individuals.'

The toads have been found as far as 400 kilometres from Santiago. They seem to be advancing from the capital at a speed of roughly 10 kilometres per year. During periods of heavy rain they make mass migrations, pushing deeper into new territory. In one such period, Claudio told me, a ranger observed a biblical scene of two thousand toads crossing a road.

African clawed toads are voracious predators. They swallow everything in their path, laying waste to populations of indigenous fish, frogs and tadpoles. This unstoppable amphibian army boasts a secret weapon with which to annihilate the indigenous froggy fauna: many of the fugitive *Xenopus* in Chile test positive for the chytrid fungus to which they appear to have developed immunity. But the extent to which *Xenopus* have contributed to the chytrid pandemic has not been clear until quite recently.

In a cunning piece of scientific detective work, Claudio, along with a handful of other international investigators, tested a pickled line-up of *Xenopus* specimens from museums around the world. They discovered individuals collected as early as 1933 had been carrying the fungus – the earliest recorded incidence of the disease, locating it to the time when the toads were first exported out of Africa to be used as pregnancy testers. Many of these toads didn't stay locked up in a lab. When the Hogben test was usurped by the little blue strip, thousands of redundant toads were released by well-meaning staff, who hoped to give them their freedom after a lifetime of good service. Countless others have escaped from labs or been liberated as unwanted pets. Invasive populations of African clawed toads have been recorded advancing across four continents, and the latest research has linked some of these invasions, such as those in Chile and California, with the arrival of chytrid fungus and the disappearance of native frogs. Other widespread invasive amphibians like the American bullfrog – which is farmed internationally for its fleshy legs – may have also carried the disease, but it appears as though the toads' exodus from Africa could have been the trigger for the global outbreak.

It's a sorry situation. We owe much of our understanding of fertilization and embryonic development to *Xenopus*, but in gaining this knowledge, we have inadvertently caused the disappearance of fabulously freaky species like the mouth-brooding northern Darwin's frog. The high-altitude home of the aquatic scrotum frog has been infected by the fungus too. 'We are living in a time of homogenization of our wildlife,' Claudio said with a heavy sigh.

'Thanks to globalization and human population growth there are even more chances for the translocation of wildlife around the world – and their diseases.'

Claudio mentioned that the modern industrial farming method of creating dams favours the lifestyle of *Xenopus*, which thrives in still and stagnant water. The farmer we visited, Jurgen, had one small irrigation pond on his farm that he referred to as 'the hell hole'. Staring at this putrid pool of fetid water squirming with toads, I thought how their sudden appearance might be more plausibly explained by Aristotle's outlandish spontaneous generation than the bizarre globe-trotting, pregnancy-testing, pathogen-infested truth.

In five thousand years the frog had come a long way. The ancient Egyptian farmers may have worshipped it for its fecundity, but in Jurgen's eyes, *Xenopus* was more akin to an embodiment of the curse bellowed by the Omnipotence in Exodus: 'I will plague your whole country with frogs. The Nile will teem with frogs. They will come up into your palace and your bedroom and onto your bed, into the houses of your officials and on your people, and into your ovens and kneading troughs.'

There is another creature in the Bible who 'knoweth her appointed times'. The stork's association with fertility led to a different set of worries and confusions. Its mysterious comings and goings inspired myths of shape-shifting, submarine and space-travelling birds – in addition to paranoid political persecutions.

## CHAPTER 8

# STORK

Species *Ciconia ciconia*

*In diverse sorts of fowl their absence is such, that*
*we know not whither they go, nor whence they*
*come, but are as it were miraculously dropped*
*down from Heaven upon us.*

Charles Morton, 'An Essay into the Probable Solution
of this Question: Whence Comes the Stork', 1703

O N AN OTHERWISE UNREMARKABLE morning in May 1822, Count Christian Ludwig von Bothmer was out hunting in the grounds of his castle in Klütz, Germany, when he shot a rather unusual white stork. The bird in question had already suffered a near fatal attack – not from a gun, the count's weapon of choice, but a wooden spear, almost a metre in length, which still skewered the stork's long, thin neck like a kebab. The count brought the spiked stork to a local professor, who deduced that the primitive weapon, roughly hewn from exotic hardwood with a simple iron blade at the tip, had been thrown from 'the hands of an African'. How extraordinary. The animal had not only survived being lanced, but then had somehow summoned the strength to fly thousands of kilometres to Europe wearing its extravagant neck piercing, only to be shot dead by the count upon arrival.

What was undoubtedly a rather bad day for the gutsy bird turned out to be a significantly better day for science. The examination of the impaled stork helped to solve one

*This famous Pfeilstorch, or 'arrow-stork', shot down in Germany in 1822, provided irrefutable evidence that birds migrate over Africa – and wears a suitably weary look for its heroic sacrifice to science.*

of the longest-running mysteries of the natural world: the seasonal disappearance of birds.

The white stork, *Ciconia ciconia*, is a conspicuous creature. Adults have arresting white and black plumage and stand well over a metre tall on long scarlet legs. Everything about them is showy, not least their gigantic nests, which can measure up to 2.5 metres wide and teeter in plain view on top of the tallest buildings in towns all across Europe. They also have a habit of clattering their big scarlet bills together in clangorous glee when greeting their partners during their nuptial dance at the start of each spring.

These are big, boisterous birds – which makes their absence, come autumn, all the more evident. After a summer spent raising their chicks in plain view, they vanish for several months, reappearing early in the new year. It seems obvious to us today that in the meantime the birds have migrated 20,000 kilometres to southern Africa in search of more favourable feeding opportunities. But the nature of the stork's disappearing act, along with that of all other migratory birds, was the subject of several of natural history's most enduring prevarications.

Aristotle was the first person to ponder seriously why some birds apparently vanished into thin air at the arrival of a new season only to reappear, as if by magic, at the start of another. The great thinker hedged his bets with a trio of theories. Some birds, he supposed, such as cranes, quails and turtle doves, sought out warmer climes during the cool European winter. He even noted that the birds fatten themselves up prior to their journey. He should have stopped with this one winning idea. But perhaps because of the fantastic nature of this biological endurance act, the grandfather of zoology felt the need to come up with two more explanations, which were not only wrong, but lingered in the scientific realm well beyond their sell-by date.

Aristotle's more creative alternative was that of transmutation. His epic *Historia Animalium* declared that certain species of bird transformed into different species from one season to another. Summertime garden warblers, for instance, became wintertime blackcaps, and winter robins became summer redstarts. These birds shared a superficial likeness, being similar in size and coloration, and, most suspiciously to the philosopher, they were never completely present at the same time (just like Clark Kent and Superman). Redstarts migrate to sub-Saharan Africa at a time when robins, who breed further north, come to winter in Greece. So Aristotle concluded they were avian shape-shifters.

The philosopher's idea of transmutation was tame in comparison to the fantasies that followed in its wake. Alexander of Myndus, another Greek, asserted four hundred years later that elderly storks transform into humans. This was reported with solemnity by Claudius Aelianus as fact. 'In my view, this is not a fairy tale,' he stated in his second-century animal encyclopaedia, *De Naturis Animalium*. 'If it were, why would Alexander tell it to us?' he wrote somewhat defensively. 'He has nothing to gain by inventing a story such as this. It would not do at all for a person so intelligent to tell a lie in place of the truth.' It's worth noting that in the same book, Aelianus – who must surely rank as one of history's most gullible encyclopaedists – also described sheep that changed colour according to which river they drink from, tortoises that absolutely 'hated' partridges and octopuses that grew as big as whales.

Storks weren't the only birds thought to transmutate. There were even more fantastic stories involving the barnacle goose, a bird which we now know migrates from obscure Arctic seas to the coasts of Britain every winter. Its most northerly breeding grounds on the high cliffs of Greenland were, of course, never observed by the European authors of the medieval bestiaries, who instead promoted the rather unlikely story that barnacle geese grew out of the rotting timbers of ships.

'Nature produces them against nature in the most extraordinary way,' wrote the twelfth-century chronicler Gerald of Wales with no overstatement, considering the theory he was propounding. 'They are produced from fir timber tossed along the sea.' The medieval clergyman claimed to have actually witnessed the bird's phenomenal genesis during an expedition to Ireland. 'Afterwards they hang down by their beaks as if they were a seaweed attached to a timber, and are surrounded by shells in order to grow more freely. Having thus in process of time been clothed with a strong coat of feathers, they fall into the water or fly freely away into the air.'

What Gerald had observed were actually goose neck barnacles, from the taxonomic order Pedunculata. As their name suggests, these finger-sized filter feeders bear a resemblance to a small beak sitting atop a long, naked neck as they strain out of whatever they've attached themselves to in the tidal zone. So great was the human mind's power of association that the esteemed sixteenth-century botanist John Gerard claimed to have cut specimens open to have inside 'found living things that were very naked, in

CHAP. 171.

*Of the Goose tree, Barnacle tree, or the tree bearing Geese.*

*Britannica Conchæ anatiferæ.*
The breed of Barnacles.

*Barnacle geese were said to grow from trees as well as from rotting timber, which meant the birds often featured in plant books and (more important) conveniently qualified for consumption on the many meat-free fast days of the medieval calendar.*

shape like a bird'. Some of these supposed beings were said to be 'covered with soft down, the shell half open, and the bird ready to fall out'.

There was, however, a more convenient motivation for the popularity of the myth: it sanctioned the consumption of roast goose during fasting days, when the eating of meat was strictly forbidden. Growing out of rotting ships meant these geese were not classed as flesh 'because they are not born of flesh,' explained Gerald. Such sneaky logic meant that 'bishops and men of religion make no scruple of eating these birds on fasting days.' Given that three days of the medieval week, not to mention the whole of Lent, were designated fast days, it's easy to see how famished men of the cloth would be keen to propagate the fable that this big, juicy bird was in fact a viable vegetarian menu item.

But what of the noisy white stork? Where did it go in winter?

Aristotle's third theory about the disappearing birds was less fantastic but significantly more enduring. In the *Historia Animalium* he proposed that storks, along with a number of other species, escaped the cold by going 'into hiding', which makes them sound like some kind of avian fugitive. Aristotle went on to explain they were in a state of 'torpor'. Many mammals – which are warm-blooded, like birds – had been observed by early natural philosophers to hibernate, including bats, which were then often classed as birds. So why not storks too?

It's a good question, one that modern science doesn't have a definitive answer for. It's probably down to a combination of factors: a relatively high metabolism and heart rate, and the struggle to store sufficient fat, would probably make hibernation physically challenging for the stork. Not to mention the fact that a stork lacks the equipment to dig a burrow suitable to sleep in. Instead, it possesses a pair of perfectly good wings that can carry it away to somewhere more favourable.

There are a handful of birds – hummingbirds, mouse-birds and swifts – that have been discovered to enter brief spells of torpor, but so far modern science has confirmed one sole species of truly hibernating bird: the common poorwill – a type of nightjar that is most common in the desert-like habitats of western North America. Some poor-will do migrate to avoid winter food shortages but find themselves competing with numerous other migrating birds in the all-too-popular wintering hotspot of Mexico. The rest avoid the competition by lowering their metabol-ism and sleeping out the winter amongst the rocks, an evolutionary adaptation that earned them a Native Hopi name meaning 'the sleeping one'.

Despite the lack of evidence of hibernation in all other birds, ornithologists argued about this from ancient times well into the nineteenth century. The bird at the centre of the sleepy academic storm wasn't the stork but another well-known harbinger of spring, the barn swallow.

Aristotle claimed these tiny birds hibernated in holes whilst 'quite denuded of their feathers'. The idea that swal-lows would spend their winter months sleeping naked in order to survive the cold is quite silly, but the theories that followed over the course of the next two thousand years were sillier still. Some of the greatest minds of the Age of Enlightenment, no less than the fathers of modern zoology, sincerely believed that swallows spent the winter hibernat-ing at the bottom of lakes and rivers, like fish. 'It appears certain that swallows become torpid during winter, and even that they pass the season at the bottom of the water in the marshes,' stated Georges Cuvier in his highly influential nineteenth-century tome, *Le Règne Animal.*

It may come as little surprise that the scissors-wielding biologist Lazzaro Spallanzani had been intrigued by the bird's Houdini act and brought his trademark sadistic flair to the numerous experiments looking to find proof of it. He tried to encourage swallows to hibernate by imprisoning them in wicker cages which he buried under snow, leaving just a small hole through which the birds might breathe. The swallows skipped torpor and went straight to death in less than two days. Over in France, the Comte de Buffon attempted a similar experiment, placing swallows in an icehouse, with equally fatal results.

In America the barbarity peaked with a physician by the name of Charles Caldwell, who, with the assistance of his 'invaluable friend' Dr Cooper, attached ballast to a pair of swallows' legs before chucking them in a river. In his manifestly sinister write-up of his experiment, Caldwell reported that the birds, which he referred to as 'our two little prisoners', sank like stones, 'showing the anxiety and convulsions of animals in a drowning state'. After three hours, the birds were removed and the men of science attempted to resuscitate them. They were forced to state, without a hint of irony, that the swallows were in fact 'reduced, not to a state of torpidity, or suspended animation, but of absolute death'.

For many years, one German university offered a

reward of the bird's weight in silver for each swallow found underwater and revived. The prize was never claimed. Nonetheless the legend, unlike all those experimental swallows, failed to die. How had this mad submarine swallow rumour started?

An obscure sixteenth-century Swedish bishop by the name of Olaus Magnus appears to be the culprit. Magnus did not entertain the idea of migration, despite intimations from other quarters that it might be the proper explanation. 'Although the writers of many natural things have recorded that the swallows change their stations, going, when the winter cometh, into hotter countries,' he wrote in *Historia de Gentibus Septentrionalibus* ('History of the Northern Peoples'), 'yet, in the northern waters, fishermen oftentimes by chance draw up

*The Swedish bishop Olaus Magnus was not one to let the truth get in the way of a good story. His 1555 bestseller* History of the Northern Peoples *is chock-full of ridiculous fables presented as fact, like these fishermen hauling hibernating swallows out of a riverbed.*

in their nets an abundance of swallows, hanging together like a conglomerated mass.' This giant bird ball, the holy Swede tells us, formed when swallows descended like tiny line dancers into the depths. 'In the beginning of Autumn, they assemble together among the reeds; where, allowing themselves to sink into the water, they join bill to bill, wing to wing and foot to foot.'

Unfortunately for the swallows, Magnus's magnum opus was a massive bestseller. All twenty-two volumes of his encyclopaedic extravaganza mixed fact with fable, painting his frozen homeland as an otherworldly place where mice rained from the sky and giant serpents prowled the seas offshore. The Swedish bishop's sensationalist tales appealed to the new wave of readers who now had access to books following the development of the printing press in the mid fifteenth century. His tome was translated into a dozen or so languages, spreading his fantastic legends all over Europe.

But it was the nascent Royal Society of London that gave the story of the submarine swallows a stamp of credibility. In 1666 – a short six years after its founding – this fellowship of the world's most eminent natural philosophers decided to investigate the matter and establish 'what truth there is . . . concerning swallows being found in winter under waters congealed, and reviving, if they be fished [out] and held to the fire'. Their conclusion: 'it was most certain, that swallows sink themselves towards autumn into lakes.' A somewhat surprising result from this storied scientific body until you learn that the man tasked with examining the matter was not a naturalist but an astronomer whose analysis involved little more than consulting an acquaintance of his who just happened to be a professor at the University of Uppsala, former hometown of one Olaus Magnus. The chance of getting an unbiased answer from the loyal alma mater was about as likely as finding a swallow wintering underwater. The legend was so deeply entrenched in local folklore in Sweden that even Carl Linnaeus – another Uppsala alumnus – still referred to it as fact a hundred years later.

Not everyone bought the hibernation story. One fierce opponent was Charles Morton, the Oxford-educated author of a highly respected seventeenth-century compendium of physics that was standard issue at Harvard for almost half a century. Morton pointed out with the unflinching logic of a physicist that freezing temperatures and the lack of air meant the idea of swallows 'lying in clay lumps in the bottoms of rivers' was utterly ridiculous. He proposed the more rational hypothesis that swallows, as well as other seasonal birds like the stork, migrated to the Moon.

'The stork, when it hath bred, and the young fully fledged ... all rise together, and fly in one great flock ... first near the earth, but after higher ... till at last this great cloud ... appears less and less by distance, till it utterly disappears,' Morton mused, before turning to the crux of the matter: 'Now, Whither should these creatures go unless it were to the Moon?'

Whither, indeed. Morton's evidence for this celestial sojourn was a little on the slim side. He reasoned that since no one knew the whereabouts of migrant birds during the winter months, they simply must be hiding somewhere off the Earth. Further evidence could be gleaned from the bird's demeanour. At their departure the bird's 'cheerfulness seems to intimate, that they have some noble design in hand' – to boldly go where no bird had gone before, perhaps, 'namely, to get above the atmosphere, hie and fly away to the other world.'

His outlandish hypothesis was a reflection of the times. The scientists of the seventeenth century were fascinated by the Moon. Using one of the first telescopes, Galileo had observed that the lunar surface wasn't smooth like a marble but was instead punctuated by mountains and valleys, just like Earth. John Wilkins, a former colleague from Morton's university days and a founder of the Royal Society, wrote *The Discovery of a World in the Moone*, an enthusiastic account of how lunar geography was much like Earth's, complete with seas, streams, mountains – and possibly life forms. To Morton, the Moon, far from being a lifeless lump of rock devoid of atmosphere, was an alluring winter destination.

The notion of space migration had wider support, with proponents arguing amongst themselves via letters to the Royal Society about which celestial body was the most likely destination for the birds. The Puritan minister Cotton Mather thought the Moon a little too distant. He suggested that birds instead flew 'to some undiscovered satellite accompanying the earth at a near distance'. Mather was famous in New England for erudite sermons, and for fanning the flames of hysteria around the Salem witch trials, including a spirited defence of 'spectral evidence'. So it should come as little surprise that he also believed in space-travelling birds.

Charles Morton was singular in his pursuit of the idea, however. He made painstaking calculations, which are at times quite well-reasoned, on behalf of his avian astronauts, exploring the parameters of their extraterrestrial migration.

He divided the year into three parts. The round trip to the Moon occupied four months, or sixty days each way; this gave the birds four months living on Earth and four months living on the Moon. As the Moon took one month to revolve about the Earth, the birds launching straight at the Moon, by Morton's reckoning, 'will find it in the same line of direction, where it was when they began their journey' – which was wonderfully convenient.

Fuel for their two-month mission was provided by excess fat, and the impetus for leaving Earth were changes in temperature and the availability of food. All of which holds some truth for earthbound migrating birds.

Morton estimated the distance to the Moon as 179,712 miles. Not such a terrible guess – the closest stage of the Moon's elliptical orbit is in fact around 226,000 miles.

During their lunar flight, Morton assumed the birds to

be unaffected by gravity, so that they encountered no air resistance and were able to cruise at speeds of around 125 miles per hour, a fair clip compared to their more typical 20 miles per hour. Here, he failed to account for the fact that the velocity required for his space-travelling storks to leave Earth's gravitational pull would be some two hundred times his calculated top speed, a feat unachievable without the help of jet packs strapped to the birds' backs. Then there were those small problems of the life-sucking vacuum, radiation and extreme temperatures the birds would encounter in space – lethal to any animal other than the bizarre microscopic creature revived by Lazzaro Spallanzani, the decidedly indestructible tardigrade.

For Morton's generation, of course, space travel was still very much a dream. It would be three hundred years before anyone could confirm or deny the presence of storks, swallows or any other birds orbiting the Earth like satellites en route to the Moon. Yet, this was also the great Age of Discovery, and keen-eyed European explorers were beginning to report sightings of their seasonal homeland birds whilst navigating foreign seas and probing faraway lands. In 1686, for example, the survivors of a Dutch ship wrecked off the coast of South Africa reported that storks were 'found during the time they are not in Holland, although not in great numbers'.

Such eyewitness accounts were easily dismissed by nonbelievers. The Right Honourable Daines Barrington, a staunch anti-migration fellow of the Royal Society, was one of the most vehement voices. He relished in rebuffing the explorers' claims, legitimizing his own solely with his imperious delivery. In response to a sighting by Sir Charles Wager, First Lord of the Admiralty, of a great flock of swallows settling on the rigging of his ship, Barrington slyly twisted the evidence to his side. It simply showed the birds were not fit for long-distance migration, he said. 'They are, in fact, always so fatigued, that, when they meet a ship at sea, they forget all apprehensions and deliver themselves to sailors.'

Barrington, a former judge, could argue black was white and had a frankly absurd answer for every sensible suggestion he heard. He dismissed the idea of migration on the grounds that it was too dangerous to believe, and said there were not enough witnesses of these 'highly improbable' events to give it any credence. Those who suggested the birds were flying too high to be seen (which they do in order to hitch a ride on favourable air currents) were shot down for being 'destitute of any ocular proof'. Those who hypothesized, quite correctly, that migration happened at night (as a way of avoiding predators) were dismissed as ridiculous since, according to the judge, everybody knew that birds, like humans, sleep at night (also untrue).

With such rabid anti-migration bulldogs as Barrington primed to criticize all claims, what was needed to end the debate was some cold hard evidence. And that's where Count Christian Ludwig von Bothmer's elaborately pierced stork comes in. For here was a bird caught carrying an irrefutable souvenir of its stay overseas, evidence which ultimately led to a paradigm shift in ornithological understanding.

The count's heroic stork proved to be no lone freak. It was just one of twenty-five similarly stoic so-called Pfeilstorchs – storks skewered by arrows – to be shot down in Europe during the nineteenth and twentieth centuries. Ornithologists took inspiration from these lanced birds and started their own tagging system, using something a little more user-friendly than an arrow – a branded aluminium band that could be fixed around a bird's leg. This small ring revolutionized bird studies, eventually revealing conclusive proof of the storks' and other birds' seasonal migrations.

The most significant of the early bird ringers was Johannes Thienemann, an unusually flamboyant Protestant minister from Germany. Thienemann wasn't the first person to ring birds – that prize had been won by a Danish school teacher a few years before – but he was the first to do so on a grand scale, and to tag birds that made long-distance migrations into Africa. Thienemann was a colourful character, with a predilection for hunting and sporting tweed plus fours, but no bog-standard boffin. Indeed, he had zero formal training. Nonetheless, between his boundless enthusiasm and knack for self-promotion he was able to found a new form of scientific establishment: on 1 January 1901, Thienemann opened the doors to the world's first permanent bird observatory.

Dedicated to the study of migrating birds, the centre was

located in Rossitten, a remote corner of East Prussia. Thienemann's favourite study species was the white stork – the
'pre-destined experimental bird' – on account of it being
highly conspicuous, a predictable migrant and extremely
popular with the general public.

Thienemann's infectious passion for birdwatching and
his PR smarts helped him to corral an army of civic volunteers across Germany to help him tag two thousand storks
with a unique number and the location of their tagging.
That was the easy part; the rest was somewhat out of his
control. All Thienemann could do was watch the storks fly
away and wait and hope that someone in the vast Dark
Continent would find the bird, notice the ring and send
news of this oblique discovery in such a manner that it
found its way back to his tagging HQ in Prussia.

The gung-ho ornithologist's grand vision was not without its opposition. The editor of the influential science
journal *Kosmos* mounted an especially vociferous attack.
He posited that the aluminium rings would harm the birds
and described the exercise as 'vain scientific humbug',
predicting it would end in the 'mass murdering of storks'.
But Thienemann wanted all the publicity he could get,
even the negative sort, so that word would spread far and
wide of his ambitious experiment. There were few tele-
phones and no such thing as television; Thienemann had
to rely upon international newspaper dispatches and the
bureaucratic corps of the African colonies if he was to hear
anything about his precious stork tags. Having some

missionary or colonial officer looking out for piles of stork corpses wasn't going to hurt.

Lo and behold, the first information about a tag made its way back to Thienemann just a few months later. Along with the bird to which it was attached. Now rather dead. This wasn't quite how the minister had envisaged his tags would turn up, but it was still a kind of success.

The northern journey of the tags to Thienemann was no less momentous than their initial southern migration. They passed through the hands of missionaries, colonial officials, traders and newspaper editors before making it home to Rossitten, creating something of their own mythology along the way. Many were discovered by African hunters who thought the mysterious metal objects were of 'heavenly origin'. One chief was said to have carried a stork tag on the shaft of his spear as a lucky charm; he considered it sufficiently precious that it only made its way back to Thienemann after the chief's death.

Between 1908 and 1913, Thienemann received news of forty-eight recoveries, which he plotted on a map, revealing for the first time the extent of the stork's impressive migration down the Nile and onwards to the southern tip of Africa. But just as the riddle of the stork was being solved, the birds themselves began disappearing from towns and villages across western and northern Europe. And this time they seemed to be disappearing permanently.

Being migrants was becoming dangerous. Their annual flight path took them over nations that were now at war, places where people were starving and eager to hunt a big bird for their pot (hence the reported increase in storks arriving in Europe with souvenir arrows). In 1930, Thienemann wrote with dismay about the decline of 'our dear storks', which were suffering the effects of hunting by natives.

He also speculated that the poisoning of grasshoppers by the South African government was to blame for the dwindling numbers of his favourite study subject. He was right. Modern industrialized agricultural methods were the enemy of the white stork. It was a sorry fate for a bird nicknamed the 'farmer's friend' after its gluttonous appreciation of common pests.

A solitary stork has been clocked devouring up to thirty crickets a minute; another dispatched forty-four mice, two hamsters and a frog in a single hour. A flock is estimated to be able to hoover up a plague of Tanzanian army worms – over 2 billion grubs – in a day. So the introduction of pesticides not only made the birds redundant, it also gave them a terminal case of indigestion.

Pesticides, pollution and the drainage of wetlands for farmland forced Europe's stork population into sharp decline over the twentieth century. The last breeding pair was seen in Belgium in 1895, in Switzerland in 1950 and in Sweden in 1955. Many villages were quite bereft when the storks stopped returning. The birds' very public vanishing act had firmly embedded them in ancient folklore. They were harbingers of spring, talismans of good luck. All across

Europe, people encouraged storks to nest on their roofs in the belief that the birds brought harmony, health and prosperity to a household.

Quite how lucky the human hosts felt once storks had taken roost is debatable. Generations of white storks will return to the same nest, adding to it every year. Nests are mostly made of twigs, but an inventory made by Thienemann of objects found in storks' nests included 'a ladies glove, a man's mitten, horse droppings, an umbrella handle, a child's skittle ball and a potato'.

And the resulting nests are big. Stork super-nests can weigh up to 2 tonnes and measure over 2.5 metres deep, a structure which would struggle to be supported by modern let alone medieval residential engineering. Yet nests survived for centuries (albeit with more than a little human help). One perched on top of a tower in the German town of Langensalza stood proud for four hundred years. A document from 1593 noted the sum given for the repair and upkeep of the nest, suggesting that the human residents were under a certain obligation to maintain the 2-tonne pile of twigs weighing down their home.

Storks are most famously associated with fertility. In many European countries, it was believed that a couple with storks nesting on their house would shortly be blessed with a baby. Even today in Germany, a wooden model of a stork carrying a bundle in its beak is often placed outside a house where a baby has just been born and pregnant women are referred to as having been 'bitten in the leg by a stork'. The prevalence of this belief can cause some confusion. The US TV network Fox News recently reported on a German couple who attended a fertility clinic because they had failed to have children, only to be told that in order to have a baby, they had to actually have sex first. They thought the stork was enough.

The big white birds' reputation as baby-bringers has its roots in pagan culture. The birds reappear every spring, and spring was generally a bumper time for births. The summer solstice on 21 June was a traditional pagan holiday of marriage and fertility. Many romantic liaisons would take place then and, nine months later, coinciding with the return of the storks, their babies would arrive. The two events became connected, with the result that people thought the storks brought the babies.

Europe's birth rate has been in decline for several decades, and so too has the population of the continent's storks (though the two are unrelated). The last thirty years, however, have seen concerted conservation efforts. On a torrential day in June 2016, I made an exceedingly damp trip to Diss in Norfolk to investigate one of these projects. Conservationist Ben Potterton picked me up from the railway station and drove me along the flooded country lanes to Shorelands Wildlife Gardens, home to his very own, highly imaginative scheme to reintroduce storks to the British landscape.

Ben has a magic touch with animals. He has coaxed the rarest, most reluctant breeds into reproducing and thus

regularly supplies stock for zoos and conservation programmes. He has a weakness for 'the little brown jobs' – his
term for uncharismatic species that get overlooked by the
big campaigns. His wildlife centre is a chaotic, cacoph-
onous place awash with obscure cocoa-coloured oddities
from pygmy marmosets to red-breasted geese, many of
which are allowed to roam free. My first encounter was
with a particularly vocal duck that was aiming to deny its
nature and escape the rain. She sat with us in the shelter of
the cafe as Ben outlined his vision for the future of British
white storks.

Back in 2014, Ben was contacted by a Polish animal rescue centre that had a surfeit of white storks needing a new
home. Most were the victims of power-line electrocutions, an
occupational hazard of their daredevil habit of nesting on the
top of electricity pylons. These lame birds could no longer
migrate and would perish in the cold of a Polish winter, but
the rescue centre had been struggling to find someone willing
to take on twenty-two handicapped storks. It occurred to Ben
that the Polish birds could produce perfectly able-winged
babies to repopulate Britain's stork-less shores. So he went to
Poland, packed the birds in flat-pack wardrobe boxes – which,
he informed me, are 'perfect for a stork since they can be
transported individually' – and drove the birds to England.

Ben and I braved the rain to meet his immigrant storks.
The majority were busy stalking the perimeter of a nearby
field in a big, bedraggled group. Two of the birds, however,
had hived themselves off from the crowd to build a

nest. With great pride Ben showed me the messy pile of twigs perched atop a muddy mound around the back of the whooper swan enclosure. The pair's unusually terrestrial set-up was home to the first British-born chicks for some six hundred years.

Storks were last recorded nesting in Britain way back in 1416, when they were spotted on top of St Giles' Cathedral in Edinburgh. Ben told me their disappearance in this country was not just down to the dangers of migration, but risks much closer to home. For, unlike other countries in Europe, where storks were so deeply revered that people harming them could even be sentenced to death, Britain actively persecuted its storks.

'There was a deliberate plan by the church and our rulers, the politicians of the time, against the stork,' Ben told me. 'The church did not like that they were baby-bringers because *God* brought babies.' The birds were dangerously associated with un-Christian, heathen beliefs that the local church was keen to stamp out. Unlike in the rest of Europe, where a nest on the roof was considered good luck, in England it became a sign that someone in the household was committing adultery. Given that the medieval punishment for extramarital sex was at best banishment (for the man) and at worst the removal of nose and ears (for the woman), a pair of noisy nesting storks would have been far from welcome guests.

The storks were also under fire for their political 'preferences': there was a persistent rumour that the birds bred only in republics or countries with no king. Religious differences played a role too. Storks were an important symbol in Islamic culture, and it was believed the birds migrated to Mecca just as the devout did. The Scottish writer and traveller Charles MacFarlane, visiting the Ottoman Empire in 1823, reported that 'these sagacious birds are very well aware of this predilection' and showed their allegiance to the Muslim Turks by building their nests on mosques and minarets 'but never on a christian roof!'

In England vagrant storks flying over from the continent were viewed with suspicion and shot on sight. One such insurgent turned up on the doorstep of the Norfolk home of the great myth-buster Sir Thomas Browne in 1668, shortly after England's own flirtation with republicanism, courtesy of Oliver Cromwell. Browne took in the wounded stork, nursing it back to health with hand-fed frogs and snails, and formed quite a bond with the bird. His neighbours were more wary. Hopefully the bird would not foretoken a new commonwealth, they joked nervously. The ever logical Browne dismissed these 'vulgar errors' as no more than 'a petty conceit to advance the opinion of popular policies', adding for good measure the list of monarchies, from ancient Egypt to modern France, where the bird was known to nest.

Ben hoped his birds would be better accepted in Norfolk today. The week I visited his wildlife centre, Britain voted to leave the European Union amidst hysterical fears over human immigration, and it was all too easy to imagine these immigrant birds once again being viewed as intruders.

'Polish storks coming over here, stealing our frogs,' the headlines might read. Yet it struck me that in many ways these broken Polish birds were helping to recreate Ye Olde England that the Brexiteers seemed to hanker for; there is archaeological evidence that storks populated England as far back as the middle Pleistocene (350,000 to 130,000 years ago). But Ben told me once the UK leaves the EU, rewilding efforts like his that depend on animals from overseas will be mired in bureaucracy and much harder to achieve.

The big question is whether Ben's birds will migrate to Africa. Eminent zoologists including Charles Darwin believed migration was strictly an innate instinct, but scientists now believe that for soaring species like the white stork, social learning also plays a significant role; fledglings may have an imprinted urge to fly south, but it's not terribly efficient. The intricacies of their route, most crucially where to stop off and feed, are learned by following their parents. This is a luxury unavailable to Ben's storks, but he remains optimistic. Every year the coast of Norfolk receives a few transient white storks, like Thomas Browne's, from Denmark. Ben's hope is that these Danish storks would take off on their natural migration and his birds would follow them all the way to Africa.

There is no guarantee, however, as new research has revealed that Europe's storks are changing their migratory habits. Many are shunning their traditional long-haul lifestyle in favour of a more sedentary existence, staying home and eating junk food.

A couple of years ago, Dr Andrea Flack, a researcher at the Max Planck Institute for ornithology in Germany, spent a month migrating alongside a muster of fledgling storks. 'We tagged sixty juveniles before they left their nests,' she told me. 'I followed a flock of twenty-seven individuals, chasing them every day in my car.'

With the help of local firefighters, Flack began by placing small GPS locators on fledglings near her research centre. This was no easy task; the possessive parents were less than keen on Flack interfering with their chicks and would attack her with their beaks, whilst she wobbled on the end of a very long ladder. But once the birds fledged, Flack could follow them wherever they flew.

Storks, like vultures, glide on thermal currents. So they travel during the day when the sun is high and can cover great distances under the right conditions, but not necessarily along convenient motorway routes. 'It was a lot of driving,' Flack told me. 'I'd wait until eight or nine o'clock in the evening, then I would jump in my car and drive hundreds of kilometres to catch up with them.' She was often driving in the dark and into the unknown. 'I'd drive along dirt roads for hours and hours and then suddenly I'd end up at a pig farm and find hundreds of storks.'

One has to admire her bravery, creeping around alone at night in the middle of nowhere in a foreign country. 'The scariest thing was the dogs, which of course are there to protect the farm and you just hear a lot of barking in the dark.' Flack usually slept in her car until dawn and then tried to explain to the farmer, with whom she didn't share a language, that she wasn't *trespassing*, merely following a flock of storks who'd arrived at his farm in search of food.

As Flack travelled further south, the human population dwindled. The birds became harder to locate. She found them in secret oases, unmarked on her map. 'Especially in Spain, it's a very arid area – very dry and dusty. You drive for a very long time through nothing and then you end up at this really beautiful pond that's so green and nice and surrounded by flamingos and storks,' she said. 'They can find these really small ponds in the middle of nowhere.' Flack doesn't know for certain, but she suspected the birds locate these secluded spots by spotting other storks circling high in the sky, riding thermals.

Flack's unorthodox road trip revealed that white storks are truly opportunistic feeders, finding pit stops to refuel on everything from frogs to pig feed. The big white birds' gastronomic tour of Europe was full of surprises, but none more so than their final feeding joint: the giant landfills of Spain.

Spain's biggest cities – Madrid, Barcelona and Seville – are surrounded by massive garbage dumps, whose mountains of organic waste and associated insects and rodents make for the ultimate smorgasbord. 'Once they reach these places, the storks stay for a couple of weeks, maybe even a month,' Flack discovered, 'and sometimes they don't even migrate any further.'

Content with this high-calorie fast food, half of Flack's

birds didn't bother pushing on to Africa. They just stayed put, eating junk food all winter. And when spring came some of her storks didn't even head back to northern Europe. They stopped migrating altogether. Given that migration is probably a series of evolutionary steps from stagnation, whereby the ancestors of Flack's storks gradually shifted either their breeding grounds or winter feeding spots to leave competitors behind or chase ephemeral food bounties, it may be that some of Europe's storks are now reversing their long-distance trajectory.

I've witnessed this profound change in the storks' behaviour myself. But unlike Flack, I haven't been racing to and fro across Europe to do so. I've done it all from the comfort of my sofa in London – and so can you. The Max Planck Institute have developed the highly addictive Animal Tracker app, which receives GPS data from Flack's tagged storks, along with data for a host of other animals, and plots their movements on your phone. Since 2015, I've followed a stork called Odysseus who was tagged in Germany and appears to have turned his back on his wandering nature and name. Since arriving at the landfills of southern Spain in September 2015, he's barely moved. Occasionally he has hopped over the Strait of Gibraltar to feast at the landfills of northern Morocco, but that's it. His brother Felix, tagged in the same nest, has been doing much the same.

These new tracking technologies are ushering in a golden age of migration studies, with potential to reveal the full life journey of not just the white stork but all 1,800 known species of long-haul migrating bird. Some of these studies are starting to confirm otherwise inconceivable acts of migrant endurance. Swifts have recently been tracked spending ten months on the wing, eating and power-napping in the air to and from South Africa, their feet never touching the ground even after they arrive. Arctic terns win the long-distance record for an annual round trip of almost 100,000 kilometres from England to Antarctica – a journey more than twice the circumference of the planet from a bird that weighs less than an iPhone. During their lifetime this diminutive aeronaut racks up around 3 million flying miles, which is the equivalent of four round trips to the Moon – which makes Charles Morton's space challenge seem slightly less ambitious.

Other studies, like Flack's, are exposing radical real-time changes in migratory behaviour. In the UK, Aristotle's blackcaps could no longer be mistaken for transmuting garden warblers; the country's recent warmer winters, and a steady supply of food from bird feeders, have removed the urge for this traditional summer migrant to ever leave Britain's shores. Swallows are also becoming increasingly reluctant to leave the UK and return to Africa. Their numbers, along with those of dozens of long-haul bird migrants across Europe, Asia and America, are in perilous decline, thanks to the combined effects of global warming, habitat destruction, hunting and pesticides. Some scientists have suggested that long-haul migration could soon become a thing of the past. These amazing avian vanishing acts, which puzzled us for so many genera-tions, could themselves magically disappear, just as they've finally been demystified.

Our couch-potato influence on the stay-at-home stork is quite the opposite of the effect we've had on the next animal we'll meet, the hippopotamus. This massively mis-understood monster has become an unlikely globetrotter, all because of the whims of a world-famous cocaine baron.

## CHAPTER 9

# HIPPOPOTAMUS

## Species *Hippopotamus amphibius*

*Some say that hee is five cubites high, and hath ox-hoofs, three teeth sticking out each side of his mouth, greater out then any other beasts, eared, tayled, and neighing like the horse, in the rest like the Elephant; he hath a mane, a snout turning up, in his inwards not unlike an horse, or asse, without hair.*

Edward Topsell, *The History of Four-Footed Beasts*, 1607

IN HIS BESTSELLING BESTIARY, the seventeenth-century clergyman Edward Topsell had little trouble accepting the existence of unicorns and satyrs, which he described in great detail. He was, however, decidedly sceptical about the hippopotamus. And who can blame him? At the time, few if any naturalists would have clapped eyes on one, and the fantastic accounts of the hippo being bandied about bear little resemblance to the animal we know.

Since the days of the Roman Empire, the hippo, *Hippopotamus amphibius*, had been portrayed as a monstrous, maned 'river horse' that could 'vomit fire' and which oozed blood. The Greek writer Achilles Tatius described it 'opening its nostrils wide and snorting out a reddish smoke as if on fire'. One could be forgiven for thinking he had been smoking something himself to fire up the imagination in this way, but it's likely he'd just been perusing his Bible. The mighty, chaos-causing Behemoth from the Book of Job bears an uncanny resemblance to these ancient hippos and is widely considered to be its inspiration: 'Under the lotus plants he lies, in the shelter of the reeds and in the marsh. What strength it has in its loins, what power in the muscles of its belly!' bellowed God in the telling of Job's sorry story.

The biblical description of this mythical monster no doubt added to the far-fetched speculation surrounding the hippo's size and fire-breathing abilities. Accounts of blood-sweating were a more credible mistake, however, and probably based on actual observation. The Roman naturalist Pliny the Elder provided an imaginative analysis in *Naturalis Historia*, his great encyclopaedia completed in AD 77:

> When the animal has become too bulky by continued over-feeding, it goes down to the banks of the river, and examines the reeds which have been newly cut; as soon as it has found a stump that is very sharp, it presses its body against it, and so wounds one of the veins in the thigh; and, by the flow of blood thus produced, the body, which would otherwise have fallen into a morbid state, is relieved; after which, it covers up the wound with mud.

What reads as a tragic tale of a self-harming hippo with some serious weight issues was in fact a portrayal of the ancient art of bloodletting – a procedure used in the treatment of an array of ailments for almost three thousand years. If you were a feverish Greek or a bubonic medieval Brit then your doctor's top-line treatment would be to puncture a vein and drain some of your blood. If you were *very* lucky, leeches might be used instead of a sharp wooden stick. Bloodletting was practised by the Egyptians but, according to Pliny, that other famous resident of the Nile, the hippo, had shown the way. 'The hippopotamus was the first inventor of the practice of letting blood,' he announced, not once but twice, in his encyclopaedia.

We may scoff at Pliny's notion that the hippo invented one of the ancient world's most popular medical fads. But the truth is that this big amphibious beast has pioneered a pharmaceutical fashion, one that's practised in our time rather than Pliny's (and, crucially, one that actually works).

The liquid the ancients observed seeping from the hippo's hide does look remarkably like blood; it completely fooled me the first time I saw it. But it isn't blood – nothing like it. Instead, this crimson goop is produced by special glands tucked underneath the animal's thick skin. For many years it was thought to act like a sort of sticky red sweat to keep the hippo cool. Scientists have recently discovered it does something much more remarkable.

The slime's blood-like appearance is the product of red and orange pigments, unstable polymers that start out clear but change shape and colour as they absorb and reflect UV light. This is rather handy, because it means the hippo is essentially secreting its very own sunblock – an innovative evolutionary adaptation for a massive, hairless mammal regularly exposed to the blazing sub-Saharan sun.

The slime is also believed to contain antibacterial agents – the reason why a hippo's war wounds hardly ever get infected despite its predilection for wallowing in water

*This Italian medical manual (1642) credits the hippopotamus as the inventor of phlebotomy. The animal (said to be the 'size of a Friesian horse') instinctively pierces a vein, lets out blood 'until it feels revived' and then wallows in the mud until the wound is healed. How terribly hygienic.*

awash with its own faeces. And despite their fondness for a poo party, flies tend to leave the hippo alone, suggesting this super-goop could be an insect repellent to boot.

This three-in-one formula is significantly more sophisticated than your average overpriced sun-slop from Boots. In fact, it's such a revolutionary substance that Christopher Viney, a biomimicry scientist in California, has been trying to turn hippo sweat into the next big thing in sunscreen. 'It is the unusual combination of properties that makes it so enticing: sunblock, bug repellent, and antiseptic all rolled into one,' he told me.

'Nature's most successful materials have had plenty of time to become optimized for purpose. If Nature makes a good skincare product, we will be hard-pressed to improve on it,' said Viney. There are some issues to be worked out. 'The challenge', he noted, 'is to get a sample that is not contaminated by faeces' – which would perhaps fail to evoke the same smell of summer holidays fabricated by pharmaceutical rivals.

Undeterred, I decided to put the professor's research to the test by smearing my own skin with fresh hippo slime. The hippo in question was an overly tame orphaned baby called Emma, resident of a rescue centre in South Africa. I was feeding her when I noticed rivers of red running down her back and collecting in the folds of fat on her neck. So I decided to help myself. The liquid had the tacky consistency of egg whites and lathered up into a creamy foam; on application, my skin quickly absorbed it.

Sadly my hands were so sun worn it was hard to deduce its SPF powers, but one hand was now noticeably silkier than the other. The owner of the sanctuary was also a fan of its moisturizing qualities. She told me she regularly uses hippo goo as a lip salve and swears by it.

No other mammal is known to secrete its own sun-block. They don't need to; hair or fur generally does a pretty good job of protecting the skin. But the fact that this so-called river horse is so sensitive to sunlight that it evolved a sophisticated super-sweat to protect it, hints that the hippo's classification was another of Pliny's blunders.

*Emma the orphaned hippo being bribed with food, just before I swiped some of the crimson slime oozing out of her hide to test out its SPF value on my own skin.*

This is entirely understandable, as the hippo hides a family secret so outrageous that it has, until very recently, continued to court controversy.

As a zoology student in the early 1990s, I was taught the hippo was more closely related to the pig than the horse. This seemed plausible – but it was, unfortunately, also wrong. Their next of kin on the taxonomic tree are a group of animals so unlikely, my former university tutor, Richard Dawkins, wrote in his book *The Ancestor's Tale* that it was 'so shocking that I am still reluctant to believe it, but it looks as though I am going to have to'.

The hippo's closest relatives are, in fact, whales.

For centuries, scientists had been attempting to classify the hippo by doing the usual studies of teeth and bones. But it turned out that there was another way to get a hippo to spill its shocking secret: to *talk* to it.

Dr Bill Barklow devoted twenty years of his life to figuring out what hippos are saying to each other, making him the world's leading expert – indeed the world's *only* expert – in the lonely field of hippo communication.

I met Bill in Uganda whilst researching animal communication for a TV series. He was now in his late sixties, but I managed to cajole him out of retirement to teach me a few phrases in hippo – no mean feat, since I can barely speak five words of French, despite years of trying. Bill is fantastically good company and does the best impersonation of a hippo's comical grunts, snorts and bellows you are ever likely to hear, perfected after many years alone with these amphibious beasts.

His twinkly blue eyes lit up when he talked about his part in the hippo classification coup. 'As a scientist you dream of that Eureka moment, where you think of something no one else has ever thought of before,' he told me as we motored upriver, towards the source of the Nile, on a sultry African afternoon. 'But few people ever get it.'

It had happened quite by accident back in 1987. Bill was studying loons – the North American feathered variety, famous for their haunting human-like calls – when he decided to treat himself to his fantasy holiday: an African safari. One morning, whilst watching hippos for the first time, he noticed something rather puzzling. When one of the males would make his raucous territorial call, within a few minutes other hippos would surface from the depths and call back. 'I thought, how can they do that? They're breaking the laws of physics!'

The density of water compared to air makes sounds above or below water reflect off the boundary, so sounds made above water can't be heard underwater, and vice versa. And yet it appeared to Bill that the hippos underwater could hear the noise the male made above, because they responded to his call. 'When I got home I went straight to the library to check the literature on hippo sounds and communication. I dug deep, but found nothing.'

Like any true scientist with a fresh bug in his brain, Bill waved goodbye to his loons, moved to Africa and dedicated the rest of his life to finding out how hippos defied physics. It took him the best part of ten years, but he eventually stumbled upon the answer: hippos are amphibious communicators.

When wallowing in the shallows (with just their nose, eyes and ears exposed), hippos' bellows are broadcast above water by their nostrils, but the sound is also transmitted below the water, through a large blob of blubber on their throat. Fat has roughly the same density as water, so the sound is transmitted directly from the vocal chords, through the fat and out into the river with little distortion. Submerged hippos pick up these sonic rumblings through their jawbone, which is linked to their inner ear.

Bill demonstrated this to me by playing a recording of a hippo's hello out of the large loud speaker on our tiny boat. We had positioned ourselves as close as we dared to a small pod of semi-submerged hippos chilling out in the shallows of the river. It was late afternoon, and the air was hot and soporific. The harsh recording of the grunt roaring out from our boat shattered the peace. It was probably less than a minute before the first hippo bellowed back. Then, as if by magic, a series of solitary hippo heads bobbed above the surface of the water and joined the chorus. The effect rippled all the way downriver as far as the eye could see, with a dozen or so hippos rising out of the muddy waters, one by one, to say hello.

As Bill continued his research, he learned that these amphibious beasts, famous for raucous bellows as loud as thunder, carry on *most* of their communication below the surface of the water. Using a separate underwater speaker and a microphone crudely strapped to a long pole so that it could be submerged, Bill showed me how he entered the secret sonic world of the hippo. Using a submarine set-up like this, he had recorded a surprising cacophony of croaks, clicks and squeaks produced by the hippos forcing air over their vocal chords or fluttering their nostrils. These decidedly un-hippo-like sounds, along with the way they were transmitted through fat and received through the jawbone, struck Bill as remarkably similar to a faraway group of underwater mammals: cetaceans, aka the whales and dolphins. Could they be related? He thought so.

Bill's breakthrough caught the attention of a molecular biologist by the name of John Gatesy who had been trying to piece together a molecular case for hippos sharing their closest common ancestor with whales for some time. This radical rethinking of the taxonomic tree had set off some suitably big waves in zoological circles. Gatesy was on the hunt for physiological evidence to support his theory. He was seeking *synapomorphies* – traits shared by hippos and whales and no other species that might have been handed down to both animals by a common ancestor. Bill had just what he was looking for.

'I had discovered that hippos make clicks or click trains underwater very similar to those that all cetaceans use for sonar,' Bill said. 'Hippos are also hairless, give birth and nurse underwater, and have a repertoire of underwater sounds. All of these could be synapomorphic, and, as such, evidence for traits inherited by both hippos and whales from their common ancestor.' The resulting 'whippo theory' – which placed cetaceans and hippos in a shared evolutionary group – was met with derision by certain palaeontologists, who had a bone to pick with both the molecular and synapomorphic evidence. The taxonomic tussle persisted for decades, pitting scientists studying the past against those searching for clues in the present.

One of the major issues was the incomplete fossil record of the hippopotamus line, which seemed to disappear some 20 million years ago. Fossilized evidence of ancient whales dated back much further. But in 2015, a handful of ancient Hippopotamidae teeth were found in a Kenyan canyon, providing a key stepping stone in the animal's ancestry: the molars unambiguously united the hippo with the whale family tree.

It was an ironic footnote to the hippo's heredity tale that the infamous Behemoth would turn out to be the brother of that other great chaos monster from the Book of Job, Leviathan (widely considered to have been a whale). And so too that the Bible's most Brobdingnagian beasts would both have evolved from what was probably a rather diminutive ancestor, little more than the size of a spaniel.

The hippo's strong link with myth and legend led to such confusion over the centuries that the celebrated French naturalist Georges-Louis Leclerc, the Comte de Buffon, attempted to wipe the slate clean with his description of the hippo when he sat down to write his magnum opus, *Histoire Naturelle*, published in 1795. 'Although this animal has been celebrated from the earliest ages it was imperfectly known to the ancients,' stated Buffon. 'It is only

*The natural history illustrators of the past struggled with the hippo as much as they did with the sloth, as is evident from this bizarre hairy-lipped and human-eyed beast – the 'heppepotame' that featured in* The Gentleman's Magazine *(1772)*

towards the sixteenth century that we have been able to procure any accurate information on the subject.'

Buffon's encyclopaedia was of course the first attempt to classify the natural world according to modern scientific principles. He made an effort to remove the superstitious folklore that plagued the medieval bestiaries. His haughty tone is a little unfortunate, given that almost everything he went on to say about the hippo was wrong. It's worth looking at his claims in some detail, however, because they influenced thinking about the animal for such a long time.

To begin, he observed that 'the hippo swims well and eats fish.' Wrong. Hippos are vegetarians, and they can't do as much as a doggy-paddle. Instead, rendered almost weightless by water, they bounce along the riverbeds, doing a sort of submarine moonwalk.

He went on: 'His teeth are very strong and of so hard a substance that they strike fire with a piece of iron. This is probably what gave rise to the fable of the ancients that the hippo vomited fire.' Nice try, Buffon, but also wrong. Hippo teeth have been prized as ivory since Egyptian times and, although harder than an elephant's tusks, they are still easily carved by hand and have the advantage of not turning yellow with age. In fact, if the Comte had lost his teeth he might even have found himself wearing a pair of hippo dentures; they were all the rage in the 1700s – even George Washington had a set. (Though as far as I know, no one ever reported the first American president 'vomiting fire' through them.)

There was more. 'Thus powerfully armed he might render himself formidable to every animal', Buffon wrote, 'but he is naturally gentle.' Again, wrong, very wrong. Hippos are famously bad-tempered, highly territorial brutes with absolutely no problem using their massive tusks for battle. They weigh much the same as a family car and despite their size, can accelerate almost as fast, easily outrunning a human. Their charging capacity combined with a penchant for attacking boats has led to a fearsome reputation as Africa's most dangerous animal. I suspect this oft-quoted legend may be an internet myth, as it seems unlikely that such a statistic could have been assessed across all hippo-dwelling African nations. But having been charged by a hippo myself (my fault for straying too close to the Behemoth's pond for comfort), I can attest to the fact they are a long way from gentle.

Finally, Buffon put forward that 'these animals are confined to the rivers of Africa.' Wrong again – as it now transpires. But not even Nostradamus could have predicted the latest twist in the hippo's inscrutable evolutionary tale: that a remote corner of Colombia would become a haven for hippos in the twenty-first century.

A couple of years ago, I flew to Medellín to investigate. Nestled 1,500 metres up in the Andes, Colombia's second city is surprisingly cool and damp for a spot so close to the equator. My heart sank slightly as I stepped off the plane to see heavy grey skies identical to those I thought I'd left behind at Heathrow. I was met by Carlos Valderrama, a handsome thirty-something veterinarian who has come to know hippos only too intimately, for reasons I'll explain shortly. Our safari began with a four-hour drive through lush emerald hills, down into the Magdalena River Valley and deep into cowboy country. The trek gave Carlos plenty of time to fill me in on the backstory.

Back in 2007, the Colombian Ministry for the Environment began receiving calls from rural Antioquia reporting sightings of a very peculiar creature. 'They said it was really big, with small ears and had a very large mouth,' Carlos remembered.

The locals were scared and so Carlos, a specialist in animal–human conflict, was sent in. He found himself faced with the task of explaining to bemused locals that this strange beast was an animal from Africa – a hippopotamus.

An equally confused Carlos wondered where they had come from. The locals all told him the same thing: Hacienda Nápoles.

Strategically located halfway between Medellín and Colombia's capital, Bogotá, and sprawling over nearly 20 square kilometres, Hacienda Nápoles was built by the infamous drug baron Pablo Escobar. It was from here that he controlled the export of 90 per cent of America's cocaine, a trade that made him one of the richest men in the world, estimated at one time by *Forbes* magazine to be worth over $3 billion. The ranch was his personal playground. Here he threw lavish parties, amassed his collection of vintage cars and built a dinosaur park for his son, complete with life-sized asbestos dinosaurs. Like many other megalomaniacs, Escobar also fancied having his very own menagerie, and he went about creating it as only a billionaire drug baron would.

Legend has it that Escobar got his hands on a massive Russian cargo plane that he ordered be flown to Africa and like some modern-day, twisted Noah, filled with (sedated) illegal wildlife. The 'Ark' then had to fly back to Colombia before the animals woke up, a task made significantly trickier when he discovered the runway at the hacienda, built for small private jets loaded with cocaine, wasn't long enough. He ordered that it be rapidly extended to ensure the plane and its drowsy passengers could land.

Over the years, Escobar smuggled in lions, tigers, kangaroos and, most crucially to our story, four hippos – three females and one very randy male he called El Viejo, a popular Colombian Mafia nickname meaning 'Old Man'. The hippos were introduced into a small lake next to the hacienda's mansion. And they're still there. Although when I paid a visit to meet El Viejo, his harem was considerably bigger than three.

Escobar was shot by military police in the early 1990s. His empire fell and his entire menagerie was rehoused in zoos across South America – except for the hippos. Transporting an animal that weighs up to four and a half tonnes is an all too hefty challenge for even the most ardent wannabe hippo owner. So for the next two decades, the hippos wallowed in their pond as their master's massive ranch was looted to the point of dereliction, and then transformed by the government into the unlikely combination of Pablo Escobar theme park (open to Escobar fans and complete with waterslides) and high-security prison (open to Escobar wannabes and without waterslides).

All the while, the hippos flourished. Carlos said their numbers were doubling every five years and there may now be more than sixty hippos. I only counted about twenty of them in El Viejo's pond. The rest, Carlos told me, had bust through the flimsy barbed-wire fence that surrounded the hacienda and were running riot in rural Colombia.

Hippos are highly territorial. So as soon as one of El Viejo's sons reaches sexual maturity, the Old Man chases him out of the family pond, away from his harem. The surrounding Magdalena valley is laced with mighty rivers that act as hippo superhighways, allowing these horny young males to travel hundreds of kilometres into the Colombian countryside. In Africa this would be perfectly normal; young males leave the pod and head off on their own in search of some hippo love. But in Colombia there are no hippos out there, and these frustrated Don Juans are causing havoc.

Carlos took me to meet one such lovelorn hippo, a large adolescent male languishing in a pool just 100 metres from a village school. As I approached to get a closer look, the hippo opened his mouth wide in a threatening gape and bellowed aggressively. Whilst I was trying to recall Bill Barklow's hippo language lessons, the hippo started barrelling towards me at such speed that large waves rippled out from around his body. The meaning of the call was abundantly clear: intruders were not welcome. I wasn't surprised to hear the kids from the school no longer bathe in the pond, and one boy told me that in the previous week, his grandmother had been chased by this lovesick beast until she nearly collapsed.

Not everyone was scared though. The BBC reported a boy telling the local paper: 'My father has captured three. It is nice because you have a little animal at home. They have a very slippery skin, you pour water and they produce a kind of slime, you touch them and it's like soap.'

Carlos believed that Colombians are more vulnerable to hippo attacks than Africans because they have grown accustomed to the image of hippos as cuddly animals, the star of Disney movies. 'Everyone thinks they are cute animals because they look chubby,' he said. 'But they're not.' Carlos regarded Colombia's hippo population as 'a ticking time bomb'.

It was not just human safety that worried Carlos. Hippos have the power to radically reshape their environment, and the effect these eco-engineers might have on the local flora and fauna was what worried him most.

In Africa the hippo life is tough. They have to survive a severe dry season. Their pools dry up, food becomes scarce and they must protect their young from hungry crocodiles and hyenas. No such challenges for Escobar's ex-menagerie. Steamy Colombia receives year-round rain. The hippos have all the grass they can eat, plenty of shallow pools to wallow in during the day, no predators and comparatively little competition from other hippos. Living the good life is changing their behaviour. In Africa hippos usually become sexually active between the ages of seven and eleven, but Escobar's hippos are breeding as young as three. And females are reported to be giving birth to a calf every year instead of every two years, the way they do in Africa. As Carlos put it, the Magdalena valley is 'a hippo paradise'.

The normal solution for dealing with an invasive species that's running amok and threatening native species is to extinguish it. Governments around the world have gone to elaborate lengths to eradicate rats, ants, mussels and a host of other alien invaders. The government of Guam was praised for its ingenuity in parachuting a fleet of commando cats onto an island to eradicate unwelcome brown tree snakes. And the government of the Galápagos used so-called Judas goats (a reference to Christ's betrayer) to lure invasive goats out into the open, where they were shot by snipers in helicopters. The US government has happily tried everything from itching powder to poison pellets in a futile attempt to annihilate starlings, which a New York pharmacist with a misplaced dream of introducing every bird mentioned by Shakespeare into America released into Central Park. Since 1890 his original sixty birds have swelled into a menace numbering in the tens of millions.

When the Colombian military shot their first rogue hippo, however, there was public outcry. The story then reverberated through the international media. For a country eager to turn the page on its bloody past, shooting the star of Disney movies was a PR disaster. The eradication programme was shelved.

Carlos was the man given the onerous task of implementing Plan B: a radical castration programme. Neutering one of nature's most deadly animals is a truly demented idea, but Carlos – clearly a man with serious *cojones* – gave it a shot. Thus far, the Colombian vet has managed to castrate one solitary male, discovered terrorizing fishermen 250 kilometres downriver from the hacienda. The operation took over six hours and was complicated by a number of unforeseen quirks of hippo biology. 'A normal castration takes thirty minutes,' Carlos informed me, 'but hippos are difficult in every way possible.'

For a start, despite their size hippos are tricky to anaesthetize. They require a large but precise dosage, and because of their high fat content (fat absorbs the drug), they are easy to overdose. It took five darts for Carlos to send the animal to sleep. Administering the drug was also a challenge. Several darts bounced off the hippo's thick hide, and those that pierced it only served to make the famously cantankerous creature even more irate. 'We had decoy cowboys to distract the animal's attention, but he still chased us a couple of times,' Carlos told me. 'It was a very scary situation.' An understatement if ever I heard one.

Once he had got the animal to sleep, his problems were by no means over. These massive mammals are prone to overheating when out of the water, and since underwater surgery wasn't an option, Carlos needed to work fast – as fast as he could, that is. Hippos have internal gonads, hidden beneath several inches of skin and fat (much like their cousins, the whales). To complicate matters further, hippo testicles have been described as 'highly mobile' due to their habit of wandering about, especially when under threat. Their position can vary by as much as 40 centimetres. Carlos told me he blunted three scalpels during the procedure. It took him a couple of hours to locate these moving targets – even though they were the size of melons – and another hour to sew the bull back up.

Afterwards, Carlos had been loaned an old Russian helicopter to airlift the neutered male back to Hacienda Nápoles. Napolitano, as the hippo was christened, now lives in the big pond. The enormous eunuch is apparently no longer a bother to El Viejo, making the lengthy ordeal an unlikely triumph.

Unfortunately, the operation cost the Colombian government over $150,000 – a prohibitive price tag for a developing country with more than its fair share of money-draining problems. Carlos thought there was little chance they would do many more hippo castrations. The hippo problem was apparently being passed from one government department to another, with no one wanting to take responsibility for it. It looked like the hippos are in

Colombia to stay. If they carry on thriving in genetic isolation, they will, in time, become a new subspecies of Colombian hippo, perhaps with the name *Hippopotamus amphibius escobarus* – a most unexpected legacy of a billionaire drug lord as well as a fascinating glimpse into the kind of random event that causes one species to divide into two.

The hippo isn't the only great big beast with a dangerous character. The moose has almost as fearsome a reputation, especially when it's drunk. But as we'll discover in the next chapter, the animal kingdom's most notorious tippler helped save America from being branded a land of natural degenerates and does not (entirely) deserve its reputation for being a reprobate.

## CHAPTER 10

# Moose

Species *Alces alces*

*The Germans call this Beast Ellend, which in*
*their language signifieth miserable or wretched . . .*

Edward Topsell, *The History of Four-Footed Beasts*, 1607

THE MOOSE ACQUIRED A reputation in ancient times for being nature's misery guts. 'It is a melancholic Beast,' wrote the naturalist Edward Topsell in his great animal almanac. So mournful in fact that it had the power to spread its sadness by being eaten. 'The flesh', he warned, 'engendereth melancholy.'

Moose have much to be moody about. Their common American name translates from Algonquian as 'twig eater', which isn't exactly a great lifestyle advert. This largest species of the deer family has evolved to survive the most inhospitable sub-Arctic climes – from North America through to Europe and Asia – on the most miserable of diets. They are, however, unlikely to be any gloomier than your average beaver or bison. They just appear that way.

Evolution doesn't care about human aesthetics – just ask the blob fish. Its long and winding road creates the most practical, if not pretty, solutions to survival. The moose needs to be able to travel long distances in deep snow in order to sniff out its twiggy dinner. Evolution's solution to this ecosystem challenge is decidedly goofy-looking. With its spindly, stilt-like legs, hunched back and long, droopy muzzle, the moose has a certain long-suffering, lugubrious look that invites human misinterpretation.

Topsell attributed the moose's melancholy, quite randomly, to chronic epilepsy. 'It is in a most miserable and wretched case, for every day throughout the year it hath the falling sickness,' he wrote. This spurious affliction was especially unfortunate for the moose on account of the long-legged creature allegedly having been denied any knees. They have no 'joints in their legs to bend', according to the clergyman-cum-naturalist, which led to some

*pag.246. Book 1 Vol.2.*    *of Animals*    *Plat*

The Elk

*The Elk falling down in an Epileptick fit being pursu'd by y Huntsmen.*

A Compleat History of Druggs *(1737) features an elk having an epileptic fit. The afflicted animal was said to self-medicate by sticking its cloven foot in its left ear. This too became a standard cure for 'the falling sickness' in humans, which is just what every fitting person needs – a dirty great hoof shoved in their lughole.*

rather undignified consequences. 'When they are down on the ground, they can never rise again.'

Their spurious lack of leg hinges was, however, first described by a man unlikely to have been taken to task for telling tall tales – the great Roman general Julius Caesar.

Caesar had encountered moose in the great Hercynian forest. *Alces*, as the Romans called them, were widespread throughout Europe at this time. 'They have legs without joints and ligatures,' the general wrote in his *Commentarii de Bello Gallico*. 'Trees serve them as beds. They lean themselves against them, and thus reclining only slightly they take their rest.'

Moose actually have rather supple knees – far more so than any other member of the deer family. Their powerful legs can kick in all directions, even sideways. The Roman's response to the moose's non-existent disability was to round them up and throw them in the Colosseum. Amongst the 5,000 exotic beasts set to bloody, fatal combat in AD 244 were 60 lions, 32 elephants, 30 leopards, 20 zebras, 10 moose and 1 hippopotamus. The bookies must have had a field day.

Such unmitigated misfortune would be enough to turn an animal to drink. And the miserable moose has indeed earned its reputation for being the animal kingdom's number one alcoholic.

September is a busy month for the Swedish police force. It is the season of falling fruit, and for police officer Albin

Naverberg, that means just one thing: drunk moose on the loose. 'Just as humans like wine, the moose like fermented fruits,' he told me as we drove across Stockholm to investigate the latest of their rowdy misdemeanours.

Sweden is home to around 400,000 moose, which, like the rest of Europe, they prefer to call elk, though they are the same species, *Alces alces*. (This causes no end of confusion since Americans have decided to call an entirely different species of deer, 'elk'.) Sweden's elk/moose spend most of the year hiding away deep in the forest, far away from the country's enthusiastic hunters, but in the autumn they appear to undergo an alcohol-induced Jekyll-and-Hyde transformation. Gangs of marauding moose invade towns and villages, terrorizing the locals like the original stag party. 'It's a big problem at this time of year,' Albin confirmed. 'We get around fifty moose calls every autumn in Stockholm.'

Albin and I arrived at a smallholding on the outskirts of the capital. It was a slice of bucolic heaven – a rustic wooden cottage nestled in a modest-sized orchard. The heady scent of overripe fruit filled the air. Albin picked up an apple and handed it to me. 'This is what they've come for,' he said, 'but they don't eat the green apples. They only pick out the soft brown ones that have started to ferment.'

The homeowners reported that a mother moose and her calf had staked out their garden for a couple of days, gorging themselves on fallen fruit. On the third day, they came out to find the calf dead and its mother absconded.

'They stay in people's gardens for long periods – one or two weeks,' Albin said, 'and they won't leave the fermented fruit. They think that it is theirs. They get angry if they think anyone is trying to take their fruit away. They can be violent.'

You don't mess with a moose. Whilst they may have been unfairly pitted against a pride of lions in the Colosseum, make no mistake: the largest member of the deer family is a badass beast when under threat. The biggest bulls weigh close to a tonne, stand over 2 metres tall and sport a pair of antlers big enough to swing a small hammock between. They use those huge antlers for duelling other males during the rut, or mating season. For us humans it's the legs you've got to watch out for. With the force of four jackhammers, these nimble-kneed ninjas can provide a pummelling worthy of Mike Tyson. One biologist's advice: 'Assume every moose is a serial killer standing in the middle of the trail with a loaded gun.' Which sounds somewhat alarmist, but in the state of Alaska moose are said to attack more humans than bears (although I've struggled to verify any data on this).

According to Albin, they are most dangerous when drunk. In recent years, mobs of boozed-up moose have terrorized a group of Norwegian hikers and laid siege to a care home of Swedish pensioners (armed police had to chase the horned hoodlums away). In one particularly curious case a man was sent to jail for murdering his wife, a crime that later turned out to have been committed by a moose that had apparently overindulged on fermented apples.

Moose are not the only members of the deer family accused of druggy delinquency. Reindeer have long been rumoured to seek out hallucinogenic fly agaric toadstools, which are alleged to make them 'behave in a drunken fashion, running about aimlessly and making strange noises'. It's hard to imagine how such trippy behaviour could create an evolutionary advantage. Perhaps, if the rumour is true, some of the other toxins in this famously poisonous red-and-white mushroom help kill off the internal parasites that these ruminants are especially prone to.

The indigenous Saami shamans of Scandinavia are said to use the toadstool's trippy powers in their ceremonies, with their preferred method of intake being a sip of the urine of a reindeer that has been indulging in the fungi. The toadstool's most toxic chemicals are broken down by the reindeer's intestinal system, whereas the psychoactive elements remain intact, making it a 'safe' (if fairly unappetizing) means of getting a fly agaric fix.

The moose's apparent lack of inhibition is much beloved amongst the Swedish press, who delight in ribald headlines relating their latest intoxicated antics. 'Swede Shocked by Backyard Elk "Threesome"' went the headline in *The Local* newspaper. In the article, a thirty-four-year-old marketing manager called Peter Lundgren was quoted complaining that the elk 'were eating apples and then suddenly they assumed the position'. He had witnessed a young male moose mounting an older female that was otherwise orally engaged with the rear end of another young male.

But what may be shocking behaviour by human marketing manager standards is not necessarily exceptional for elk. A Swedish zoologist told the paper that though it was 'extremely rare' to see moose mating in a residential area, it was not unusual for them to have sex whilst others look on. 'Usually there are several males in the area competing to be with the in-heat female. The strongest one usually wins, and the others are left to watch,' said the moose sex consultant. 'It's quite normal behaviour.'

This public moose-shaming shares strange moralistic parallels with the medieval bestiaries, whose interest in the animal kingdom wasn't intended to educate about the lives of animals so much as to employ animals as a means of teaching important moral lessons – which is arguably how many animal stories are regarded by the tabloids today. Ironically, the moose was chosen by the medieval scribes to lecture people about the evils of alcohol.

Back in the Middle Ages, moose were far more widespread than they are today. They roamed all across North America, eastern Asia and Europe, as far south as France, Switzerland and Germany, and were known by an even more confusing variety of names, including *alg*, *elch*, *hirvi*, *tarandos* and *javorszarvas*. The twelfth-century *Book of Beasts*, written in Latin, refers enigmatically to an 'antelope' that historians now believe was most likely a moose.

This 'antelope' was praised for its 'incomparable

celerity. So much so that no hunter can ever get near it' – a statement the stuffed moose heads hanging over many a fireplace would solemnly disagree with. Whilst they may not be able to outrun a bullet or an arrow, moose are indeed swift; faster even than a greyhound and capable of clocking a top speed of just over 55 kilometres per hour.

A combination of their speed, especially in deep snow, and surprising susceptibility to being tamed, led the moose to a brief if somewhat unlikely career in the seventeenth century as royal postmen. According to the Scottish naturalist Sir William Jardine, the court of King Charles IX of Sweden employed moose to pull the sledges of his couriers. The monarch even considered founding a moose cavalry, which would have won points for novelty value on the fields of battle, if nothing else.

*The Book of Beasts* went on to explain that the moose 'has long horns shaped like a saw' which 'can cut down very big trees and fell them to the ground'. This claim is more odd. Moose are not known for their lumberjack skills, though the bulls do have a habit of vigorously rubbing their antlers against trees to remove their soft velvet coating just before the rut. The bestiary's author did all he could to find a religious allegory in this deer behaviour, relating the elk's two antlers to the two testaments of the Bible, which, he said, can be used to saw off 'all fleshly vices', including 'drunkenness and lust'. Beware 'the shrub Booze', the author warned. Its long branches can entangle

*The 'antelope' featured in the Northumberland bestiary (1250–60) is depicted getting his comeuppance (death at the hands of the hunter) after getting caught up with the corrupting 'shrub Booze'.*

the elk's antlers and cause this otherwise swift creature to become trapped, leading to death at the hands of a hunter.

Beware indeed. In a strange case of life imitating art, Albin told me that drunk moose frequently have to be rescued from all manner of entanglements. 'I have seen elk that have fallen down hills and end up hanging from trees,' he reported. 'They often get caught in football nets and washing lines.' These usually do not result in a loss of life, but there is a significant loss of dignity for all involved.

In Anchorage, one local moose, nicknamed Buzzwinkle, could regularly be found staggering around town trailing long trains of Christmas lights in his antlers after a big night out of hitting the apples. In Sweden, one bedraggled individual achieved international fame after being caught with its gangly frame entwined amongst the branches of 'the shrub booze'. A snapshot that seemed to capture its especially humiliating hangover ended up on CNN and went viral, taking moose-shaming to a new level.

Drunk moose stories have been described as 'the best thing on the internet'. But just because these big gangly beasts with their squiffy eyes – which can naturally point in opposite directions – look like they're wasted, doesn't mean they actually are.

Moose aren't the only animals that have been accused of getting plastered on fermented fruit. Newspapers abound with stories of all types of inebriated beasts from pissed parrots falling out of trees in northern Australia to orangutans getting blitzed in Borneo on the sickly liquor produced by overripe durian. There was even a report of a badger in Germany disrupting traffic by lurching around a main road after allegedly overindulging on alcoholic cherries.

When I looked into them, I found that most of these stories were purely anecdotal – and about as reliable as the word of a drunk moose. One story kept rearing its drunken trunk, however. African elephants have long been alleged to get wasted on the fermented fruit of the marula tree which, according to an old hunting bible from 1875, makes them behave like teenagers hitting the town centre on a Saturday night. They 'become quite tipsy, staggering about, playing huge antics, screaming so as to be heard miles off, and not seldom having tremendous fights.'

*Modern morality fables as told by the popular press: this unfortunate moose found international fame after becoming entangled in an apple tree in Gothenburg, Sweden, in 2011. It was allegedly drunk on fermented fruit and had to be rescued by firemen (who were unable to salvage the animal's self-respect).*

A natural history documentary entitled *Animals Are Beautiful People* achieved notoriety in 1974 for capturing the drunken antics of elephants, ostriches and scores of other animals on camera. The film absurdly anthropomorphized its subjects as it showed scene after scene of them getting loaded on marula and then reeling around with hooded eyes and wobbly legs, all set to a *Benny Hill* soundtrack. The footage was sufficiently compelling to have found a second life on YouTube, where the video has been watched by over 2 million people.

The first person to delve into the truth of this story was the legendary psycho-pharmacologist Ronald K. Siegel. Amongst scientists, Siegel has form in the animal intoxication department. As associate professor at the University of California, Los Angeles, he spent a career experimenting with the effects of alcohol and drugs – mostly on human volunteers he called his 'psychonauts', but also sometimes making the occasional foray into the wider animal kingdom. He has given monkeys cocaine chewing gum and claims to have taught pigeons 'how to tell us what they were seeing while under the influence of LSD'. To which the somewhat mundane answer was: blue triangles.

In 1984, Siegel undertook a significantly more treacherous study into what happens when you give a group of captive elephants 'with no history of alcohol use' access to unlimited alcohol. He discovered they were more than happy to drink the equivalent of thirty-five cans of beer a day, enough to partake in 'inappropriate behaviours' such as wrapping their trunks around themselves, leaning against things with their eyes closed and dropping their trunkhold on each others' tails, which Siegel described as 'the trained elephants' version of walking in a straight line'.

Playing bartender to a herd of elephants was not without its risks. One lairy customer, a large bull named Congo, chased Siegel's jeep after the professor tried to cut off his beer, attacking Siegel with the empty barrel. On another occasion, Siegel had to break up a fight between Congo and a sober rhino that happened to wander into the elephant's favourite waterhole at the wrong moment. 'I knew a life-threatening clash was imminent.' Siegel decided to drive his jeep between the two animals, only narrowly avoiding becoming part of the fight himself. 'I should have known better,' he wrote later. Valuable lessons were learned by all that day, which we can only hope included not giving dangerous animals access to inebriants in the name of science.

Siegel's rather whimsical conclusion from his elaborate drunken circus was that the elephants did indeed drink until drunk, doing so perhaps to forget 'the environmental stress' of their ever-shrinking homeland and the competition for food. But just because elephants can get drunk when supplied with a steady stream of alcohol, doesn't mean they are getting similarly wasted on fermented fruits in the wild.

Whilst attending a physiology conference in South Africa, a group of British biologists decided to get to the bottom of this legend. They took a more sober scientific approach to the investigation than had Siegel, and instead of dosing elephants irresponsibly with unlimited booze, they used statistics to find their answer. They created various mathematical models based on an average elephant's weight and the alcohol content of the marula fruit and calculated that an elephant would have to eat marula at 400 per cent its normal feeding rate to get looped. 'These models were highly biased in favour of inebriation,' the researchers said, 'but even so failed to show that elephants can ordinarily become drunk.' The biologists branded the marula story as yet another zoological myth driven by our desire to humanize animals. The boozed-up stars of *Animals Are Beautiful People*, had, it seems, been injected with veterinary anaesthetic in order to elicit their woozy behaviour. 'People just want to believe in drunken elephants' was the researchers' final conclusion.

The same would seem to be true of the moose. One Swedish professor told me that there had never been a test confirming high blood alcohol in an elk. 'When you show me a study presenting data on alcohol content in an apple-consuming moose, I will take it more seriously. At this point I think the idea rather reflects our Nordic–Germanic problematic relationship to alcohol.'

A Canadian biologist said a more likely explanation was that the moose are suffering from apple acidosis, brought on by suddenly consuming an unnatural amount of irresistible, sugar-rich food. This causes a build-up of lactic acid in their gut, a condition that can result in symptoms that include dilated pupils, a struggle to stand and severe depression – all of which sounds remarkably like the early naturalists' portraits of the moose. It seems the animal they were describing was neither alcoholic nor melancholic, but instead suffering a case of acute indigestion.

Which is not to say no moose has ever been blotto. Indeed, there appears to have been at least one – a pet belonging to the sixteenth-century Danish astronomer

Tycho Brahe, whose accurate pretelescopic observations laid the foundations of modern astronomy.

It may sound a little unusual to have a pet moose, but there was very little about Tycho that might be described as normal. He lost his nose as a student in a duel over maths and was forced thereafter to wear a false one fashioned from brass. He built his very own castle, complete with underground laboratory, on the island of Hven and invited the great and the good to join him there for lavish parties. There they were entertained by a psychic dwarf called Jepp and Tycho's pet moose, which, according to the astronomer's diaries, was an exceedingly good sport: 'It prospers, runs about, dances and is of good cheer . . . just like a dog.'

Though he was clearly very fond of his pet, Tycho agreed to gift it to his patron in an effort to increase the astronomer's standing in society. It died en route, at a castle in Landskrona, where it was alleged to have consumed a quantity of beer, becoming quite legless, before taking a fatal tumble down the stairs.

Perhaps this was the only case of a genuinely drunken moose. But it's worth considering that a sober moose might have had some trouble going down the stairs as well.

Given their reputation for drunken delinquency, it's poignant that the ASBO-bearer of the animal kingdom would find itself playing a starring role in saving the newly independent American colonies from being branded a nation of degenerates. But in the late 1780s, a rather dilapidated dead moose became the unlikely defender of the United States' honour.

The Old World was deeply suspicious and decidedly threatened by the New. These defensive sentiments were crystallized into a neat scientific doctrine by none other than the imperious Georges-Louis Leclerc, Comte de Buffon, who outlined the highly contentious 'Theory of American Degeneracy' in his *Histoire Naturelle*. 'In America', he proclaimed, 'animated Nature is weaker, less active.' Not only were there fewer species to be found in the New World, but 'all the animals are much smaller than those of the Old Continent.' Of those found on both continents, the ones of the New World were more 'degenerate'. And America boasted no showstopping giants: 'No American animal can be compared with the elephant, the rhinoceros, the hippopotamus, the dromedary, the camelopard [giraffe], the buffalo, the lion, the tiger.'

Buffon had never actually set foot in the New World but, as usual, that was no impediment to his theorizing. His knowledge of the diminutive nature of American animals was mostly gleaned from stuffed specimens and travellers' tales, neither of which were known for excessive accuracy. He had, however, developed an idiosyncratic system of accountability: if he read the same 'fact' in at least fourteen travellers' tales then, according to his peculiar probability calculations, he was able to be certain of its 'moral certitude'.

The cause of America's inherent dwarfism, he decided,

was environmental. The continent had only recently lifted itself up out of the sea and was mostly swamp; unlike Europe it was still drying out. That's why American animals and plants were smaller, weaker and less diverse. The only creatures that grew to any size were insects and reptiles, 'all the animals which wallow in the mire, whose blood is watery, and which multiply in corruption, are larger and more numerous in the low, moist, and marshy lands of the New Continent.'

The dogs of America were, for instance, both diminutive and 'absolutely dumb'. And in a uniquely French insult, the Comte proclaimed that the lamb raised there was 'less juicy'.

The Native American peoples were, according to Buffon, equally degenerate – weak of mind with hairless bodies, a lack of 'ardour' and 'small and feeble' genitals. Although he stopped short of actually saying it, the suggestion was that any European going to America would suffer the same diminishing effects, since any animals transported to America 'shrink and diminish under a niggardly sky and an unprolific land'.

Buffon's theory was a massive slap in the face for the developing nation. The prospect of giant insects and shrivelling genitals wasn't exactly a great advert for a country desperately trying (in those days) to appeal to immigrants. What's more, these scurrilous schoolyard jibes were delivered with unquestionable authority. The Comte was the most famous naturalist of his time, a leading light of the

Enlightenment whose encyclopaedia was an international bestseller. As a result, his 'Theory of American Degeneracy' caught on like wildfire, providing Europeans with a handy scientific justification for believing that their continent remained superior to this Brave New World.

In the name of American virility, something had to be done. Enter Thomas Jefferson, future president of the United States, who somehow found time in between authoring the Declaration of Independence, holding office as governor of Virginia and serving as ambassador in Paris, to take on the Comte's withering claims. Jefferson loved nature almost as much as he loved politics. So he was perfectly placed to retaliate against the belittling of his beloved nation with hard evidence of American greatness.

Jefferson wrote to his fellow Founding Fathers urging them to head out into the wild with a pair of calipers and start measuring American animals so that they might counter the French naturalist with their own set of diplomatic data. The political men responded to this novel task with great gusto. James Madison, for example, sent Jefferson a lengthy missive in which he first debated the merits of different forms of representative government, and followed it up with an extraordinarily precise description of a local Virginian weasel, measuring each and every part in three dimensions right down to the 'distance between the anus and the vulva'. Madison concluded that the weasel's statistics 'certainly contradicts his [Buffon's] assertion that, of the animals common to the two continents, those of the new are in every instance smaller than those of the old'.

Whilst Jefferson was serving as the US ambassador to France, he received an invitation to the Comte's summer home in Paris. It must have been a tense soirée. After initially trying to ignore each other in the garden, they collided in the library. Jefferson had his hard-earned intellectual ammunition prepared, but before he could dazzle Buffon with his comparative weasel stats, Buffon plopped a massive manuscript in front of him, the latest version of his encyclopaedia, stating, 'When Mr Jefferson shall have read this, he will be perfectly satisfied I am right.' The evening then dissolved into an argument about moose.

Buffon said he was 'absolutely unacquainted' with the American moose and thought it was simply a miscategorized reindeer. Jefferson told the Comte, somewhat rashly, 'that the reindeer could walk under the belly of our moose'. Buffon scoffed at him, and rightly so. Finally, the French aristocrat relented and threw down a giant gauntlet: if Jefferson could present him with a moose 'with horns one foot long' he would retract his 'Theory of American Degeneracy' in the next volume of his natural history tome.

Jefferson had known for some time that moose were his trump card. He'd already circulated a sixteen-question survey to gather information on them, covering such pertinent issues as, 'Do they make a rattling sound when they run?' He had also begged his political allies to shoot, stuff and post him their largest specimen, 'seven to ten feet tall' with 'horns of a very extraordinary size' – the very definition of a tall order.

One General John Sullivan had emerged as Jefferson's main moose man. So after the encounter with the Comte, an obsessed Jefferson wrote to General Sullivan with increased urgency. 'The readiness with which you undertook to endeavour to get for me the skin, the skeleton and the horns of the moose,' he wrote from Paris on 7 January 1786, 'emboldens me to renew my application to you for those objects, which would be an acquisition here, *more precious than you can imagine*' (emphasis his).

Jefferson went into minute detail about how the animal should be prepared in order to preserve its greatness. 'Leave also the bones of the head in the skin with the horns on,' he explained in his lengthy set of instructions to Sullivan, 'so that by sewing up the neck and belly of the skin we should have the true form and size of the animal.' Sadly, when Sullivan finally procured a seven-foot moose for Jefferson, it had already been on the road for fourteen days. The general was no taxidermist and he struggled to fix the toll taken by the bumpy road on the animal's carcass, which was in 'a state of putrefaction'. The moose's magnificent antlers were also crucially absent. So Sullivan was forced to send the corrupt creature with a smaller, surrogate pair. 'They are not the horns of this moose', he confessed to Jefferson, adding breezily, 'but may be fixed on at pleasure.'

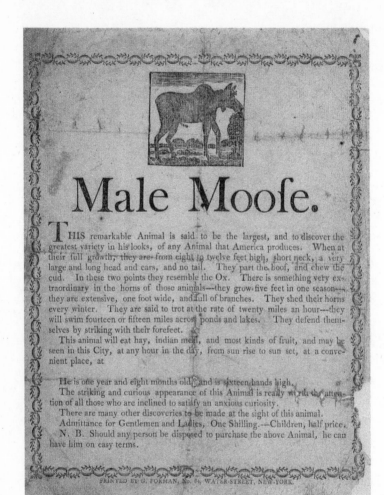

# Male Moofe.

THIS remarkable Animal is said to be the largest, and to discover the greatest variety in his looks, of any Animal that America produces. When at their full growth, they are from eight to twelve feet high, short neck, a very large and long head and ears, and no tail. They part the hoof, and chew the cud. In these two points they resemble the Ox. There is something very extraordinary in the horns of those animals—they grow five feet in one season—they are extensive, one foot wide, and full of branches. They shed their horns every winter. They are said to trot at the rate of twenty miles an hour—they will swim fourteen or fifteen miles across ponds and lakes. They defend themselves by striking with their forefeet.

This animal will eat hay, indian meal, and most kinds of fruit, and may be seen in this City, at any hour in the day, from sun rise to sun set, at a convenient place, at

He is one year and eight months old, and is sixteen hands high.

The striking and curious appearance of this Animal is really worth the attention of all those who are inclined to satisfy an anxious curiosity.

There are many other discoveries to be made at the sight of this animal.

Admittance for Gentlemen and Ladies, One Shilling.—Children, half price.

N. B. Should any person be disposed to purchase the above Animal, he can have him on easy terms.

PRINTED BY G. FORMAN, No. 64, WATER-STREET, NEW-YORK.

*This 1778 advertisement boasting the greatness of the male moose was probably an attempt to crush the Comte de Buffon's withering 'Theory of American Degeneracy', which accused New World creatures of being weak and feeble. It claims that 'this remarkable animal' might be as much as 12 feet high – a tall tale indeed.*

After yet more mishaps, including almost getting lost at the docks, the moose finally arrived in Paris in October 1787. By then it was in a decidedly forlorn state: misshapen, virtually bald and minus its massive antlers. Jefferson was nevertheless optimistic and forwarded the animal to Buffon with a note excusing the unusually pathetic appearance of this great beast, in particular its horns, which 'are remarkably small'. He even found the gumption to brag that 'I have certainly seen of them which would have weighed five or six times as much.'

Jefferson wrote in his journal that Buffon did indeed receive the moose and, despite its miserable appearance, 'he promised in his next volume to set these things right.' But the timing was tragically off. The Comte died shortly afterwards, in 1788, with no word of a retraction to be printed in his epic encyclopaedia. Still, Jefferson's degenerate dead moose cannot be denied its influential role in defending America's greatness. The Founding Father went on to develop his argument and published a comprehensive table of comparative New and Old World animal statistics in his *Notes on the State of Virginia*. The book became a bestseller in its own right, and the degeneracy theory fell into a state of dissolution.

The moose wasn't the only animal to have had a dance with international relations. In the next chapter we'll meet the panda, the planet's preeminent political animal, whose expert diplomatic skills have helped spread an entirely false image of this misrepresented bear.

## CHAPTER 11

# PANDA

## Species *Ailuropoda melanoleuca*

*Pandas are bad at sex and picky about food . . .*
*Females are in heat only for a few days a year;*
*males have the savoir faire of pimply prom dates.*
*These genetic misfits might have died out long ago,*
*had they not been so adorable.*

*The Economist, 2014*

OVER THE COURSE OF the twentieth century, it has become commonplace to pity the giant panda as some kind of evolutionary mishap – an animal incompetent in even the most basic functions for survival. It is considered a joke of a bear, universally adored for its cute comic-strip looks but ridiculed for an apathetic approach to sex and deviant vegetarian diet. Even respected naturalists have declared that 'it's not a strong species' and dared call for its demise. No other animal has been forced to justify its existence as much as the panda, which, without our help, would surely join the dinosaurs and the dodo on evolution's scrap heap.

Or would it?

This image of the pathetic panda is a very modern myth. There are, in fact, two pandas. The one that lives in zoos and gets celebrity treatment in the media is a cartoon of our own creation, a benign bungling comedy act that does indeed need human help in order to exist. The other panda is a splendid survivor that's endured in its current, natural form for at least three times as long as humans and is perfectly adapted to its (admittedly) eccentric lifestyle. This wild panda is a secret stud, fond of threesomes and rough sex, with a taste for flesh and a fearsome bite. But it inhabits an impenetrable forest in a cryptic country, which has allowed an imposter to take centre stage and ensured that one of the most recognizable animal brands is nothing but a fraud.

For an animal as phenomenally famous as the panda, it is surprisingly new to science. As little as 150 years ago, it languished in virtual anonymity, with remarkably few references to its existence even within its native China. That changed in 1869, when a French missionary set off the rhetorical rocket that would launch the panda into global superstardom.

Father Armand David loved nature almost as much as he loved God. 'It is unbelievable that the Creator could have placed so many diverse organisms on the earth,' he wrote in his diaries, 'only to permit man, his masterpiece, to destroy them forever.' The good father indulged both of his devotions by exploring China – a country where he could convert plenty of 'infidels' to his particular flavour of Catholicism whilst searching for new species to send to the natural history museum in Paris. We do not know how many Chinese souls he managed to save, but the keen-eyed missionary certainly had an impressive strike rate in uncovering new species: 100 insects, 65 birds, 60 mammals, 52 rhododendrons and 1 frog ('that barks like a dog') were all first discovered by his hand. His most enduring legacy might have been giving the world gerbils – an unquestionably prolific species – if it hadn't been for a chance encounter that guaranteed his place in zoological history.

One afternoon, whilst taking tea at a hunter's house in the mountains of Szechuan, Father David stumbled upon the pelt of 'a most excellent black and white bear' that he believed might prove 'an interesting novelty to science'. A few days later his 'Christian hunters' brought him back a specimen which the priest noted 'does not look very fierce' and had a stomach 'full of leaves'. He named it *Ursus melanoleucus* (literally 'black and white bear'), and sent its skin to Alphonse Milne-Edwards, director of the National Natural History Museum in Paris, for classification.

The animal was unknown to science, and quite a find. But Milne-Edwards was not convinced by the priest's assessment. The teeth and unusually hairy underpaws resembled those of another bamboo-munching mammal recently discovered in the same Chinese mountains, a relative of the racoon which had been named the red panda (*Ailurus fulgens*). So Milne-Edwards declared that this black-and-white bear should join the red panda in its own family, the *Ailuropoda* (meaning 'panda foot'), quite distinct from the bears.

So began over a century of taxonomic toing and froing over the status of the anomalous giant panda. As would be the case with all issues panda, the arguments ranged from the scientific to the highly subjective. The molecular biologists tussled over mitochondrial DNA and blood proteins; others, who should have perhaps known better, took a more instinctive approach – including esteemed biologist and conservationist George Schaller, who, despite overwhelming evidence to the contrary, continued to insist that 'even though the giant panda is most closely related to the bears, I think that it is not *just* a bear.' Schaller felt in his gut that lumping the panda in with the other *Ursus* destroyed its uniqueness. 'The panda is a panda' was his professional opinion on the matter. 'Just as I hope there is a yeti but that it will never be found, so I would like the panda to retain this minor mystery.'

Alas for Schaller, the geneticists poured irrefutable ancestral evidence all over his dreams. When the panda's genome was sequenced it unequivocally exposed the animal's bear necessities. Father David had been right: the panda was not a panda but the most ancient of all the bears, an early offshoot from the *Ursus* lineage that diverged from the rest some 20 million years ago. But the panda name stuck, promoting its mythical otherness.

Once you scratch beyond the surface, the giant panda is not so different from its bear brethren. The panda's quirky reproductive cycle, boasting a brief fertility window and an ability to delay implantation of the foetus, is also found in other bears. Panda babies are born decidedly undercooked – blind, pink and roughly the size of a mole – like all bears, whose tiny newborns are less than 1 per cent of their adult body size. This fact led early naturalists, such as

*This bear from this French bestiary (c.1450) may look as if it is indulging in a little casual coprophagy, being rather sick or both. It is instead illustrating the myth that bear cubs are born as unformed lumps that are 'licked into shape' by their mothers.*

Claudius Aelianus, writing in the third century, to the conclusion that a bear 'gives birth to a sort of misshapen lump, with no distinctive form or features' and the mother then 'licks it into the form of a bear' – an imaginative mistake that provided the source of the phrase 'lick into shape'.

Aelianus had a way with words, which he put to effective if inaccurate use in his descriptions of bear behaviour. He observed that bears like to hibernate without food or water, causing their intestines to 'dehydrate and atrophy', which the bear reactivates by eating wild arum. This he said 'makes her fart', before she goes and 'eats a bunch of ants' and 'enjoys a fine defecation'. Pandas neither hibernate nor self-medicate but, strictly speaking, no bears do. A handful of species – the black, brown and polar bears – do enter the long winter sleep known as torpor, during which their body temperature drops, they fast and refrain from excreting, but it's not considered a true hibernation. How much they 'enjoy' their first post-sleep poo is something we will likely never know.

The panda's vegetarian diet may be 'picky', but that is not so terribly freaky. Most bears, despite being classed as carnivores, are actually opportunistic omnivores, with plants accounting for at least 75 per cent of their diet. The panda has taken this to an extreme and dines almost exclusively on bamboo, which is more than plentiful in their native mountains. Other bears are equally choosy about their food. The sloth bear is adapted to eat only termites (and has lost its front teeth to simplify sucking them up with an extra long tongue), and the polar bear has a preference for feasting almost exclusively on ringed seals. This dietary specialism doesn't, however, mean that the panda has lost its taste for flesh. When George Schaller was studying pandas in the wild, he would bait the traps with goat meat, as he soon learned this was a sure-fire way to attract them, and I've seen footage of a wild panda chowing down on a dead deer. Panda eats Bambi is a decidedly less

Disney depiction of every kid's favourite cuddly veggie, but it is the bare, if unpalatable, truth.

Still, it's the giant panda's sexual appetite that is the most misconstrued. This modern mythology has been created by a parade of pandas parachuted into foreign zoos where, thanks to us, they've acted out a sexual farce worthy of a 1970s sitcom, making them and their laughable sex lives very famous indeed.

The first of the monochrome bears to grace foreign soil landed in the US just before the start of the Second World War, bringing a dose of much-needed joy to Americans weary from years of suffering under the Great Depression. First came a roly-poly baby named Su-Lin, meaning 'a little bit of something cute'. Her anthropomorphic antics and extreme exotica were only amplified by her chaperone – fashion designer and socialite Ruth Harkness. This unlikely female explorer had faced bereavement, bandits and bewildering bureaucracy, not to mention the indignity of travelling by wheelbarrow, in order to pluck the black-eyed ball of fluff from the mountains of China with her own bare hands. The deliciously scandalous story of her panda-snatching, complete with rumours of illicit romance and the advent of a dastardly competitor (who allegedly tried to smuggle a panda out of China before Harkness by dyeing the bear brown), had fed the newspapers for months. So when the explorer and the bear finally stepped off the boat, Su-Lin received a welcome worthy of a movie star.

The Shirley Temple of the animal world did not disappoint. Humans are preprogrammed to want to nurture anything with neotenous, or baby-like features – namely, a big bulging forehead, large, low-set eyes and round protruding cheeks. It's a neurochemical insurance policy to ensure we take good care of our unusually vulnerable babies, themselves a result of our big brains, which require a birth in early development in order to allow our relatively humongous heads to exit the birth canal safely. It's such a deeply hardwired but rather imprecise impulse, we will even respond lovingly to inanimate objects that vaguely exhibit these characteristics – like the VW Beetle.

Pandas, with their unique markings and decidedly human-like way of sitting and eating, could have been genetically engineered as the perfect trigger for this nurturing instinct. They fool our brains into firing off the reward centre, the same part that responds so delightfully to sex and drugs. So baby giant pandas, with their clumsy, child-like movements, are essentially cute crack. The sight of Su-Lin being bottle fed by her human 'mother' and acting up like a naughty toddler for the assembled cameras left America in a warm and fuzzy puddle.

Su-Lin was soon followed by Mei-Mei, her 'little sister', and finally a potential beau named Mei Lan. Attempts by the Chicago zoo to get them to mate were hampered by the fact that all three were actually male. So as the world watched with bated breath for a budding romance, the two male pandas did nothing but disappoint, and the press reported their every failed move. 'Panda Love: Mei-Mei Courts Her Beau and Gets Nowhere at All,' shouted a typical headline from *Life* magazine, sowing the first seeds of the sex-shy myth.

A similar fate befell the Bronx Zoo's 'breeding pair', which arrived to much fanfare in 1941. Pan-dee and Pan-dah – an early example of the 'Boaty McBoatface' rule of never naming anything of any importance via the medium of public contest – were not a little boy and girl but two females. 'The external differences that the Bronx officials studied were obviously individual characters rather than true sexual ones,' explained the zoologist Desmond Morris helpfully in his 1960s book *Men and Pandas*.

Sexing pandas would prove to be a notoriously difficult art, with countless other cases of mistaken gender leading to further sexual disappointments. The truth didn't help the panda's case much either. Needless to say, being in possession of a penis that is virtually indistinguishable from female genitalia has done little to promote the panda's virility to those judging the bear by human standards.

When a male and a female panda did find themselves in a cage together the results were frankly no more fulfilling, and certainly no less public. One of the most influential of these failed liaisons starred a panda called Chi-Chi.

The young Chi-Chi arrived at London Zoo in 1958 and found herself the star of a hit TV programme that documented her every move to an adoring public. After several years of carefully staged bubble baths and football games with her keeper, the soap opera of Chi-Chi's life demanded a love interest. The only other panda in captivity outside of China was An-An, a resident of Moscow Zoo. So at the height of the Cold War, an unlikely East–West union was planned, much to the glee of the international press corps.

Chi-Chi, however, was less than keen. Once she'd made her rendezvous in Moscow, she repeatedly fought with An-An, spurning each of his clumsy advances. Chi-Chi, it transpired, wasn't attracted to pandas; her desire appeared to be directed towards humans, especially ones in uniform. When the Soviet zookeeper entered her cage, Chi-Chi 'raised her tail and rear-end in sexual response', reported Oliver Graham-Jones, the London Zoo's curator of mammals – much to the Russian's 'intense embarrassment'.

This was not the first time this had happened. 'Sexually, Chi-Chi appeared to be somewhat warped,' recalled Graham-Jones. She was more attracted to zoo staff and 'even complete strangers' than she was to her own kind. It was the 1960s, the era of Free Love, but after three failed attempts at panda romance, it was clear there would be no sexual fulfilment for the zoo's superstar. The Zoological Society of London was eventually forced to issue a statement declaring: 'Chi-Chi's long isolation from other pandas has "imprinted" her sexually on human beings.'

Chi-Chi and An-An's doomed romance was no one-off.

*A romantic scene from 1959 – Chi-Chi with her true love, London zookeeper Alan Kent, as he tenderly feeds her bamboo from his own mouth. A decade later, the zoo was forced to admit their famous female panda had sexually imprinted on the wrong species.*

Shortly after it fizzled out, another high-profile pair of pandas, Hsing-Hsing and Ling-Ling, arrived at the National Zoo in Washington with an important mission – to save their entire species. Chi-Chi had inspired the World Wildlife Fund's famous logo, and the growing panda conservation movement was exceptionally focused on breeding the bears in captivity as part of their survival plan. Unfortunately, the bears had not read the conservation memo and their high-profile romance was confined to yet more underproductive antics. Hsing-Hsing exhibited an 'orientation problem', which resulted in Ling-Ling's ear flap, wrist and right foot being the targets of his amorous attempts. But now these weren't just personal failures; they spoke to the fate of the species. The press reacted with much ribaldry. The public responded by sending the pandas a waterbed.

For the next two decades, top zoologists delved into the biology of the Washington pandas in search of answers, whilst the press and public bayed for babies. Ling-Ling's oestrus was exposed to last less than two days every year – a frustratingly narrow fertility window that took much of the blame. Then, when the capital couple finally did manage to get it on, their offspring did not survive more than a few days. One cub perished after Ling-Ling sat on it, which did little to promote her fitness for motherhood.

Each of these very public dramas added to the perception that pandas are simply not built to procreate *or* parent, and have somehow been denied the fundamental instincts required for survival. The calls to take human control of the situation and find some way to force pandas to reproduce in captivity became increasingly urgent.

Breeding wild animals in captivity is rarely easy. And it takes just a little common sense to see why: a concrete enclosure is not a sexy place for a wild animal. Their desire to procreate has to be stimulated by a range of behavioural and environmental cues – the animal equivalent of a nice glass of wine and a bit of Barry White. Often zoos have no idea what is required to get their animals in the mood. The white rhino, for example, was proving impossible to breed in captivity, because zookeepers were simply plonking a male and female in a pen together and hoping for the best. This didn't take into account that rhinos are herd animals, and for a male to get the horn, as it were, he has to flirt with *several* females before choosing the lucky lady. In giant pandas, it is the reverse – the female is the picky one.

In the 1980s, George Schaller was the first person to discover that these notoriously solitary creatures are not loners when it comes to sex. He observed complex mating rituals in their mountain homeland, in which lone females climbed trees and moaned like Chewbacca as several males fought for their attention below. The winning male would take advantage of his prize by having sex over forty times in a single afternoon – which, according to a recent pop-science survey, is roughly the amount of sex your average Japanese adult has in a year, but nobody's suggesting the Japanese are about to go extinct. The semen of the giant panda is also said to contain 'prodigious amounts of high quality spermatozoa', ten to a hundred times more than a human male. There is no denying that these are virile animals.

Panda sex itself is a rough-and-tumble affair with plenty of biting and barking. The male probably learns the right amount of submissive–dominant behaviour from playing with his mother and observing her in the act; baby pandas stay under their mother's care for up to three years. This gives them the opportunity to witness at least one breeding season and learn the ins and outs of the female panda's preferred Kama Sutra.

Pandas occupy sizeable home territories of around 4 to 6.5 square kilometres, and they sniff out sex parties by leaving scented status updates advertising their identity, sex, age and fertility on specially designated trees – the panda equivalent of Tinder. When a female comes into season she arouses male interest by rubbing her anal glands at the base of one of these communal message boards. Her smelly signal attracts males from far and wide, who then compete for her affections in a sort of urinary Olympics. Female pandas prefer the males that can leave their sexy scent marks the highest up a tree. Scientists have described males adopting a selection of athletic poses – 'squat', 'leg-cock' and, most remarkably, 'handstand' – in order to squirt their pee as high as possible. Males are also thought to use their own bodies as sexy-scented advertising boards by dabbing urine, like aftershave, on their ears, which act as a pair of fluffy beacons broadcasting the bear's availability on the mountain breeze.

Bears are famous for their highly developed sense of smell. So the female's short fertility window is no impediment to reproduction in the wild. Indeed, it could even be an evolutionary adaptation to control population size, precisely because male pandas are so accomplished at procreating, which helps ensure the birth rate never exceeds what the bamboo forests can support. A wild female will raise a cub on average every three to five years, which is not an unusual reproductive rate. If they reproduced any more quickly, they would quickly outgrow their habitat.

This wild sex is a world away from being thrown into a concrete enclosure with a random panda and being expected to publicly perform. Yet, despite the differences, in the last couple of decades the Chinese have cracked the captive breeding conundrum to produce bumper crops of baby pandas, which make for images so cute they should come with a public health warning. Dozens of baby pandas lined up in a row are all but an overdose of cute crack – and have guaranteed these conservation 'success' stories get attention around the globe. So back in 2005, I flew to China to find out how they were doing it.

My destination was the Szechuan capital of Chengdu, home to the most bountiful of China's specially built panda breeding centres. I was expecting the heart of panda country to be a green and pleasant land, but I was instead greeted by a sprawling city of 14 million people that dwarfs London. The first panda I saw was on a packet of cigarettes, which seemed oddly appropriate given the amount of smog that hung in the heavily polluted air. There is a saying in Chengdu that the dogs bark when they see the sun. They were resolutely silent during my entire visit.

I was researching panda breeding for a documentary, so I had privileged, behind-the-scenes access to the catchily named Chengdu Research Base of Giant Panda Breeding, starting with a tour from one of the senior scientists working there. As we wandered around the grey concrete buildings he told me about some of the more imaginative approaches they'd taken to getting pandas in the mood for love in this astoundingly bland and brutalist environment. Aware that the young male pandas had not received the necessary sex education from their mothers (most were hand-reared by humans from birth), they were experimenting with plonking them in front of a portable TV playing a VHS recording of captive pandas humping away on it as a kind of coming-of-age present. I tried not to snigger at the surreal image of baby boy pandas watching porn on their third birthday, but given the panda's notoriously poor eyesight, and the difficulty any animals (other than humans) have wrapping their brains around the concept of seeing themselves on TV, panda porn seemed unlikely to do anything more than raise a laugh. As did their experiment with using sex toys to stimulate the female pandas. Viagra had also been used at other panda breeding centres; one underperforming sixteen-year-old named Zhuang Zhuang ('strong strong') had been given the first experimental dose, but nevertheless failed to live up to his name.

It was as if Ann Summers had taken over as scientific consultant. I almost expected to turn a corner and catch a panda in a pair of red satin suspenders and glittery nipple tassels. I couldn't understand how such human-centric solutions to the panda problem could have contributed to the extraordinary boom in babies. And it turned out they hadn't. The strategy that was paying baby panda dividends involved something significantly less saucy hen party and more J. G. Ballard nightmare: artificial insemination (AI).

AI has become standard practice for coaxing reproductive success out of all sorts of captive animals. All you needed is some viable sperm and a sleepy female. Sometimes the semen is collected using 'digital manipulation', euphemistic science-speak for an animal hand job – surely one of the most desperate jobs in conservation, but by no means unusual. The last pure Pinta Island tortoise, a Galápagos native named Lonesome George, had his very own personal 'digital manipulator' – an attractive young Swiss zoologist whose task was to bottle as much of this living relic's seed as she could possibly extract. She managed to hone this skill sufficiently to relieve the slow-moving centenarian in under ten minutes, earning her the nickname 'George's girlfriend'.

I once witnessed a prizewinning Shire horse being 'harvested' for his 'liquid gold'. It is something my eyes will never un-see. Such exploits are not without hazard for the designated manipulator. A senior scientist at a conservation centre in Berlin sustained a serious black eye from trying to manually massage a bull elephant's flailing metre-long penis to orgasm, which must have taken some explaining down the pub afterwards.

A safer and more dignified solution for the human, if not the animal, is electro-ejaculation. This is as terrifying as it sounds and involves inserting an electric probe up an animal's rectum and cranking up the voltage until the animal climaxes. Dr Kati Loeffler, an American veterinary scientist who spent several years working at the Chengdu centre and Smithsonian, explained to me that this technique was developed for the intensive breeding of farm animals. It is now standard practice for pandas in China, which are dosed up with trance-inducing ketamine to help mitigate the discomfort associated with being anally raped with an electrified truncheon. According to Loeffler, these factory-farming techniques were the reason the captive panda population had soared to almost five hundred individuals in the last couple of decades.

The results are far from a conservation success story, however. Whilst these black-and-white balls of fluff look like pandas, they don't grow up to *behave* like pandas. Inseminated females frequently give birth to twins, which are kept alive by switching them between their mother and an incubator so both get a chance to suckle her milk and develop physically, with the necessary immune system for survival. Then, at three to four months they are removed from their mother completely so she can return to the captive breeding conveyor belt. The babies are subsequently raised by humans in an unnatural pack, until they get too big and belligerent, at which point they get placed in solitary confinement.

'Cubs in breeding centres and zoos are raised in a human-intensive environment in which opportunities for normal social and behavioural development are severely

*2016 saw a bumper crop of baby pandas for the Chengdu breeding centre, seen here being wrestled into position for the all-important 'cute crack' photo opp that will send the story of their 'conservation success' worldwide.*

compromised,' Loeffler said. 'Young pandas never have a hope of learning to become a normal panda.'

Their lack of panda-ness is further exposed when this next generation of animals is thrust together in public breeding situations and struggle to perform. We've fulfilled the myth of the sex-shy panda by artificially breeding them.

When attempts have been made to reintroduce these offspring into the wild – which is the much-heralded purpose of these captive breeding efforts – the results are little better. Recent studies have shown that these so-called solitary animals are quite social, even outside of the breeding season. 'In the wild, bears have to be very savvy socially,' said Loeffler. 'They learn these very sophisticated social negotiations that allow them to work together and share a food resource as well as at mating time.' A socially awkward panda risks more than just going hungry or not getting laid, as one young male named Xiang Xiang found out.

Xiang Xiang was the first panda to be reintroduced to the wild from a captive breeding programme in China. Loeffler told me it was no accident they chose a male to experiment with. 'They need to keep the females because they're the ones that make the golden eggs.' She said he did OK for the first few months, 'but then came the time for the breeding season and you have all these males gathering around the oestrus female and of course he had no idea what to do – he'd been raised in isolation behind bars – and of course they beat him up so badly that he was nearly killed.' He was eventually found dead, savaged to death by wild pandas. To date, of the ten pandas released into the wild, only two remain there.

Releasing captive-born animals into the wild is a bit like chucking a Chihuahua into a pack of wolves. In recent years, one of the Chinese breeding centres has made efforts to better prepare their pandas for wild life. Designated mothers are permitted to stay with their babies in semi-wild enclosures. Their human handlers wander around in panda onesies, pushing about taxidermy leopards mounted on wheels in an attempt to teach the babies about predators. The surreal scene makes for a great photo opportunity, but Lü Zhi, professor of conservation at Peking University, has called the reintroduction efforts 'as pointless as taking off the pants in order to fart'.

Dr Sarah Bexell, a conservation scientist with a CV that includes successful reintroduction schemes for golden lion tamarins and black-footed ferrets, explained why. 'For one thing, there are no longer leopards in panda habitat,' she said. There are more fundamental issues too. 'Humans cannot teach animals how to be animals. Only their mothers, or other conspecifics' – meaning, members of the same species – 'can be the teachers.' Since these panda mums have been reared by humans, they have little or no experience themselves of life in the wild to transfer to their cubs.

The biggest issue of all is the panda's shrinking habitat, something I noticed on the long drive from Chengdu to the Qinling Mountains, where wild pandas are said to still roam. It took several hours to emerge from the city. We passed miles of sprawling urban detritus, then factories belching cement dust over entire villages like something out of a dystopian sci-fi movie. Finally, once we reached the mountains, we were greeted by monstrous dams. And that was more than a decade ago.

The Chinese government have created over fifty panda reserves that claim to have witnessed an increase in pandas – so much so that the panda's status was recently downgraded from 'endangered' to 'vulnerable'. But Kati

Loeffler isn't convinced. She told me the authorities had zoned these 'protected' areas to allow farming, roads and even mining inside them. 'We are so arrogant that we think we need to breed pandas and put them back in the wild because they are too stupid to manage on their own,' she said. 'If we just gave them back their habitat they would do the job themselves, like any other species. There is nothing terminally wrong with these animals that we need to fix; the only thing we need to fix is to give them their home back.'

Sarah Bexell agreed. 'I really worry that it is wildlife conservation's way of saying, "See, guys, we can do this, we are scientists and we're fixing this huge biodiversity crisis problem and we can right the wrongs of our entire species by doing these little projects." It's a feel-good story. The public feels good and sits back and eats their potato chips in their La-Z-Boys and drives their SUVs, has a five-bedroom house and three kids, and says, "Great, those scientists are out there fixing this problem for me,"' she told me. 'But science is not going to save biodiversity; a shift in human behaviour is the only thing that is going to save it. I think there needs to be more effort, first and foremost, in getting the human population under control globally, and for people to start contemplating not being such mass consumers.'

Paradoxically, the pandas themselves have helped grease the wheels of China's explosive expansion, and the associated environmental cost, with their extraordinary diplomatic skills – the one thing these mythical bears are not apparently hopeless at.

A few years ago, I spent some time with two such political pandas: Tian Tian and Yang Guang, aka Sweetie and Sunshine. They had arrived in Edinburgh in December 2011 on board their very own private Boeing 777 airliner, complete with a giant panda painted on the side. Flag-waving school children lined the streets to greet them, bagpipes played and a specially commissioned panda tartan was unveiled in their honour (I'm sure it made the pandas feel very welcome). The whole event was covered by live rolling news. Sweetie and Sunshine's job was to spread a bit of panda magic at the local zoo's flagging ticket office, with the aim of boosting sales by some 70 per cent. But their arrival was also underpinned by other, less publicized economics: a set of trade deals through which Scotland would provide China's burgeoning middle class with factory-farmed salmon, amongst a suite of contracts worth an estimated £2.6 billion. In recent years, globetrotting pandas have accompanied similar arrangements for uranium (with Australia) and seal meat and petroleum (with Canada).

'The panda can be used to seal the deal and signify a bid for a long and prosperous relationship,' Dr Kathleen Buckingham, lead author on a study of 'panda diplomacy', told the BBC. 'If a panda is given to the country, it does not signify the closing of a deal – they have entrusted an endangered, precious animal to the country; it signifies in some ways a new start to the relationship.' China, she said, was interested in having 'soft power influence through a global visual seal of approval'. The panda seems tailor-made for the part.

Panda diplomacy is not new. Way back in the seventh century, the Tang dynasty presented a pair of live pandas (along with seventy of their skins) to the rulers of Japan. The policy was resuscitated in 1941 when China sent Pan-dee and Pan-dah to the Bronx Zoo as a thank-you gift for American aid during the Second Sino-Japanese War. Chairman Mao was a huge fan of the diplomatic power of these iconic black and white bears. During his time in power, pandas were dispatched to long-term Communist partners like North Korea and the Soviet Union as well as new political allies. When Nixon brought a close to twenty-five years of antagonism between the US and the People's Republic with his landmark trip to China in 1972, the sexually underperforming Hsing-Hsing and Ling-Ling were dispatched to Washington and sparked a general 'Panda-monium'.

In exchange, the White House also presented China with a pair of animal ambassadors. The Americans could have chosen stately bald eagles or powerful grizzlies to represent their country, but instead a couple of shaggy, smelly musk ox were forced to step up. The notoriously belligerent beasts failed to elicit quite the same commotion in China as the pandas had in America. Milton, the male, was prone to excessive mucus and suffered from a skin condition which had left him partially bald. His partner Mathilda was in a similarly wretched state. 'One can only hope that a century from now "musk ox" will not be Chinese slang for a useless object that can't be disposed of,' commented a *New York Times* editorial at the time.

Countless animals, from polar bears to platypuses, have been shuffled around the planet as political pawns, with varying degrees of success. In 1826, France received a giraffe from Egypt which put Paris 'in the grip of an intense giraffe-driven craze'. The animal's distinctive coat influenced high fashion, with women even wearing their hair *à la girafe*.

Still, pandas have remained the preeminent diplomat of the animal kingdom. 'The giant panda's exclusive natural existence … and its visual identity make it a perfect tool to attract people around the world and to create – at least temporarily – a good image of China,' wrote Falk Hartig, a scholar of diplomacy who has studied the subject extensively. 'While it is, of course, debatable whether China is as peaceful and friendly as the panda may suggest, the message that it sends out in the name of China is also undeniable.'

China's fluffy diplomats no longer come for free, however. Pandas are loaned to zoos at a cost of $1 million a year and tied into their captive breeding programme. When I visited Edinburgh Zoo in 2014, the director of pandas, Iain Valentine, was hoping for the pitter-patter of tiny panda feet. Valentine's life was, as a result, dominated by panda urine. Pandas have cryptic pregnancies and the only way to gauge if Tian Tian was about to give birth was by monitoring her hormones in forensic fashion. She had been trained to urinate on command but was not always keen to oblige, which meant a daily charade of scrabbling around her pen trying to siphon up some of her prognostic pee. Valentine confided that had he known how much time would be spent trying to get his hands on the panda's precious pee, he would have designed their enclosure with it in mind.

In the end, Tian Tian disappointed everyone by reabsorbing her foetus. This sounds like something out of a horror movie but is probably one of the panda's adaptations to ensure it only gives birth in favourable conditions. Had Sweetie delivered a baby panda, it would, however, have been the property of China and subject to its own $1 million dollar rental fee. Any babies have to be returned to Chinese breeding centres after two years – even sooner if the politics demand it. In 2010, two days after the US decided to go forward with a meeting between President Barack Obama and the Dalai Lama, the Chinese government registered their disapproval by forcing the return of the two American-born cubs to China.

'It's all about politics and money,' Kati Loeffler told me. 'Panda breeding is a full-time, multi-million dollar industry, particularly if one can convince the public that pandas are incapable of reproducing on their own.'

It's not just pandas in foreign zoos that rake in the dollars. In China, panda tourism increased fivefold after the newly minted middle class embraced domestic tourism, and it's now a significant moneymaker for the city of Chengdu. At the breeding centre, ardent fans pay $170 a pop for the chance to have their photo taken holding a baby panda; even more, bizarrely, for the opportunity to muck out their pen. Not all baby pandas have appreciated the adoration of their fans. In 2006, a tourist who paid to frolic with baby pandas suffered the painful embarrassment of her new fluffy friends suddenly turning on her. 'She made the mistake of stroking them on the head a little too enthusiastically – and found herself suddenly knocked to the ground,' the papers said. The woman was rescued, weeping and wailing, from the baby panda pen with only a damaged pride. A few months earlier, at the same centre, another snap-happy tourist lost her thumb in pursuit of the perfect Kodachrome moment.

The panda's bamboo-munching lifestyle has equipped it with a fearsome bite, to crack its way into the tough sheath of the plant's stem. The powerful muscles in the panda's cheeks, which ironically give the bear its adorable big round head, deliver a bite-force quotient that placed the panda in fifth place, wedged between the lion and jaguar, in a recent study of the top bite-forces amongst carnivores.

A website entitled 'When Pandas Attack' has catalogued the surprisingly numerous victims of the panda's 1,300-newton bite, painting a very different portrait of the bumbling bear. The wounded include a keeper at a Hong Kong amusement park who was mauled by a panda named Peace; a former French president who had to be rescued from the jaws of a male named Yen-Yen (narrowly avoiding a major diplomatic faux pas); and a drunk man who fell into a panda enclosure at the Beijing zoo and tried to give a repeat offender called Gu Gu a hug. The man woke up in hospital having nearly lost his leg. 'I always thought they were cute and just ate bamboo,' he later told CNN. Which just goes to show how perilous the great modern panda myth can be.

Until recently these panda attacks had been confined to captive pandas. But in 2014, an elderly Chinese man required over fifty days in hospital after his leg was ravaged by a wild panda running rampage through his village near the Baishuijiang National Nature Reserve. Who knows, with the pandas' homeland being increasingly invaded by humans, maybe we'll start to see more of these wild attacks, which, seen through anthropomorphic eyes, could be the bear's bloody revenge for decades of misrepresentation, ridicule and rectal probes.

My guess is this savage side of the panda is unlikely to ever tarnish its wholesome image. We like our pandas harmless and helpless. Such is the power of cute. In the next chapter, we'll meet the penguin, another animal that's much loved for its adorable anthropomorphic antics. But this enchanting star of so many children's cartoons hides a sex life so shocking it was kept secret for almost a century by those in the know. Get ready for the outrageous X-rated tale of Pingu the pervert.

## CHAPTER 12

# PENGUIN

## Order Sphenisciformes

*All the world loves a penguin: I think it is because
in many respects they are like ourselves, and in
some respects what we should like to be.*

Apsley Cherry-Garrard,
*The Worst Journey in the World*, 1910

MY FIRST ENCOUNTER WITH a wild penguin was an unexpected affair. For a start, I was in Australia. Not all penguins spend their lives skidding around on the ice; half of the existing species inhabit far cosier climes as far north as the equator. Nevertheless, it still seemed odd that my first rendezvous with Antarctica's most famous resident would be on a balmy golden sand beach, just a short drive from Melbourne. But then very little about the penguin's perceived public image turns out to be true.

The southern coast of Australia is home to several colonies of fairy penguins. If you could genetically engineer cute in a lab, it would probably take their pocket-sized form. Standing at just over 30 centimetres tall, they may be the planet's most petite penguins, but they have the biggest number of fans.

Tourists have been flocking to Phillip Island to watch the fairy penguins since the 1920s. I joined several hundred ardent fans, some clutching freshly purchased penguin stuffies several times larger than the real thing, to wait for the arrival of the island's famous penguin parade, a nightly carnival in which the tiny, shiny blue birds totter up the beach from the surf to their sandy burrows as soon as the sun goes down.

Evolution has done a splendid job of equipping the penguin for a life chasing fish in the frigid sea. But bird biology dictates that they must return to dry land to lay their eggs and raise their chicks. This is awkward to say the least. Penguins are basically built like a Thermos flask, which is fine if you live on the sea ice. For those penguins that inhabit more tropical locations, waddling around in a thick-feathered wetsuit can be a perilous sport.

These birds have evolved creative, if somewhat convoluted, strategies to avoid getting overcooked. Some species stand around panting like dogs, others are forced to seek out shade. Yellow-eyed penguins trek up to 1 kilometre inland (quite a marathon for those little legs) to raise their chicks in the cool of the New Zealand rainforest. Galápagos penguins avoid the brutal equatorial sun by nesting in uncomfortable-looking cracks of coastal lava rock. Humboldt penguins arguably have it even worse. Living on the barren coast of Peru they are forced to improvise shade by carving castles of crap from piles of their own mature manure. Fairy penguins solved the problem by shunning the sun altogether and becoming nocturnal. Hence their nightly procession back to their nests on Phillip Island.

The penguin parade was billed with great pride by the local tourist board as 'a waddle on the wild side'. The diminutive birds did not disappoint. As the warm

Australian sun dipped below the horizon, the ocean surf began spluttering out dozens of pint-sized penguins, which worked the crowd like professional entertainers. They shuffled up the beach, and it was impossible not to watch them and smile.

The penguins' farcical walk is quite deceptive. Those stiff feet, so ill at ease on land, act as a rudder underwater allowing penguins to make hairpin turns at speeds of over 50 kilometres per hour. They are the fastest manoeuvrers and deepest divers of any bird; emperor penguins can reach depths of over 500 metres (the height of the new One World Trade Center in New York City). These sea-birds spend 80 per cent of their lives as slick predators that are more James Bond than buffoon. But we only get to see the 20 per cent spent staggering around on land like Charlie Chaplin.

'Our perception of animals is based on where we are able to observe them,' Dr Rory Wilson explained. He's the genius that has fitted hundreds of penguins with speed-o-meters, beak-o-meters and even bum-o-meters in an attempt to uncover their underwater life. 'Seeing penguins stumble around being failures on land is like seeing the world's greatest athletes stumble around in the dark and never realizing what they are capable of,' he told me. 'It's impossible to swim like a penguin *and* run like a cheetah on land.'

The muscles that control penguins' feet have to stay warm to function, so they're hidden under feathers way up in a penguin's leg. They manoeuvre their extremities by a remote 'pulley' system that's about as efficient as operating a Muppet and which gives the penguin its distinctive wobble. This inadvertent act of pathos has blinded us to the penguin's true story – a shocking tale of prostitution and perversion that would make Pingu's feathers curl.

The first penguin to be described by Europeans wasn't a penguin at all. It was a great auk. To be fair to the sixteenth-century captain who goofed up, the physical ID of a great auk does sail pretty close to that of a penguin. They were similarly fat, flightless, black-and-white birds that inhabited large rookeries on isolated rocky islands, albeit in the polar opposite, *northern* hemisphere. And they shared one other crucial characteristic: they were very easy to catch.

These portly birds became a boon for the starving sailor. Sir Francis Drake wrote about an island in the Strait of Magellan where he had killed three thousand 'fowl which could not fly' and which were 'the bigness of geese'. Mythical 'Penguin islands' featured on maps like buried treasure, such was their significance to the survival of men at sea. From the time of Drake onwards, the word 'penguin' became common currency for waddling ready meals whether they were found on islands in the northern or southern hemisphere. According to connoisseurs, these 'penguins' tasted like fish if cooked with their fat. If the fat

*One of the earliest maps of the Strait of Magellan (16th century) features a mellow-looking penguin out for a stroll – an indicator that these fat, flightless ready meals were up for grabs along those shores.*

was removed, their flesh (perhaps with a little wistful imagination) could pass as beef. They boasted the added novelty of their fatty carcasses being so flammable that their bodies could be used as their very own barbecue. Wrote one able seaman in 1794: 'You take a kettle with you into which you put a Penguin or two, you kindle a fire under it, and this fire is absolutely made of the unfortunate Penguins themselves. Their body's being oily soon produce a Flame; there is no wood on the island.'

Despite their superficial form, and perhaps flavour, great auks were part of a completely different family of bird, more

340

closely related to guillemots and puffins than penguins. Their similarities are skin-deep – and a great example of convergent evolution, namely, when two very different and unrelated animal groups evolve the same solution to a survival dilemma. In this case, both birds evolved to fly underwater to feed on small fish and sea creatures. They ditched the large, fragile wings and light-boned bodies that favour conventional airborne flight to become blubber bullets with short, powerful flightless flippers and squat, streamlined bodies – a shape so effective that nothing designed by humans has ever managed to beat the penguin's low drag coefficient. They also developed the same tuxedo-like livery for camouflage: their white front disguises them from predators and prey looking up at the sun-bleached surface of the water, and their black back conceals them from predators above against the murky depths below. Add to this the same webbed feet and short legs that waddle so ineffectively on land, you can see how mistakes might arise, especially amongst sailors semi-delirious with hunger.

Great auks were eventually christened, somewhat unhelpfully, *Pinguinus impennis*, meaning 'featherless penguin' – of which they were neither. This inappropriate name did nothing to quell confusion between the two monochrome seabirds, which burbled on for centuries. This so annoyed Georges-Louis Leclerc, Comte de Buffon, that he proposed the penguin be renamed. The French aristocrat could have chosen 'arse-feet', which was the moniker adopted by certain sailors after watching the birds swim along with their legs trailing behind them. But for reasons best known to himself, he decided on *manchot*, or 'one-armed' in French. As the penguin, like all birds, has two quite distinct wings, or arms, the name failed to catch on. Luckily for the Comte (if not for the birds), great auks were eventually eaten to extinction, bringing some form of closure to his personal penguin stew.

There was further confusion surrounding what type of animal the penguin was. Some early explorers thought they were part bird, part fish. Others saw them as some kind of missing link between dinosaurs and birds. Having spent many hours marvelling at their peculiar reptilian feet, which appear to have been stolen from a crocodile, I can understand why. But this turned out to be a surprisingly dangerous misconception. It led to what can only be described as the world's most harrowing egg hunt, costing two men their lives and one his sanity.

The chief architect of the theory was the polar explorer Edward A. Wilson, who had served as ornithologist on Captain Robert Falcon Scott's famous expedition to Antarctica on the *Discovery* in 1901–4. Edward Wilson was a highly respected pioneer of penguin research whose enquiring observations helped crack the mystery of the emperor's rather unenviable reproductive cycle. This sees the male weathering the brutal Antarctic winter with an egg on his feet and nothing to eat whilst the female, her reserves dangerously depleted from egg-laying, spends two months gorging herself at sea. The male and female then take turns raising the chick and feeding themselves – a relay of extreme endurance that Wilson described as 'eccentric to a degree rarely met with even in Ornithology'. He believed the emperor was a relic species whose eggs held the secret to their evolution. In his report on the Antarctic mission he declared: 'the possibility that we have in the emperor penguin the nearest approach to a primitive form not only of penguin but of a bird makes the future working out of its embryology a matter of the greatest possible importance.'

Wilson's ideas on embryology were influenced by the German biologist Ernst Haeckel. In 1868, Haeckel had devised the rather neat (if sadly not true) notion that all animal embryos go through stages of development that mirror their evolution from distant ancestors – that, as he would be famously paraphrased as saying, their ontogeny (individual development) recapitulates their phylogeny (species development). This grand 'theory of recapitulation' was artfully illustrated by the zoologist himself, whose exquisite, if controversial, drawings of developing foetuses were a highly persuasive piece of promotion.

Assuming Haeckel was right, Wilson believed the emperor penguin's egg would be a time machine, transporting him back to lost transitional stages in the evolution of reptiles to birds. 'The earliest bird, the *Archaeopteryx*, had teeth,' Wilson explained in a lecture on penguins in 1911. 'One hopes to find real teeth in the embryo of the emperor penguin, though none are present in the adult bird.' Wilson also wanted to see if the papillae that develop into penguin

*Ernst Haeckel's fine drawings of comparative embryos – in this case, a hog, calf, rabbit and man – provided persuasive PR for his flawed recapitulation theory (which sent a trio of explorers to the ends of the earth, with only one coming back).*

feathers corresponded to those that become a reptile's scales. This was just fifty odd years after Darwin's shocking theory of natural selection was first published, and not everyone was converted. Wilson hoped that the emperor egg was just what was needed to crush the naysayers and prove Darwin's theory to be true.

He somehow managed to persuade Captain Scott that his far-fetched mission should be an essential part of the scientific endeavours of the explorer's second Antarctic expedition. So in June 1911 Wilson, Henry 'Birdie' Bowers and Apsley 'Cherry' Cherry-Garrard set off on a quixotic crusade to find lost dinosaur teeth in an emperor's egg at the ends of the earth. Their 200-kilometre side trip from base camp was later coined 'the worst journey in the world' by Cherry, its sole survivor. And he wasn't exaggerating. His unflinching memoir of the same title recounts the full horror of this ill-fated egg hunt.

Emperors nest in the middle of the Antarctic winter, so the three men were forced to make their expedition to the only known rookery, located at Cape Crozier, the eastern-most point of Ross Island, in pitch darkness, navigating only by candlelight. No easy task when being battered by Antarc-tic gales. The team took turns tumbling into the copious crevasses that littered their path. Temperatures dropped below -60 degrees Celsius and made the snow so sticky they could only pull one sledge at a time. They were forced into a trudging relay, gaining only one mile for every three they walked. Sweat turned their clothes into an icy armour and their breath froze their balaclavas to their faces. Cherry's teeth chattered so violently they shattered, and the liquid in his blisters turned to Popsicles.

So horrific was the schlep that by the time they reached their goal, Cherry had lost the will to go any further. 'I for one had come to that point of suffering at which I did not really care if only I could die without much pain. They talk of the heroism of dying – they know little – it would be easy to die . . . the trouble is to go on.'

The frozen trio forced themselves forward, scrambling up 60-metre ice cliffs in complete darkness to reach the rookery.

The penguins weren't exactly pleased to see them. 'The disturbed emperors made a tremendous row,' recalled Cherry, 'trumpeting with their curious metallic voices.' The explorers snatched five eggs from between the rowdy penguins' legs and skinned a few of the birds for their fatty fuel. But before they could say 'mission accomplished', their fortunes took a turn for the worse.

The group became lost. Groping around in the dark trying to locate their trail, Cherry's frozen fingers dropped two of the eggs. By some fluke the explorers found their way back to their camp at the foot of (the aptly named) Mount Terror, and they immediately set about trying to get warm. It was the eve of Wilson's birthday and they fired up the penguin blubber stove, but, as if the birds were seeking their revenge, 'it spouted a blob of boiling oil into Bill's eye'. Wilson was blinded and he lay all night 'unable to stifle his groans, obviously in very great pain'.

'I always mistrusted that stove,' said Cherry. But worse was still to come. A furious storm, 'as though the world was having a fit of hysterics', blew their tent and most of their supplies away. The trio were forced into a makeshift shelter with a canvas roof 'whipped to little tiny strips' by the force 11 gales. They spent Wilson's birthday 'face to face with real death'. With no food or fire, they huddled in their sleeping bags singing hymns and dreaming of tinned peaches whilst occasionally thumping the birthday boy to check for signs of life.

After two days, there was a lull in the blizzard and by some miracle Bowers found their tent. 'Our lives had been taken away and given back to us,' wrote Cherry.

The three men staggered back into base camp on 1 August 1911. Their frozen clothes had to be cut from their bodies and their fingers were virtually dead. They looked as if they had aged thirty years in the five weeks since their little egg-collecting expedition had begun. Cherry never really recovered psychologically from the ordeal and wrestled with PTSD for the remainder of his life. Wilson and Bowers somehow bounced back. This only brought them worse luck, since it enabled them to join Scott's doomed polar trek. Both men perished along with the rest of the party on the return journey from the South Pole, leaving Cherry as the sole guardian of the three precious emperor eggs and the associated honours of evolutionary science.

With the weight of two dead men on his shoulders, Cherry took his responsibility as 'Custodian of the Sacred eggs' extremely seriously. When he made it back to London, he took them in person to the Natural History Museum in South Kensington. He may have anticipated a hero's welcome. Instead, he was met by a junior jobsworth who showed absolutely no interest in the specimens, famously barking, 'Who are you? What do you want? This ain't an egg-shop,' at him. Cherry later wrote to the museum to complain about his reception. 'I handed over the Cape Crozier embryos, which nearly cost three men their lives and cost one man his health, to your museum personally and ... your representative never even said "*thanks*".'

Unbeknownst to the explorer, the source of this curatorial insouciance was a rather untimely paradigm shift in evolutionary thinking. Whilst Cherry and his colleagues risked their lives for science on the sea ice, Haeckel's recapitulation theory had itself capitulated. Science had marched selfishly on, rendering the emperor eggs redundant.

Cherry spent much of the rest of his life pushing to have the embryos studied, but twenty-one years would pass before any results were published. And the results were not worth the wait. For one, the zoologist James Cossar Ewart surmised from microscopic slides of the embryos that scales and feathers do not, as Wilson had hoped, share a common origin. Then a final blow came in 1934, when the anatomist C. W. Parsons concluded cuttingly that the eggs, harvested rather too early in their development,

348

didn't even 'add to our understanding of penguin embryology'.

Having lost his toenails, teeth and much of his sanity to the penguins, the polar explorer could be forgiven for harbouring a certain amount of resentment towards them. Yet Cherry remained resolutely enchanted. His writing exudes nothing but warmth and respect for these human-like birds. 'The Adélie penguin has a hard life, the Emperor penguin a horrible one,' he noted at the end of his tumultuous memoir. 'I challenge you to find a more jolly, happy, healthy lot of old gentlemen in the world. We must admire them: if only because they are so much nicer than ourselves!'

Such is the anthropomorphic power of the penguin. 'They are extraordinarily like children,' wrote Apsley Cherry-Garrard, 'full of their own importance and late for dinner, in their black tail-coats and white shirt-fronts – and rather portly withal.' He was not alone in seeing them this way. Such child-like analogies became the lingua franca for penguins soon after they were first spotted. Even the most earnest eighteenth-century scientists writing to the Royal Society waxed lyrical about how the seabird had 'at first sight, the look of a child, waddling along with a bib and apron on'. Even the seamen of the seventeenth century, capturing penguins for the pot, were charmed by how they 'stand upright like little Children in white aprons'.

As with the panda, the penguin's wobbly vulnerability

seemingly mimics a toddler's first steps and triggers our innate desire to nurture. Add to this a long-suffering life at the edge of existence and a natural aptitude for clownish physical comedy and you have a recipe for anthropomorphic superstardom.

The potent mix of stoicism and slapstick made the first penguins to leave Antarctica an instant hit. *The Times*, reporting in 1865 on the penguins at the zoological gardens in London's Regent's Park, revelled in the birds' clumsiness, which was accompanied by a 'ridiculous air of gravity'. Their dignity in the face of endless icy pratfalls, combined with their unexpected love of tobogganing, made them stars of the moving image from the moment it was invented. The Charlie Chaplins of the animal kingdom were perfect fodder for children's books; their naturally iconic black-and-white suiting was (like the panda's) an ad agency's dream. Penguin logos adorned everything from books to biscuit tins. The birds were even adopted by the American religious right as a paragon of Christian family values, thanks to the Oscar-winning documentary *March of the Penguins*.

'This is the incredible true story of a family's journey to bring new life into the world. In the harshest place on earth, love finds a way,' intoned the voice of Morgan Freeman over a series of shots of a perfect-looking emperor penguin couple caring for their impossibly fluffy chick. From that moment, the film played pretty fast and loose with the truth. The scripted narration interpreted the emperor's annual hormone-driven trek across the ice floes to breed as an epic love story. It wasn't true, but it made for a box-office smash. Christian fundamentalists flocked to the message, holding up the emperors' struggle as an allegory for spiritual striving and their behaviour as an example for humans.

The conservative film critic Michael Medved declared *March of the Penguins* to be 'the motion picture that most passionately affirms traditional norms like monogamy, sacrifice and child-rearing'. A group called the 153 House Churches Network set up a *March of the Penguins* Leadership Workshop for members to discuss the impact of the film on their lives. 'Some of the circumstances [the penguins] experienced seemed to parallel those of Christians,' declared the organizer. Churches block-booked cinemas for their members, and at the time of writing the film remained the second most-viewed documentary in US history (sandwiched somewhat uncomfortably between *Fahrenheit 9/11*, Michael Moore's critical dissection of the Bush administration's 'War on Terror', and *Justin Bieber: Never Say Never*).

Penguins may actually be models of upright social behaviour – in a literal, biomechanical sense. Choosing a flightless, fish-eating bird as a moral role model is, however, far from ideal. Not only do most penguins fail to uphold traditional Christian family values, but some of their sexual activities would challenge even the most liberal of communities.

Most penguins, for a start, are far from monogamous. The worst offenders are those 'romantic' stars of the big screen, the emperors, with a whopping 85 per cent switching partners from one year to the next. They do, however, have a reasonable excuse: since they carry their eggs around on their feet, there is no nesting site, and therefore no obvious rendezvous point to meet a mate at the start of each breeding season. They must instead try to locate their previous year's partner by shuffling around in a massive scrum and yelling. At a party of several thousand penguins, all dressed the same, and with a severely limited window within which to locate a mate, one can appreciate the difficulty in staying faithful.

Monogamy, when it does occur, can be a rainbow-coloured affair. In his comprehensive compendium of animal homosexuality entitled *Biological Exuberance*, the Canadian biologist Bruce Bagemihl reported on lifelong same-sex partnerships amongst Humboldt penguins. Bagemihl's book celebrated a spectrum of natural sexual liberation in over 450 species from gay gorillas to boto river dolphins with a penchant for casually boffing each other's blowholes. Many of his observations had been kept in the closet by zoologists for years, as they did not fit into neat Darwinian thinking. Incidents of mutual fellatio amongst male orangutans, for example, were explained away by one prudish biologist as 'nutritively rather than sexually motivated'. It is only very recently that the natural diversity of sexual behaviour found in the animal kingdom has been accepted, with new theories about how such sexual activities defuse tension, benefit child-rearing or simply might be *fun*.

Same-sex penguin partnerships have been particularly well-documented in zoos, with some couples becoming famous for flying the rainbow flag. Dotty and Zee, two males at the Bremerhaven zoo in Germany, recently celebrated their tenth anniversary together and have even adopted and raised a chick together. But though the penguins' celebration of sexual diversity may not sit well with buttoned-up Christian conservatives, it has also brought some disappointment to their more liberal champions. Roy and Silo, probably the penguin world's most famous gay couple, inspired a children's book, *And Tango Makes*

*A couple of gay Humboldt penguins at Bremerhaven zoo in Germany were caught trying to incubate rocks as if they were eggs. The zoo flew in females from Sweden to 'test' the penguins' sexual orientation – a move which enraged gay rights activists. The 'Swedish strumpets' could not, however, break up the couple, who went on to foster their own chick.*

*Three*, much loved by the LGBT community, after they too raised a chick, in New York's Central Park Zoo. A few years later, Silo forsook his partner of six years and ran off with a female named Scrappy, which, according to the *New York Times*, 'rocked the gay scene'. Proving that the penguin's struggle with lifetime fidelity is very real, whatever the flavour.

Penguin divorce rates do tend to lower as you travel north from Antarctica, where warmer weather allows for a more flexible breeding season. This makes the penguin's mission to procreate less pressurized and they can spend more time seeking out last year's successful partner. Galápagos penguins, which live as far north as the equator, manage to be the most faithful, with 93 per cent of pairs reuniting each season. This fidelity may or may not help improve their ability to coordinate cooling efforts – and prevent the kids from turning to a crisp under the fierce equatorial sun – but you have to hope that it does.

Even those penguins that appear to stay together season after season may not be as faithful as they seem. Nearly a third of female Humboldt penguins cheat on their partners, often with members of the same sex. One in ten female Adélie penguins also have a bit on the side. Such female infidelity was generally thought to increase the genetic strength of offspring, until Dr Lloyd Spencer Davis of the University of Otago, New Zealand, discovered that their motives may be a little more complicated than that. Adélie penguins, he claims, are one of the only animals on the planet to have turned to prostitution.

Adélies are your classic, knee-high cartoon penguin. They are the southernmost breeding of any nesting bird and gather in vast rowdy crowds at the start of each brief summer to nest along the edges of the Antarctic Peninsula. Towards the end of the season, as the weather warms, there is a danger of the penguins' simple stone nests becoming flooded and drowning their eggs in meltwater. So the females go on the hunt for fresh pebbles to shore up their parental investment. Stealing is rife and scuffles are commonplace. 'They can be surprisingly vicious, pecking and beating each other repeatedly with their flippers,' Davis told me.

Some sneaky females have learned to avoid getting beaten up by possessive pebble owners by targeting the nests of unsuccessful males living at the edge of the colony. With no parental duties, these singletons are free to go on a pebble-hunting extravaganza and amass veritable stone castles. They are also extremely desperate to spread their seed. The sly female shuffles up to one of these lonely males with a deep bow and a coquettish sideways glance, as if she wants to copulate with him. The male bows back and steps aside to allow the female to lie down on his pebble castle and prepare to procreate. The sex is a swift affair, with the inexperienced male frequently misfiring and missing his target. After the deed is done, the female toddles back to her nest with a pilfered pebble in her beak.

Davis noticed that some especially cunning females

stole stones from the males without even offering sex in return. They flirted exactly as before, only they skipped the sex part and simply made off with a stone. 'She takes the money and runs,' as Davis put it. In response, the males were never seen to put up a fight – although some did make a desperate attempt to claim their conjugal rights as the female beat a hasty retreat with her booty. And the duping of these males was pathetically easy. One particularly effective hustler was recorded swiping sixty-two stones within an hour.

Davis told me that the females have learned that the males 'are not exactly dumb, as much as they are desperate'.

*Female Adélie penguins are one of the only species known to exchange goods for sex. Females dupe lone bachelors into having a quickie only to make off with some hard currency – stones – that they need to amass in order to protect their nests from drowning in frigid meltwater.*

They have big stone nests and not much to lose. If there is a chance the female will have sex, then it is worth them taking the risk. They may look foolish but, as Davis admitted, 'evolutionary-wise, it's a pretty smart move.'

Cases of transactional sex are surprisingly rare in the animal kingdom – and hotly contested. The only other concrete examples Davis could find amongst vertebrates were chimpanzees (which have been observed bartering meat for sex) and, erm, ourselves. Which makes these female penguins a little more human than we may have expected, though perhaps not in a way the Christian right would be keen to discuss in Sunday school.

The behaviour of the male Adélie is, however, even worse. So shocking, in fact, that the Natural History Museum in London refused to share with the public the first scientific account of their sexual antics.

The private lives of the Adélies would have been lost to science were it not for a chance discovery in 2009 by Douglas Russell, the museum's senior curator of bird's eggs and nests. He was sifting through boxes of ancient documents, researching Scott's doomed second expedition, when he happened upon a scientific paper from 1915 that caught his eye. Its prosaic title was 'Sexual Habits of the Adélie Penguin' but 'it had "Not for Publication" written in large unfriendly letters at the top of it,' he remembered. This, of course, 'immediately piqued my interest', he said.

His interest was repaid, so to speak. The long-lost document was a wide-eyed account of male Adélies having sex with basically anything that moves. And quite a few things that don't. Like dead penguins. Not even fresh ones at that, but frozen relics from the previous mating season.

The lurid details of this avian orgy were delivered with deadpan Edwardian horror, the penguin perpetrators identified in decidedly human terms. They were 'gangs of hooligan cocks' whose 'passions seem to have passed beyond their control' and whose 'constant acts of depravity' run the gamut of masturbation, recreational sex and homosexual behaviour to gang rape, necrophilia and paedophilia. Chicks were 'sexually misused by these hooligans', including one who 'misused it before the very eyes of its parent'. Strayed chicks were crushed and 'very often suffer indignity and death at the hands of these hooligan cocks'.

The author, Dr George Murray Levick, was a famous pioneer of penguin research. As a surgeon and zoologist on board Scott's second expedition, he'd been afforded the rare privilege of observing the Adélie penguins at Cape Adare for twelve whole weeks during the Antarctic summer of 1911–12. He is to this day the only scientist to have spent an entire breeding season studying the world's largest colony. His meticulous daily observations were published by the Natural History Museum upon his return in 1915 under the authoritative title 'Natural History of the Adélie Penguin', but the more unusual sexual proclivities of the penguins were nowhere to be found amongst the pages of Levick's definitive work.

Russell wondered why. And after a fair amount of digging he unearthed a note from the then keeper of zoology at the Natural History Museum to the curator of birds, which instructed a conspiracy of silence around the Adélie's sexual secret. Curiously, the note said, 'We will have this cut out and some copies printed for our own use.'

Levick's graphic account of the sexual behaviour of Adélie penguins was a little too ripe for the tastes of the post-Victorian academic world. This was, after all, an era in which prudery dictated that verbal or written communication about sex or emotions be couched in the language of flowers, that the word 'leg' was too naked to be used in public and that any hint of homosexuality was positively wicked. Perverted penguin sex pests were not something polite society was quite prepared for. The pamphlet was privately circulated, like some kind of under-the-counter penguin porno, amongst a select group of peers who were deemed learned and discreet enough to handle its graphic content. Only one hundred were ever printed. 'It's a miracle the copy I discovered survived,' Russell told me.

Further detective work uncovered Levick's original field notebooks, which exposed the full extent of the Adélies' behaviour and the good doctor's resulting turmoil. His initial observations of the first penguins arriving at the colony were laced with wonder. But after witnessing the penguins' 'astonishing acts of depravity', he began to encode his more lurid observations in ancient Greek – an old boarding-school trick for keeping secrets.

One coded section described a male penguin 'actually engaged in sodomy' upon one of its own species. 'The act occurred a full minute,' Levick noted conscientiously. But he made no attempt to explain this behaviour. His scientific analyses were paralysed by his outrage. He simply and solemnly concluded: 'there seems to be no crime too low for these penguins.'

Levick's observations of the Adélies were decades ahead of his time. It wasn't until the 1970s, sixty years later, that the penguins' dirty secret was discovered by another visiting scientist and made public. Then, the behaviours were recognized as a regular part of penguin life, triggered by the pressure of the short breeding season.

Adélies gather at their colonies in October. They are flooded by hormones and have only a few weeks to find a mate. The young males have no experience of how to behave, so many respond to inappropriate cues, exhibiting a somewhat flexible interpretation of what constitutes a potential mate. 'It's not as if a young Adélie penguin is wandering through the colony and sees a frozen female and thinks, "I've always quite fancied having sex with a dead frozen female",' Russell explained. To these hormonal penguin teenagers, a frozen penguin lying with its eyes half open is very similar in appearance to a compliant female. 'From an evolutionary point of view, in a species in which there is a very limited opportunity for breeding, this behaviour has purpose,' Russell said, before adding with a laugh, 'There's no romance here at all.'

The Adélies' urge to reproduce is so intense that when a researcher set out a dead penguin frozen in such a position, many males found the corpse 'irresistible'. So much so that it soon was so damaged by its repeated deployments, all that remained was 'a frozen head, with self-adhesive white O's for eye rings'. This was still 'sufficient stimulus for males to copulate and deposit sperm on the rock' – a sight that would have probably tipped poor Levick over the edge.

But it's not just penguins who are at it. 'Anyone who knows birds knows they are quite famous for this sort of thing,' Russell explained to me with an air of thinly veiled exasperation. So I checked out an online birdwatchers' forum to see what they had to say.

A thread devoted entirely to avian necrophilia had postings of all manner of shenanigans, including a 'feral pigeon' mounting 'a dead house martin', which, the witness added helpfully, is 'a much smaller bird'. Not to mention a different species. Another birdwatcher reported seeing a female house sparrow, a road victim unfortunately squished with its wings splayed out, 'as if presenting to a male'. This indeed turned out to be a deadly turn-on for the cock that flew down to mate with her and 'was duly squashed in its turn'. There was also a posting about an aggressive encounter between two cock pheasants, wherein one attacked another that had been hit by a car. 'The episode ended with the first pheasant mounting the dying one and copulating with it,' the twitcher said. ('Grim stuff, but I have photos if anyone is interested!' the person added cheerily.)

There are still great limits in our understanding of animals. 'You have to be very careful about placing value judgements on animals,' Russell emphasized. 'People are always keen to draw analogies with human behaviour, but you've got to remember, it is just a bird with a very tiny brain.'

But what might we learn about an animal with a big brain and several other genuine similarities to us humans? In my last chapter, you'll see how we've come up close, sometimes too close for comfort, to one of our closest cousins in the animal kingdom, the chimpanzee. And in the centuries during which we've probed the line dividing 'us' from 'them', we've confronted some of our own greatest fears and obsessions.

## CHAPTER 13

# CHIMPANZEE

Species *Pan troglodytes*

*A brute, but a brute of a kind so singular, that man cannot behold it without contemplating himself.*

Comte de Buffon, *Histoire Naturelle*, 1830

I'VE HAD MORE THAN my fair share of extraordinary animal experiences, but one will stay with me for ever. I was in the Budongo Forest of Uganda filming for the BBC. I had joined a research team that had been studying a particular troop of wild chimps for almost a decade, shadowing their lives from dawn to dusk every single day until they'd become habituated to the scientists' presence and now ignored them. Tagging along promised a rare peek into the intimate lives of our nearest cousins.

But first we had to find them. That meant starting our expedition at the tail end of the night in the hope we could catch the chimps as they woke in their 'sleep tree' and before they disappeared into the depths of the forest.

Sneaking into the sleeping jungle was an exercise in sensory deprivation. Under the cover of the canopy it was dark, still and uncannily quiet, the steady *thwick-thwack* beat of rubber boots – standard issue to protect our ankles from the toxic retaliation of any snoozing snakes we might disturb – providing a spartan soundtrack for our thoughts. But sunrise is fast in the tropics, and before too long the first shafts of light began to illuminate the morning fog with a warm yellow glow, revealing the riot of life all around us.

I've always felt that the rainforest is my cathedral, the place where I feel closest to my god – evolution. And Budongo is an impressive place of worship: 500 square kilometres of dense jungle that hugs the eastern edge of the Albertine Rift, part of the Great Rift Valley where man himself is thought to have evolved. It is the largest indigenous rainforest still standing in East Africa, and although many of its magnificent mahogany trees were uprooted by the Victorians to deck out the Royal Albert Hall, a smattering of old-growth trees still stand, some twenty storeys tall and almost half a millennium old.

Filing silently through the mists beneath these ancient trees felt like stepping back in time. Then came a crescendo of distant pant-hoots. This rising *whoop* that signals a chimp's excitement can penetrate the forest for miles and seems to go right through you. Hearing it gave me goosebumps – much the same effect it can have on another chimpanzee. We were getting close. I felt a flush of adrenaline. Chimps have a fearsome reputation. Although reports of them being ten times stronger than humans (with the ability to rip off a man's arm with ease) are overblown (they are just twice as strong), I still felt uncontrollably apprehensive about arriving on foot to wake them without so much as a banana smoothie as a breakfast offering.

The research team stopped underneath a towering fruit tree and pointed upwards. At first I couldn't see anything; the chimps' black bodies blended into the infinity of the forest. But my eyes gradually adjusted, and as though I were looking at a magic-eye painting, the chimps emerged from the gloom: a dozen of them studiously munching away on their morning repast. I'd seen chimpanzees countless times before, acting up at the zoo or slurping down PG Tips on TV, but this was totally different. They were somehow incredibly familiar but unfamiliar at the same time; like us, but not like us. The effect was mesmerizing and strangely emotional. I felt a lump in my throat and tears in my eyes. It was such a poignant scene, a window perhaps into our distant past, made all the more meaningful by the increasing rarity of seeing these endangered creatures in the wild today.

My reverie was shattered by the sound of a fart. Wild chimpanzees, it turned out, suffer from profuse flatulence – loud, loose and unrepentant, the sound of an animal that subsists on unripe fruit and doesn't give a fig about being polite. I was unprepared for this particular dawn chorus, which was more like a scene from a Mel Brooks movie than anything I'd seen in an Attenborough documentary. But it was apparently nothing unusual. The team told me the sound of distant trumpets is one of the best ways of locating lost chimps in the vast expanse of trees.

We can't help but look for a reflection of ourselves in the animal kingdom, but in the chimp we find a mirror image that is disorientating in its familiarity. This has promoted confusion and fear and helped ensure that our closest relative is also one of the most tragically misunderstood animal cousins. Our obsession with the line that divides us – where it lies and what happens if it is crossed – has ushered in some of the most misguided moments in science.

'The constitution of the ape is hot and since he is rather similar to man, he always observes him in order to imitate his actions,' wrote Hildegard of Bingen in the eleventh century. 'He also shares the habits of beasts, but both these aspects of his nature are deficient, so that his behaviour is neither completely human nor completely animal; he is therefore unstable.'

It is unlikely that the visionary German nun had ever clapped eyes on an unstable ape herself. To the earliest naturalists, apes were essentially mythical beasts, their descriptions cobbled from hearsay and muddled up with tales of pygmies, satyrs and weird savage men who covered their bottoms with their own long ears, all trapped in an uneasy hinterland between humans and beasts. In his great encyclopaedia, Pliny the Elder claimed that apes could play chess, whilst medieval bestiary writers highlighted their grave fear of snails. Each acknowledged the animal's eerie ability to imitate, or 'ape', man. This made them devilish, for if man had been created in God's own image, this scary, hairy imposter must be his nemesis. The illustrations that accompanied these early texts were suitably surreal. One particularly oft-copied portrait depicted a large, hairy lady standing proud whilst sporting an impressive mane, massive pendulous udders and a walking stick.

The earliest European eyewitness reports of wild apes were no less bizarre. One of the first came from Andrew Battel, an English privateer captured by the Portuguese in 1589 and incarcerated in Angola. Battel spent eighteen years yo-yoing between prison and trade expeditions for his captors in Africa. When he finally made it home to Leigh-on-Sea, the wily Essex lad had quite the story to tell. He turned his misfortune into a bestselling adventure that included a lengthy, if somewhat fanciful, description of what are widely believed to be gorillas and chimps. Battel described 'two kinds of Monsters, which are common in these Woods, and very dangerous' and then gave a fuzzy account of hirsute, human-like creatures that he called 'pongos' and 'engecos'; they built tree houses and beat elephants with clubs.

Battel was not alone in being befuddled by hairy humanoids. The Dutch traveller Willem Bosman claimed that apes in West Africa attacked people and could speak, but chose not to, so they would not be forced into working, 'which they do not very well love'. He considered them 'terribly pernicious sort of brutes, which seem to have been only made for mischief'. Others said the creatures were known to kidnap children, ravish women and keep humans as pets.

The first live chimp arrived on British soil to much fanfare. The *Speaker*, an English merchant ship, docked in

London in 1738, bringing with it 'an animal of remarkably and terribly hideous countenance ... called by the name Chimpanzee'. Unsure of how to greet this new arrival, the British did what they knew best and furnished the animal with a cup of tea. It was said to have sipped it daintily, like a human. The chimp's eating habits were, however, less suitable for the Georgian drawing room. 'It seeks food from its own excrement,' noted one report. In addition to these coprophagous tendencies, the chimp was reported to seek human females for 'illicit sexual intercourse' – a recurring insecurity amongst Victorian visitors to zoos in later decades.

It wasn't just the animal's behaviour that confused. The first attempt at dissecting a chimpanzee, conducted by the English physician Edward Tyson, revealed unsettling similarities between ape and man, chipping away at our God-given sense of superiority. Of the chimp brain, Tyson noted: 'one would be apt to think, that since there is so great a disparity between the Soul of a Man, and a Brute, the Organ likewise in which 'tis placed should be very different too.' But it wasn't. Instead it bore a 'surprising' resemblance to human grey matter.

At the time, specimens available for study were few and far between. The different great ape species – chimps, gorillas and orangutans – became confused and conflated. This made them hard to categorize. The very father of taxonomy, Carl Linnaeus, initially divided the apes into two: the more and the less anthropomorphic. The former category he called *Homo troglodytes*, which he designated as a

THE UNEXPECTED TRUTH ABOUT ANIMALS

second species of humans (the 'cave-dwelling man'), whilst the latter he called *Simia satyrus*, an altogether different set (a 'satyr monkey').

The uncomfortable proximity of man to these excrement-eating, lascivious beasts did not please the aristocratic Georges-Louis Leclerc, Comte de Buffon, who poured characteristic scorn on Linnaeus's attempts to classify them. Buffon fashioned his own, even more eccentric solution: he assumed that chimpanzees – or 'jockos' as he called them – were in fact juvenile orangutans. The fact that his adult was a giant ginger beast, and his child small with black hair, did not bother the Comte, who pointed out: 'in the human species have we not similar variety?' The Laplander and the Finn, he argued, shared equal disparity, despite living in the same climate (which may have been a sly dig at his Scandinavian taxonomic rival).

Buffon devoted endless pages of his encyclopaedia to exhaustive descriptions of the striking similarities between apes and humans, right down to their 'fleshy posteriors'. But these physical analogies didn't offend him. Instead he interpreted the apes' likeness to humankind, yet total absence of any 'power of thought and speech', to be the ultimate proof that man had been 'animated by a superior principle', which forged his preeminence over these brutes. Any system that gave the two neighbouring classifications was, in his mind, deeply humiliating. Linnaeus took his revenge on the Comte by naming a plant *Buffonia tenuifolia* – a jab at the Frenchman's *tenuous* grasp of taxonomy.

*A confusion of early apes and ape-men as featured in 'Academic Delights', edited by the great taxonomist Carl Linnaeus (1763). It was this beastly classification of man, putting us so close to creatures like Lucifer (second on the left), that made the Comte de Buffon so irate. For once, I can see his point.*

By the time Darwin published *On the Origin of Species* in 1859, the search for some characteristic that set us apart from our ape cousins had become a matter of scientific urgency. Chief amongst the protagonists in the quest was one of natural history's most notable villains, Sir Richard Owen. As Britain's most celebrated anatomist, Owen had clawed his way to the pinnacle of the scientific establishment, even tutoring the Queen's children in zoology. But he was a man of such a jealous nature and cut-throat ambition that he was openly booed by his contemporaries. He even looked the part of the bad guy. His weaselly frame, bulging eyes and bulbous, bald head make him a

371

dead ringer for *The Simpsons'* Mr Burns, only slightly less yellow.

A deeply religious man, Owen was a vociferous opposer of Darwin's evolutionary ideas. He could not accept that man was merely a 'transmuted' ape. So he made it his mission to seek out the physical source of mankind's uniqueness. His first stop was the brain, which produced a trio of likely suspects including, most crucially, a small fold of skin at the rear known as the hippocampus minor. Owen claimed this innocuous bulge only existed in man and must therefore be the seat of human reason, and the source of man's 'destiny as the supreme master of this earth and of the lower creation'. This discovery provided Owen with the confidence to elect humanity to its very own highfalu-tin class, which he christened, in no uncertain terms, *Archencephala*, or 'ruling brain'.

When Darwin heard about Owen's claims, he sarcas-tically mused in a letter to a colleague: 'what a Chimpanzee [would] say to this'.

Darwin's private words were cutting, but it was the brash working-class biologist Thomas Henry Huxley who took the dissecting knife to Owen's theory in public. Hux-ley, who referred to himself as 'Darwin's bulldog', firmly believed that science should be separate from religion, stating 'he was not ashamed to have a monkey as an ances-tor; but he would be ashamed to be connected with a man who used great gifts to obscure the truth'.

He began to systematically inspect primate brains

himself. Quickly he recognized the magnitude of Owen's error – and saw a delicious opportunity to 'nail ... that mendacious humbug ... like a kite to the barn door.'

In a series of public showdowns and scientific papers, Huxley exposed Owen as a deceitful plagiarist who had not only fabricated his theory by copying drawings of chimpanzee brains from other anatomists (whom he conveniently neglected to credit), but who had also ignored their blatant descriptions of the chimp's hippocampus minor. Huxley's own methodical dissections revealed the startling similarity between chimp and human brains. He declared Owen's theory to have been built like 'a Corinthian portico in cow dung.'

As it turned out, Owen was right that the secret to our very different lives may well reside in subtle differences in the structure of chimp and human brains, he just hadn't found them. In the face of Huxley's relentless attacks, he was forced to concede that the hippocampus minor was indeed present in apes. His reputation never recovered.

Richard Owen would by no means be the only scientist to fall from grace over the chimp. Scientific fascination with the boundaries between ape and man – and lack of boundaries – would dredge up quite an extraordinary cast of reprobates.

Around the start of the twentieth century, a Russian scientist named Ilya Ivanovich Ivanov was making a name for himself as the creator of strangely named beasts – zonkeys, zubrons and zorses – that wouldn't be out of place in the less credible corners of the medieval bestiaries. These animals were hybrids, genetic as well as linguistic bastards of a zebra and a donkey, a bison and a cow, and a zebra and a horse. Ivanov's greatest aspiration, however, was to breed a *humanzee* – a hybrid between a human and a chimp.

He wasn't the first scientist to dream of being a real-life Dr Moreau. Interest in breeding humanzees was very much in the air. When the German physiologist Hans Friedenthal experimented with mixing blood from a human and an ape in 1900, he had found their antibodies did not attack one another and postulated that interbreeding might be possible between the two. In the following two decades, Dutch zoologist Hermann Moens and German sexologist Hermann Rohleder (author of the enigmatically titled *Die Masturbation*) both tried to test this prediction by inseminating chimpanzee females with human sperm. Neither got beyond the planning stage.

Ivanov's success at manufacturing zonkeys and zorses confirmed him as a pioneer in the art of artificial insemination, and his unique expertise made him the right man in the right place at the right time. During the 1920s, the newly established Soviet Union was keen to undermine religious thinking and prove the superiority of their wilfully technocratic society. The Soviet authorities believed a hybrid would provide 'extraordinarily interesting evidence for a better understanding of the problem of the origin of man' and 'a decisive blow to the religious teachings and ... in our struggle for the liberation of working people from the power of the Church'.

It wasn't just heretical Bolsheviks who backed Ivanov's work. In 1924, the Pasteur Institute in Paris wrote to the Russian scientist to share good news: it would be 'possible and desirable' for him to conduct his experiment at their newly established chimpanzee colony in West Africa. The iconic research centre had developed something of a taste for crazy Russian scientists. They were already supporting Serge Voronoff, who was breaking equally bizarre ground in chimpanzee science – he claimed to have discovered the fountain of youth by grafting thin slices of chimp's testicle onto an ageing man's scrotum. He had come up with this

*Voronoff's rejuvenation therapy made the front page of a French newspaper in October 1922, when the Russian pioneered his technique of grafting slices of chimpanzee testicle onto an old dog. Many more old dogs followed – of the billionaire variety – keen to add a little youth to their step.*

rather imaginative 'rejuvenation therapy' after observing eunuchs and undergoing some distinctly unenviable self-experimentation that included injecting his own testicles with a cocktail of crushed guinea pig and dog gonads.

Hand-stitching slivers of 'monkey gland' using the finest silk thread was Voronoff's reassuringly expensive formula for extending human life up to 140 years. Although he insisted that 'grafting is in no way an aphrodisiac remedy, but acts on the whole organism by stimulating its activity,' the rumour was that it could restore a millionaire's flagging sex drive, as well as his memory and eyesight. In any case, it was enough to ensure that Voronoff's clinic was never empty. Hundreds of men signed up for the treatment – including Sigmund Freud who, having failed to find an eel's testicles, was clearly not afraid to experiment with his own.

Ivanov himself was in need of a little of Voronoff's monkey gland magic. The Pasteur Institute had offered him facilities but no funding, and, perilously low on cash, his humanzee project was wilting. So he stopped off in Paris en route to Africa to collaborate with Voronoff. They made headlines by transplanting a woman's ovary into a chimp called Nora and attempting to inseminate her with human sperm. No humanzees were conceived. Voronoff decided to stick with his lucrative day job of doctoring millionaires' testicles and Ivanov flew off to French Guinea with only his son, a medical student, to support him.

On 28 February 1927, Ivanov attempted to inseminate

a pair of chimps named Babette and Syvette with human sperm. Ivanov senior wanted to keep the experiment secret from his African assistants, and thus the situation was far from ideal: 'the sperm was not completely fresh, but approximately 40 per cent of the spermatozoa were moveable,' he noted in his diaries. 'The injection took place in a very nervous atmosphere and in uncomfortable conditions. The threat from the apes, the work on the open ground, and the necessity to conceal.'

The attempt was a failure. Disappointment drove Ivanov into ever more desperate directions. He decided to change tack and lobbied the local governor to allow him to impregnate hospitalized women with chimp sperm. As if the ethical challenges thrown up by such an experiment weren't questionable enough, Ivanov proposed doing this *without* the women's knowledge, under the pretext of a medical examination. The authorities actually considered his plan, but eventually rejected it, a decision that Ivanov noted in his diary came as 'a bolt from the blue' – which gives a sense of how divorced from reality he had become by then. He was forced to move his mission back home, relying on his ability to acquire imported apes and consenting women in his homeland. Indefatigable, he somehow managed to get both. But in the summer of 1930, the political winds changed, and Ivanov was arrested by the secret police, accused of counter-revolutionary activities and exiled to prison in what is now Kazakhstan. He died there two years later.

Could Ivanov's dream ever have been realized? I asked J. Michael Bedford, an emeritus professor of reproductive biology at the Weill Cornell Graduate School of Medical Sciences, who spent time in the 1970s investigating the early stages of fertilization, in particular how sperm attaches itself to the egg, with a view to developing a male contraceptive. He introduced human sperm to a range of different animal ova – from hamsters to squirrel monkeys to gibbons (a lesser ape). Bedford was surprised to find that human sperm has a high degree of specificity – the only egg it would attach to was that of the gibbon, our most distant ape relative. When I asked him what he thought would happen with a chimpanzee egg, he suspected a positive outcome: 'Given that it is closer to man than the gibbon, it seems likely that sperm of the chimp would be able to fertilize a human egg and vice versa.'

Fertilization is, however, just the first stage in a very long process fraught with potential failure. We may share 98.4 per cent of our DNA with chimps, but producing a healthy humanzee baby would, according to Bedford, be 'something of a crapshoot'. He explained that in some hybrid combinations, live young are born sterile, but sometimes they are not; in others, the embryos begin to develop and then fail at some point in pregnancy. 'It is not possible for me to predict whether the resulting embryo would survive,' he said.

We may never learn whether humans and chimps could hybridize. But a study by researchers at Harvard Medical

School and the Massachusetts Institute of Technology uncovered a ghostly secret in the human genome that suggests such liaisons may well have been part of our ancestor's past.

The scientists were comparing the genomes of humans and chimps using a 'molecular clock' to estimate how long ago we diverged – the further back two species split, the more differences will have accumulated between their DNA sequences. The team estimated that humans and chimps separated no more than 6.3 million years ago, and probably less than 5.4 million years ago, but there was a massive anomaly with the X chromosome, which contained significantly fewer differences than the rest of the genome. The most logical explanation to the team was that speciation between humans and chimps had been 'complex', which is a polite way of saying that the two emerging species continued to have sex and form hybrids for some time, in fact.

The amount of similarity on the X chromosome suggests that this wasn't just a solitary dark night at the disco but 1.2 million years of messy speciation. Nick Patterson, one of the team's lead researchers, told me how their discovery sent shock waves through the mainstream media. 'The tabloids had fun. A headline in the German paper *Bild Zeitung* was "Ur-Menschen hatte sex mit Affen" (translation hardly needed) with a picture of the ugliest chimp they could find,' he recalled. 'But those who were shocked were missing the point. This is not a case of creatures like us mating with creatures very like chimps. We are talking about two groups of apes, one group very slightly more similar to us than to chimps.'

Whilst the idea of our ancestors getting down and dirty with the ancestors of our closest cousins may not appeal to some, the Harvard–MIT team think these hybrids could well have given our species an evolutionary boost, speeding up their adaptation to a new life out of the trees and on the savannah.

Another bold experiment to blur the line between chimps and humans took place in 1960s America – but this time, the tinkering was behavioural rather than genetic. A newborn baby chimp was transplanted into a human family, to be raised as a human in isolation from its own species. The man behind this outlandish idea was Maurice K. Temerlin, a professor of psychology at the University of Oklahoma, who was particularly interested to see how the chimp, which he named Lucy, would develop socially and sexually.

There had been two previous attempts at raising chimps in human homes, but only as far as infancy, so to continue beyond puberty was uncharted territory. I don't suppose Temerlin ever imagined he would wind up being a father to a gin-drinking chimpanzee teenager that took to masturbating with a hoover. But we know that's how his 'experiment' panned out, thanks to Temerlin's earnest oversharing in his memoir, *Lucy: Growing Up Human*, which serves as an extraordinary time capsule of misguided 1960s pseudoscience.

'I am a psychotherapist. My daughter, Lucy, is a chimpanzee.' So began Temerlin's self-indulgent account of his eleven years as a chimpanzee 'father'.

Lucy joined the family in a traumatic manner, when in 1965 Temerlin's wife, Jane, snatched the chimp, aged just two days, from her mother, a Californian circus entertainer. Temerlin considered this kidnapping to be the 'symbolic equivalent of the act of giving birth', a statement many mothers may beg to disagree with. At the outset of their family 'adventure', Temerlin wondered how human Lucy would become, and whether he, a self-confessed 'Jewish mommas boy', could become a good 'chimpanzee father'. As the story unfolded, it became evident that the answer to his psychoanalytic hand-wringing was a deafening 'NO'.

Things started relatively innocuously. Lucy learned how to dress herself, use silverware and eat at the dinner table alongside the Temerlins' seven-year-old human son, Steve (who one can only imagine went on to have a fair amount of psychotherapy himself). Lucy was taught American Sign Language, eventually mastering over one hundred words, including such essential chimpanzee terms as 'lipstick' and 'mirror'. She even raised her own pet kitten. So far, so cute. But then comes a chapter entitled 'Creative Masturbation', and things begin to get quite a bit darker.

At around the age of three, Lucy had acquired a taste for alcohol after she swiped a drink from the nervous wife of a visiting academic. In the book, Temerlin père wrote self-consciously about his guilt over giving alcohol to his teenage son, but curiously not about giving it to Lucy. Every night before dinner he would 'fix her a cocktail or two' – a G&T in the summer and a whiskey sour in the winter. Lucy eventually learned to work her way around the drinks cabinet and pour her own cocktails, which she liked to enjoy whilst lying on the sofa and flicking through magazines with her feet.

It was during one of these drinking sessions that Temerlin noticed Lucy getting creative with the nozzle of their Montgomery Ward vacuum cleaner. It was an inspired example of tool use, he noted – a skill once thought to be the exclusive preserve of man and a means of drawing that all-important line between them and us, until Jane Goodall observed chimps using sticks to fish for termites. Goodall's discovery led her mentor, Dr Louis Leakey, to declare: 'Now we must redefine tool, redefine Man, or accept chimpanzees as humans.' One wonders if Leakey's redefinition would have been broad enough, in the great palaeoanthropologist's view, to include Lucy's imaginative hoover use.

The Freudian shrink in Temerlin was fascinated by his daughter's emerging sexuality, and whether Lucy was attracted to humans or chimps. So whereas many parents would have subsequently confiscated the vacuum cleaner and locked it in a cupboard, Temerlin instead dashed out to the mall to buy his daughter a copy of *Playgirl* to see if she would prefer to look at this female top-shelf staple instead of her usual favourite, *National Geographic*. Lucy did indeed take a shine to the magazine, fixating on the photos of naked men and stroking them so vigorously in key places that she ended up wearing through the pages. Pleased with his results, Temerlin next took the extraordinary step of dropping his trousers and joining his daughter in an afternoon of self-pleasure, 'to see what would happen'.

It is something of a relief to read that Lucy ignored Temerlin's looming onanism on each of his turgid attempts. Now if it were me, I might be inclined to omit this rather tawdry non-event from my memoir. But not Maurice K. Temerlin. In a chapter entitled 'Oedipus-Schmedipus', the psychoanalyst dived into solemn conclusions about how his rejected tumescence was gratifying evidence of his status as Lucy's father and of her demonstration of an inherent incest taboo (one of his major research obsessions).

Eventually Lucy's behaviour became too challenging for the Temerlins to cope with. She learned how to master all the locks in the house, often escaping into the neighbourhood or locking herself in, and her parents out, of the house (perhaps not surprising, given all of the above). Temerlin claimed that his daughter even started to lie. When challenged for crapping on the carpet, Lucy's sign language response was to point the finger at Sue, one of his grad student assistants.

At the age of twelve, a fully grown adult, Lucy completely defied her parents' control. 'Lucy was into everything,' wrote Temerlin. 'She could take a normal living room and turn it into pure chaos in less than five minutes.' So with

*Maurice Temerlin was sure to document 'his daughter' at work with her beloved hoover. His original caption for the second picture reads: 'having achieved orgasm, Lucy is enjoying a reflective moment before returning to her magazine'. Fortunately, there are no photos of dad joining in on the self-pleasure party.*

heavy hearts, the Temerlins realized their domestic experiment must come to an end and looked for a new family for their chimpanzee daughter.

And this is where Temerlin made his most catastrophic error of judgement: he decided to send Lucy home and set her free.

He packed Lucy off to a chimpanzee rehabilitation centre in the Gambia accompanied by a young scientist called Janis Carter, another of his graduate students. The African bush was a very long way from Lucy's suburban life in Oklahoma. Lucy had barely ever met another chimpanzee and had no desire to integrate into her new community. She didn't want to eat the wild leaves and fruit that the other chimps did, let alone sleep with them in the trees. She had acquired rather more sophisticated tastes and was now stranded in the jungle without a sofa or a cocktail cabinet. Janis Carter dedicated several years to trying to encourage Lucy to rediscover her chimpanzee roots in a valiant but ultimately futile effort. Eventually, the Temerlins' daughter was found dead, her hands, feet and skin removed. The suspicion was that she had been taken by poachers, whom she'd probably guilelessly approached, having no fear of humans. They took advantage of their unwitting and overeager prey. And that was Lucy's end.

Fortunately, the study of chimpanzees has moved on from the narcissistic set-ups of the 1960s and now is primarily comprised of observations of our closest cousins in their natural habitat. This is significantly more challenging than watching chimps in a controlled situation, as I discovered when I joined Dr Cat Hobaiter, of the University of St Andrews, and her team in the Budongo Forest of Uganda.

For a start, wild chimps can travel 10 to 20 kilometres a day in search of food. Keeping sight of them was like playing a game of hide-and-seek with Olympic-standard opponents (who can make a mockery of their lumbering, bipedal relatives from their treetop superhighway). Yet Cat was persistent. She believed that documenting chimpanzees' natural lives reveals not just more about them, but also provides a better template for studying the origins of human behaviour.

'I think Lucy and other enculturated apes allowed us to ask what apes could do, under *extraordinary* circumstances. The answer is that extraordinary apes can do extraordinary things in extraordinary circumstances!' Cat explained to me. 'Of course, there are very good ethical reasons why we would never want to replicate those studies today. But some of the same point holds in modern captive settings. You can test apes on puzzles, or in controlled circumstances that are not available in the wild. However, no matter how good the zoo or sanctuary, the environment these apes are in remains more human-like than ape-like.'

Cat aims to study chimp behaviour in its purest form, away from the polluting influence of humans. To accomplish this, she and any human tag-alongs, like me, had to become invisible, figuratively. That means thinking like a chimp and following strict rules, first and foremost no eye contact. Staring is an act of aggression amongst chimps and picking a fight with your study subject isn't a great move for those trying to be inconspicuous (or, for that matter, trying to avoid serious injury).

As we sat just a metre or so away from a family unit engaged in a group grooming session, the mother chimp looked up and caught me gawping at them. I followed Cat's guidance and immediately looked away, my heart thumping in my chest. I picked up a leaf and pretended to inspect it intently whilst peering out of the corner of my eye to gauge whether my eye-balling had been noted. With great relief, I saw the mother chimp was still engrossed in picking and eating the ticks off her teenage sons.

Silence was the second requirement of Cat's field-work – a state I struggle to sustain at the best of times. What I hadn't anticipated was how hard it would be to hush my body language. Most intentional chimp communication is made up of subtle hand gestures and facial expressions. Their chatter is unusually peaceful, and I was struck by how they resided in relative quiet – apart from their farting. It is these gestures that Cat was trying to decode in order to compile the world's first chimp dictionary. Captive chimps like Lucy may have made the cover of magazines by mastering up to 250 words in American Sign Language, but wild chimps have little need for words like 'lipstick' and 'mirror' in the jungle, and make do with far fewer. So far Cat had translated around 70 gestures for her groundbreaking glossary.

Many of these gestures are strikingly similar to our own. A handshake is a sign of affiliation, just as it is for any businessman closing a deal. I saw chimps use an upturned hand to beg for forgiveness and kiss to say hello. But it's dangerous to assume that our hairy black cousins are communicating just like humans. Cat constantly worked to shed her human preconceptions and think like a chimp. 'We tend to think that chimps are very much like us. It's very easy to fall into that trap when analysing the gestures – to assume, for example, that a handshake has a different meaning to an arm shake, because that makes sense to us,' she said. 'Maybe the chimps don't care what limb you shake. It all has the same meaning.'

Some of the chimps' body language registers as quite the opposite of what it looks like to a human observer. It seems those grinning chimps in the PG Tips ads weren't having such a fun time after all. 'A bare-tooth grin means I'm nervous, worried or afraid,' Cat told me. 'That's the horrible thing about all those greetings cards where you have smiling chimps – they are definitely not *smiling*.'

One of the most significant recent discoveries is that chimps tailor their communication according to what they think another chimp might already know. This insight into the minds of others – known as having a *theory of mind* – is a hot topic in animal psychology. It was long considered a unique attribute of being human, one of those key boundaries separating us from them. There have been numerous experiments probing for its existence in captive chimps. But Cat showed me how colleagues of hers demonstrated it in the wild – an exhausting exercise which tested our own ability to read the minds of chimps.

The idea itself was relatively straightforward, if a little eccentric. We had to conceal a rubber viper along the path of a group of travelling chimps and, when the snake was revealed, observe whether the chimpanzee who saw it first communicated differently according to whether it thought the other chimps had seen the snake or not. Simple and elegant. In practice, the experiment was anything but. It involved us having to predict, in a vast forest, where the chimps would next go on foot. We then had to scramble through the thick jungle to try and get ahead of the apes in order to place the fake snake in their path (without them seeing). The snake was covered with a camouflage cloth attached to a fishing line, at the end of which was a field assistant (also hidden) who was primed to pull it once the chimps ambled up. We had to hope that one of the chimps saw the toyshop snake and believed it to be real – and then figure out whether their subsequent behaviour was a warning to the rest of the group. Finally, we had to make sure we were in the right position to record the chimps' responses on a video camera. No mean feat.

The almighty struggle involved in pulling off this task made me appreciate how hard it has been to get animals to give up any of their secrets. We ran around the jungle for a whole day, getting ourselves utterly lost and savaged by ants as we crashed through the undergrowth. Only in the dying light did we finally manage to get our stars aligned. When the chimp that saw the snake (the last in the group) made an almost inaudible *hoo* – a soft warning – it suggested he 'knew' the other chimps ahead of him had already seen the snake and he didn't need to make the loud barking alarm normal for such a threat.

The researchers managed to do this experiment 111 times in order to draw their conclusions, which took them an exhausting six months of haring about the forest. I can only imagine how skinny and pimply they must have been by the end of the study.

The ability to read another's mind is extremely useful for chimpanzees whose lives are enmeshed in hierarchical but highly fluid social networks of up to one hundred individuals. Understanding the dynamics of this jungle soap opera is essential to survival, which means learning to recognize a lot of faces – or rather, in the case of chimps, bums. In a recent study, chimps were shown photos of their friends' rear ends and faces and their behaviour showed they were equally familiar with both. This makes sense for an animal that spends much of its life in a tree. 'Most of the time you are looking up at bottoms,' Cat told me. She has even developed genital photo flash cards to enable her research team to familiarize themselves with both ends of their study subjects.

After almost a decade together Cat said she had come

to know her chimps as well as her own family. 'I have watched individuals growing up and so I have all that information available to me.' By way of example, she told me about two brother chimps, Frank and Fred. 'I know that Frank, who is currently our up-and-coming alpha male, was a really outgoing young boy who would constantly push his luck with the adults when he was still young enough to get away with it. Compare with his brother who had the same mother and same rearing environment, same community, same forest but was a totally different chimpanzee. Fred was just incredibly quiet, laid back and not boisterous at all,' she recalled. 'Starting to unpick what the reasons are for that, how you get such radically different survival strategies, is fascinating.'

Cat believes that the chimp's complex social life, intelligence and long lifespan are a recipe for individuality, a quality that she said is crucial to understanding chimps and indeed other species. 'In Western science, we have a tendency to say we need to find a population of animals and we will take the average of their behaviour and get rid of all the variabilities. Variation is bad and seen as a negative thing. Whereas individual differences are fundamental to looking at human behaviour,' she pointed out. 'In our quest to get rid of variation we have totally overlooked the fact that that's a very interesting thing about animal behaviour.'

When Cat has visited chimps at other research sites across Africa, she's observed major differences between her chimps and these groups, 'just as you'd find in people from India and Scotland', she said. 'Females in West Africa, for example, are high-ranking and integrated into politics in a way that they aren't in Budongo. When a female arrives she is greeted as you would greet a male – a significant cultural difference.'

Cat explained that talking about cultural differences between chimp populations in this way is relatively new. 'There were a lot of people who treated chimp behaviour in general as if it were the same. Now we understand that we were quite biased in what we thought of as "chimp" behaviour, because for years much of [the data] came from Gombe' – where Jane Goodall did her pioneering research. 'It turns out that those things are true for Gombe behaviour, but they're not true for chimps in general. Even *within* Gombe – the group today and the group a couple of generations ago are very different, so we can see the impact of individuals, of personalities, and life history on group culture.'

Many of these regional differences relate to tool use. A population of chimps from Senegal were recently observed living in caves and fashioning spears out of sticks that they sharpened with their teeth and then used to hunt bushbabies hiding out in hollow trees. In Guinea, chimps were seen making leaf sponges to enable them to drink high-proof alcohol fermented from a palm plant. And in Uganda juvenile female chimps were documented seemingly playing with sticks as if they were toy dolls – cradling them and even making nests for them to sleep in at night.

Each of these groups had developed unique tools – which were remarkably anthropoid in nature.

But perhaps the prize for the most curious case of tool use ought to go to chimpanzees in West Africa that were recently recorded hoarding rocks in neat piles – reminiscent of those uncovered by archaeologists at human sacred sites – and then hurling them at trees in an excited ritualistic display. Within a matter of days of the scientific paper on this extraordinary behaviour being published, tabloids around the world were shouting about how chimps were 'building shrines' at a 'sacred tree'. Could this be 'proof that chimps believe in God?' asked one headline.

Dr Laura Kehoe was one of the 'baffled scientists' at the centre of the media storm. 'It was a bit ridiculous,' she sighed when I asked her about the newspapers' reaction. 'I think it's actually a really good example of how a myth can evolve and get completely out of control in a matter of days, to the point where you have religious people writing to you, thanking you for your work,' she said. 'I got this one letter – it was just amazing – from this woman in Ireland, to say how happy she was that chimps had religion and that she would be praying for me.'

The original scientific paper had merely made the comparison with ancient human stone cairns. It had then pointed out that archaeologists should perhaps exercise caution when assuming that these human sites are sacred given their similarity to the chimps' handiwork. The chimp cairns, the authors proposed, might be associated with male chimp display or communication. The same chimps were known to use tree buttresses as drums to send long-distance messages, and their rock-throwing could be serving a similar purpose. The rock piles could also indicate something more symbolic, such as the marking out of territory. The authors noted the striking resemblance with indigenous West African stone shrines built at 'sacred' trees in the same area, and how it would be interesting to explore the parallels in these behaviours.

As one of the paper's authors, Kehoe was approached by a number of online news outlets to write about the discovery and heavily encouraged to ponder big 'What ifs?' around the idea that the chimp sites had spiritual meaning. She wrote a piece, and 'the editor then changed the title from "An interesting behaviour found in our closest living relatives" to "Mysterious chimp behaviour may be evidence of sacred rituals",' she told me. 'Obviously once someone clicks on that title, that's what they want to read about and that's their whole mindset. It just got out of control from there.'

She got a ton of mail – some of it abusive and 'very little from sane people'. It's a cautionary tale for scientists encouraged to sex up their findings in order to raise awareness for their work and for the urgent conservation needs of their dwindling study subjects. Thanks to the internet, we have entered a new era of myth-making, where clickbait headlines and fake news are too often indistinguishable from the real thing.

Whilst Kehoe didn't endorse the press reports that her chimps had found God, she did think they could have the capacity to experience feelings of awe. Other primatologists have suggested the same thing. Jane Goodall has said she's observed chimps behaving in an idiosyncratic, ritualized manner around waterfalls – throwing stones with their hair erect and then sitting down and just staring at the tumbling water. Chimps cannot swim, so water is a danger. But this display is definitely not a fear response. It's something quite unique – what Goodall said might be 'perhaps triggered by feelings of awe and wonder' in an online video showing and describing the strange display. 'The chimpanzee brain is similar to ours. They have emotions that are clearly similar to those that we call happiness and sadness and fear and despair and so forth,' Goodall said. 'So why wouldn't they also have feelings of some kind of spirituality? Which is, really, being amazed at things outside yourself.'

Cat had seen a similar phenomenon in the Budongo chimps when they dance in the rain. 'It's the most beautiful thing to watch. It only happens when you get a really big storm – that thundering rain that just drowns out every other noise – and the chimps will do this weird ballet – like a display in slow motion, underwater, that's totally silent. It is totally different to any other display and they only give it in response to this very grandiose, big natural event. You know, when you hear inspiring music and you just want to move. It doesn't feel like that's anything like religion, but it seems to be about awe for natural wonder. So perhaps there's capacity for it. I don't know.'

I don't know either. It could be the seeds of spirituality, or yet another instance of us viewing the animal kingdom through the prism of our own existence. As with so many animal mysteries, we may never know the truth. But I do know that watching the Budongo chimps aroused such wonder in me, I'd love to believe they had the ability to share that awesome feeling. And I can't help but think that, given the alarming decline in chimp numbers at the hands of man, feeling connected with our closest cousins, rather than drawing more lines around what we think makes us superior, is the way forward in our relationship.

With each new discovery, the boundaries we have created around our uniqueness, century after century, continue to fade. The seventeenth-century bestiary author Edward Topsell wrote, in his definition of the ape: 'They are not men, because they have no perfect use of Reason, no modesty, no honesty, nor justice of government, and although they speak, yet is their language imperfect; and above all they cannot be men, because they have no Religion, which (*Plato* saith truly) is proper to every man.'

How much of that list remains true today of man or chimp?

# CONCLUSION

W E HAVE MUCH TO learn from our centuries of misunderstandings about animals. Historians of science like to celebrate our successes, but I think it's equally important to examine our failures – especially when we ponder why the truth *can* be so completely unexpected to us.

The magnetic urge to anthopomorphize is our major undoing, tripping us up and obscuring the truth. We are an insecure species, seeking reassurance about our behaviour from drunk moose and busy beavers, and quick to condemn those creatures that don't conform to our moral code like indolent sloths, cruel hyenas and dirty vultures. Our discomfort with the truth about these animals reveals a great deal about our hopes as well as our fears.

It's been fascinating to trace the origins of these prejudices, in many cases to one book, the fourth-century *Physiologus*. The constrictive moral codes of the ancient philosophers and the medieval bestiary authors are still perpetuated today in the popular press and natural history programmes (some of mine included) that intone praiseworthy emphasis on traditional norms: heterosexuality, monogamy and the nuclear family. Few of which really exist in nature.

That's not to say that some animals don't have a rudimentary moral compass. This is a hot topic right now, with researchers like the esteemed primatologist Dr Frans de Waal pointing out that the basis of morality – a combination of empathy and a sense of fairness – is found in species as diverse as monkeys and rats. This suggests that moralizing could be part of our fundamental biological make-up. But painting the animal kingdom with our artificial ethical brush denies us the astonishing diversity of life, in all of its blood-drinking, sibling-eating, corpse-shagging glory. We need not be afraid of these behaviours – they are not here to instruct us. Whether a penguin is gay, straight or having sex with a frozen head has no bearing on our own sexuality. Despite what we may think, we are not the centre of the animal universe.

Which brings me to my second observation from writing this book. If anthropomorphism is enemy number one, arrogance is a close runner-up. From obliterating beavers for their bogus medicinal balls to using frogs to test for pregnancy or recruiting pandas as diplomats, we have a history of viewing the rest of the animal kingdom as simply here to service our needs. This selfish standpoint has resulted in many of our most misguided mistakes. In these times of mass extinction, we cannot afford to make many more.

The quest for truth is a long and winding road, littered with deep potholes. We take two steps forward and one step back. Thankfully our methods are less brutal than those of our eye-popping past, but we are still stumbling along in the dark and making mistakes. With the rise of right-wing religious fundamentalism that often attempts to discredit science, there has never been a greater need for truth. Yet, wrong turns are an essential part of all scientific progress, which demands blue-sky thinking as it seeks out each new horizon in understanding. As long as our egos or dogmatic beliefs are not to blame, we should not be afraid to continue to make wondrous mistakes, like Charles Morton and his birds that migrate to the Moon.

# ACKNOWLEDGEMENTS

FIRST AND FOREMOST, I want to thank Will Francis for being the best literary agent in the world and holding my hand so steadily through every stage of this book. The whole team at Janklow & Nesbit have been superb – PJ, Rebecca Folland, Kirsty Gordon and the rest. Thanks to them, I have been lucky to work with two expert editors – Susanna Wadeson and Thomas Kelleher – whose experience, ambition and endless patience have made this book something I am immensely proud of. Their respective teams at Transworld and Basic Books could not have been more supportive and I feel privileged to have them on my side. Special mention has to go to Robin Dennis, Elizabeth Stein and Kate Samano for kicking the book up a notch with their meticulous copyedits, and Caroline Hotblack and Jo Ormiston for all the gorgeous images. And to Sophie Laurimore for keeping those TV plates spinning when I was buried in books.

The research for this book was immense. Matt Brierley and Joseph Russell did a great job helping me with initial forays into various animals. The Reaktion series of animal

# ACKNOWLEDGEMENTS

books were also a valuable first port of call. Thanks to the medical historian Jesse Olszynko-Gryn for being so generous with his research on amphibian pregnancy tests. And Henry Nicholls and Jon Mooallem for being not just inspirational writers but open-handed with their address books. But my greatest debt is to the scientists and conservationists who have shared their knowledge with me over the years. There are too many to mention, but you've met a few in the pages of this book. In particular I'd like to thank Dr Andrew Crawford, Dr Rory Wilson and Sam Trull (of the Sloth Institute) for casting an expert eye over various chapters. As did Dr Mrinalini Erkenswick Watsa, who, along with Marianne Brooker, helped wrestle my chaotic notes and bibliography to the ground.

The writing of this book spanned two of the most challenging years of my life (mired by cancer and death). I could not have got through it without the help of my closest friends: Bini Adams, Heather Leach, Maxx Ginnane, Wendie Ottewill, Maxyne Franklin, Lisa Gunning, Chris and Tori Martin, Sara Chamberlain, Charlotte Moore, James Purnell, Luke Gottelier and Lesley Katon. Special mention has to go to Jess Search for laughing at my stories for so many years and encouraging me to push my creative boundaries. To Rebecca and Damien Timmer for inspiring me to become the Amphibian Avenger and subsidising my metamorphosis with a home in their attic (and thank you to Jed and Samson for graciously sharing it). And, of course, a massive thank-you to

# ACKNOWLEDGEMENTS

Bruce for being Bruce, and propping me up with such thoughtfulness, hilarity and love.

For their indispensable advice on how the hell to write a book, I am grateful to Alex and Natalie Bellos, Alexis Kirschbaum and Andrea Henry (who pushed me in the right direction at a key moment). Thanks to Jet for making the trial of having my photo taken so much fun; Archie Powell and James Brown for providing me with a place to live and work during a very tough summer; Tom Hodgkinson for letting me get up on the Idler stage to rave about sloths. And Liz Bisoux for all things web.

Finally, thanks to my mother, for allowing me to be whoever I wanted, supporting my crazy dreams and giving me my sense of humour (it's her fault there are so many testicle jokes in the book). And to my wonderful Dad, for sinking that bathtub in the garden and stimulating my love of nature. Mum and I miss you terribly, but your warmth, wit and wisdom are woven through every page of this book.

# PICTURE ACKNOWLEDGEMENTS

p. 2 The author holding a sloth. (Author's collection.)

p. 7 Bishop-like sea monster. Woodcut from '*Nomenclator Aquatilium Animantium. Icones Animalium Aquatilium . . .*' by Konrad von Gesner, Zurich, Switzerland, 1560. (Granger Historical Picture Archive/Alamy Stock Photo.)

p. 19 Eel. Watercolour illustration by Adriaen Coenen from his *Visboek*, Koninklijke Bibliotheek, Jacob Visser collection, f216r, 1577–81. (Koninklijke Bibliotheek, The Hague, The Netherlands.)

p. 25 'The Beetle in the act of Parturition. The Eel full developed'. Frontispiece to *The Origin of the Silver Eel, with Remarks on Bait & Fly Fishing*, by David Cairncross, London, 1862. (© British Library Board. All Rights Reserved/Bridgeman Images.)

p. 31 Page of drawings by Sigmund Freud from a letter to Eduard Silberstein reproduced in *The Letters of Sigmund Freud to Eduard Silberstein 1871–1881* edited by Walter Boehlich, translated by Arnold J. Pomerans, first published by the Belknap Press of Harvard University Press, Cambridge, Massachusetts, 1990. (By permission of The Marsh Agency Ltd on behalf of Sigmund Freud Copyrights.)

p. 47 Beavers voluntarily handing over their castor sacs to hunter so he will save their lives. Xylograph illustrating an old edition of Aesop's tales, J. Marius and J. Francus, 1685. *Castorologia*. (Augsburg, Germany: Koppmayer.)

p. 53 A beaver. Woodcut illustration from *The History of Four-footed Beasts and Serpents . . .* by Edward Topsell, printed by E. Cotes for G. Sawbridge, T. Williams and T. Johnson in London in 1658. (Special Collections, University of Houston Libraries. UH Digital Library.)

p. 64 Detail of 'The Beaver Map' (*'L'Amerique, divisée selon Letendue de ses Principales parties, et dont les points principaux sont placez sur les observations de messieurs de l'Academie Royale des Sciences'*) by Nicolas de Fer, 1698. (Image reproduced courtesy of Sanderus Maps: www.sanderusmaps.com.)

p. 71 Beaver squashed by the tree it was felling. (© Beate Strøm Johansen.)

p. 79 Drawing of the 'Periquito ligero' (sloth) from Part One of *La Historia natural y general de las Indias* by Gonzalo Fernández de Oviedo, RAH, Muñoz, A/34, Book 12, chapter 24. Signatura RAH 9/4786. (© Real Academia de la Historia. España.)

p. 87 Sloth crossing the road. (Scenic Shutterbug/Shutterstock.)

p. 92 Engraving of sloth by Johann Sebastian Leitner after George Edwards from *Verzameling van Uitlandsche en Zeldzaame Vogelen*, 1772–1781 by George Edwards and Mark Catesby. (Image from the Biodiversity Heritage Library. Digitized by Missouri Botanical Garden, Peter H. Raven Library, www.biodiversitylibrary.org)

p. 98 William Beebe holding a sloth. (© Wildlife Conservation Society. Reproduced by permission of the WCS Archives.)

p. 109 Hyaena, called Papio or Dabah. Woodcut illustration from *The History of Four-footed Beasts and Serpents* . . . by Edward Topsell, printed by E. Cotes for G. Sawbridge, T. Williams and T. Johnson in London in 1658. (Special Collections, University of Houston Libraries. UH Digital Library.)

p. 116 Spotted hyaena mating. (© NHPA/Photoshot.)

p. 119 Hyena devouring a corpse. Detail from *The Ashmole Bestiary*, England, early thirteenth century. MS Ashmole 1511, folio 17v. (The Bodleian Library, University of Oxford.)

p. 132 Turkey Vulture from *Birds of America* by John James Audubon, 1827–38. (Natural History Museum, London, UK/Bridgeman Images.)

p. 136 'A Nondescript' drawn by T. H. Foljambe, engraved on copper (with later tinting) by I. W. Lowry, being the frontispiece to Charles Waterton's *Wanderings in South America*, London, 1825. (Paul D. Stewart/Science Photo Library)

p. 144 German Alonso with Sherlock, a Turkey vulture. (JOHN MACDOUGALL/AFP/Getty Images.)

p. 166 'The Batte or Backe or Flittermouse'. Illustration of bats from *The Fowles of Heaven* by Edward Topsell, *c.*1613. E L 1142, folio 35 recto, Egerton Family Papers, The Huntington Library, San Marino, California. (The Huntington Library, San Marino, California.)

p. 168 Author holding bat. (Author's collection.)

p. 172 Illustration of bats flying around a leg of ham from *Hortus Sanitatis*, published by Jacob Meydenbach, Mainz, Germany, 1491.

# PICTURE ACKNOWLEDGEMENTS

Cambridge University Library, Inc.3.A.1.8[37], folio 332r. (Reproduced by kind permission of the Syndics of Cambridge University Library.)

p. 194 Bat and incendiary device. (United States Army Air Forces.)

p. 200 *Telmatobius culeus*, Lake Titicaca, Bolivia. (Pete Oxford/Nature Picture Library/Getty Images.)

p. 209 Spermatozoon. Homunculus. Woodcut from 'Essay de dioptrique' by Nicolaas Hartsoeker, Paris, 1694. (Wellcome Library, London.)

p. 212 Mating frogs by Hélène Dumoustier. Ms. 972, BCMHN. (© MNHN (Paris) – Direction des collections – Biblothèque centrale.)

p. 215 Audrey Peattie working at the family-planning laboratory in Watford hospital. (Reproduced by kind permission of Jesse Olszynko-Gryn, a medical historian based at the University of Cambridge and funded by the Wellcome Trust.)

p. 227 Pfeilstorch. Lithograph by Friedrich Lenthe, 1822, Universitätsbibliothek, Rostock MK-865.55a. (Universitätsbibliothek, Rostock, Germany.)

p. 231 'The Goose tree, Barnacle tree, or the tree bearing geese'. Illustration from *The herbal or, generall historie of plantes* by John Gerard, London, 1633. (Wellcome Library, London.)

p. 235 Fishing for swallows (*'De Hirundinibus ab aquis extractis'*). Illustration from *Historia de gentibus septentrionalibus* by Olaus Magnus, 1555.

p. 261 A hippopotamus, 'the inventor of Phlebotomy'. Illustration from *Il Ministro del medico trattato breve*, part 2 of *Il Chirurgo* by Tarduccio Salvi, Rome, 1642. (Wellcome Library, London.)

p. 263 Author with hippo. (Author's collection.)

p. 269 Hippopotamus. Engraving from *The Gentleman's Magazine*, published in December 1772. (Private Collection/Photo © Ken Welsh/Bridgeman Images.)

p. 283 'The Elk falling down in an Epileptick fit being pursu'd by the Huntsmen' – from *A compleat history of druggs . . . The second edition* by Pierre Pomet, London, 1737. (© British Library Board. All Rights Reserved/Bridgeman Images.)

p. 290 'An Antelope'. Pen-and-ink drawing tinted with body colour and translucent washes on parchment from 'The Northumberland Bestiary', Ms. 100, folio 9, England, *c.*1250–1260. The J. Paul Getty Museum, Los Angeles. (Digital image courtesy of the Getty's Open Content Program.)

p. 292 Intoxicated moose, Gothenburg, Sweden, 6 September, 2011. (JAN WIRIDEN/GT/SCANPIX/TT News Agency/Press Association Images.)

# PICTURE ACKNOWLEDGEMENTS

p. 302 'Male Moose'. Broadside, printed by G. Forman, New York, 1778. (Courtesy, American Antiquarian Society.)

p. 310 Bear licking her cub into shape. Illustration from French bestiary, *c*.1450, The Hague, Museum Meermanno, 10 B 25, folio 11v. (Museum Meermanno, The Hague, The Netherlands.)

p. 316 London Zoo keeper Alan Kent feeding Chi-Chi the giant panda, 29 September 1959. (William Vanderson/Stringer/Hulton Archive/ Getty Images.)

p. 324 Staff of Chengdu Panda Breeding Base with 23 panda cubs born in 2016. Photograph dated 20 January 2017. (Barcroft Media/Getty Images.)

p. 340 'One of the Earliest Maps of the Strait of Magellan'. Engraving after sixteenth-century Portuguese map, from *The Romance of the River Plate*, Vol. 1, by W. H. Koebel, 1914. (Private Collection/Bridgeman Images.)

p. 344 Comparative embryos of hog, calf, rabbit and man. Lithograph after Haeckel from *Anthropogenie, oder, Entwickelungsgeschichte des menschen* ... by Ernst Haeckel. Published by Wilhelm Englemann, Leipzig, 1874. (Wellcome Library, London.)

p. 353 Gay penguins at the Zoo in Bremerhaven, Germany, February 2006. (Ingo Wagner,Epa/REX/Shutterstock.)

p. 356 Adélie Penguin with stone for nesting material. (FLPA/REX/ Shutterstock.)

p. 371 'Anthropomorpha'. Engraving from *Amoenitates academicae, seu dissertationes variae physicae, medicae, botanicae* by Carl Von Linnaeus. Published by L. Salvius, Stockholm, 1763. (Wellcome Library, London.)

p. 375 Serge Abrahamovitch Voronoff and his assistant operating on an old dog, according to his method of rejuvenation by grafting. Front page of *Le Petit Journal Illustré*, 22 October 1922. (Photo by Leemage/ UIG via Getty Images.)

p. 384 Lucy the chimpanzee with hoover. (Photographs taken from *Lucy: Growing Up Human* by Maurice K. Temerlin, reproduced courtesy of Science & Behavior Books, Inc.)

# NOTES

M Y READING LIST FOR this book was too long to reproduce in full. So apologies if you are hunting for the source of a specific fact, there were too many to cite every one. Instead I have given references for all direct quotations and a bibliography of key books and academic papers that informed the book. Interviews with experts were conducted in the field or while I was writing the book.

## *Introduction*
3   'the stupidest animal that can be found in the world': Gonzalo Fernández de Oviedo y Valdés, *The Natural History of the West Indies*, ed. by Sterling A. Stoudemire (Chapel Hill: University of North Carolina Press, 1959), p. 54.
4   'perhaps it will not take it up alone': Simon Wilkin (ed.), *The Works of Sir Thomas Browne, Including His Unpublished Correspondence and a Memoir*, vol. 1 (London: Henry G. Bohn, 1846), p. 326.
4   'consists of a church-door key': Sebastien Muenster, *Curious Creatures in Zoology* (London: J. C. Nimmo, 1890), p. 197.
8   'so foul that its attackers are forced to retire in confusion': Anne Clark, *Beasts and Bawdy* (London: Dent, 1975), p. 92.
8   'gentle and meek': Edward Topsell, *The History of Four-Footed Beasts and Serpents and Insects* (London: DaCapo, 1967; f.p. 1658).
8   'great hatred': quoted in ibid., p. 90.
8   'the most chaste': quoted in ibid.
9   'the lowest form of existence': quoted in Stephen Jay Gould, *Leonardo's Mountain of Clams and the Diet of Worms: Essays on Natural History* (Cambridge, MA: Harvard University Press, 2011), p. 380.

## *1. Eel*
13   'There is no animal concerning whose origin': Leopold Jacoby quoted in G. Brown Goode, 'The Eel Question', *Transactions of the American*

*Fisheries Society*, vol. 10 (New York: Johnson Reprint Corp., 1881), p. 88.

14 'proceeds neither from pair, nor from an egg': D'Arcy Wentworth Thompson (trans.), 'Historia Animalium', *The Works of Aristotle* (Oxford: Clarendon, 1910), p. 288.

17 'daily scenes of cannibalism': quoted in Tom Fort, *The Book of Eels* (London: HarperCollins, 2002), p. 161.

17 'The eel also comes out of the water in the night time': Albert Magnus, *De Animalibus*, quoted in M. C. Marsh, 'Eels and the Eel Questions', *Popular Science Monthly* 61.25 (September 1902), p. 432.

17 'a smacking sound': Bengt Fredrik Fries, Carl Ulrik Ekström, and Carl Jacob Sundevall, *A History of Scandinavian Fishes*, vol. 2 (London: Sampson Low, Marston, 1892), p. 1029.

18 'thirty feet long': Tom Fort, *Book of Eels*, p. 164.

18 'was a yard and three quarters long': Izaak Walton and Charles Cotton, *The Compleat Angler: Or the Contemplative Man's Recreation*, ed. by John Major, (London: D. Bogue, 1844), p. 179.

18 'the coffee-houses in King street Westminster': ibid., p. 194.

18 More measured measurements come from Dr Jorgen Nielsen: Fort, *Book of Eels*, pp. 166–7.

20 'which he kept long, and loved exceedingly': Walton and Cotton, *Compleat Angler*, p. 189.

21 'the scrapings come to life'; 'This is the only way they breed': Pliny the Elder, *Naturalis Historia*, book 3, trans. by H. Rackham (London: Heinemann, 1940), p. 273.

21 'electrical disturbances': Marsh, 'Eels and the Eel Questions', p. 427.

21 'reverend bishop': ibid.

21 'a lie'; 'No doubt the first founder of so damnable an untruth': Thomas Fuller, *The History of the Worthies of England* (London: Rivington, 1811), p. 152.

23 'the progenitor of the silver eel': David Cairncross, *The Origin of the Silver Eel: With Remarks on Bait and Fly Fishing* (London: G. Shield, 1862), p. 2.

23 'I could not be expected to be acquainted with the names': ibid., p. 6.

23 'employ names and terms of my own': ibid.

24 'hair eels': ibid., pp. 14–15.

24 'fall from the tails of the horses': ibid., p. 14.

24 'often did my mind revert': ibid., p. 15.

24 'looks about a bit'; 'in a very troubled state': ibid., p. 17.

24 'the beetle in the act of parturition': ibid., p. 32.

25 'may seem strange'; 'members of the vegetable kingdom': ibid., p. 5.

25 'Great Creating Gardener': ibid.

26 'They believed me . . . and rejoiced in the solution': ibid., p. 27.

27    'eel will be made more palatable': Richard Schweid, *Eel* (London: Reaktion, 2009) p. 77.
27    'dry mint, rue berries, hard yolks': quoted in ibid., p. 77.
28    'a matter of extreme importance': Goode, 'Eel Question', p. 91.
28    'cry and beg for mercy': Marsh, 'Eels and the Eel Questions', p. 430.
30    'seeing that eels keep no diaries': Sigmund Freud to Eduard Silberstein, 5 April 1876, *The Letters of Sigmund Freud to Eduard Silberstein, 1871–1881*, ed. by Walter Boehlich, trans. by Arnold J. Pomerans (Cambridge, MA: Harvard University Press, 1990), p. 149.
30    'I have been tormenting myself': ibid.
32    'thin-head short-nosed': Fort, *Book of Eels*, p. 85.
34    'pathologically ambitious': ibid., p. 129.
34    'A chance of luck': Bo Poulsen, *Global Marine Science and Carlsberg: The Golden Connections of Johannes Schmidt (1877–1933)* (Leiden: Brill, 2016), p. 58.
35    'I had little idea at the time': Johannes Schmidt, 'The Breeding Places of the Eel', *Philosophical Transactions of the Royal Society of London, Series B* 211.385 (1922), p. 181.
35    'from America to Egypt, from Iceland to': ibid.
36    'was considered sufficient': Fort, *Book of Eels*, p. 95.
36    'Here lie the breeding grounds': Schmidt, 'Breeding Places of the Eel', p. 199.
36    'No other instance is known among fishes': Johannes Schmidt, 'Breeding Places and Migrations of the Eel', *Nature* 111.2776 (13 January 1923), p. 54.
41    'It is certainly somewhat humiliating': Jacoby, 'Eel Question', quoted in Schweid, *Eel*, p. 15.

## 2. Beaver

43    'There is a very gentle animal': W. B. Clark, *A Medieval Book of Beasts: The Second-Family Bestiary: Commentary, Art, Text and Translation.* (Suffolk: Boydell and Brewer, 2006), p. 130.
45–6 'If by chance the dogs should chase': Gerald of Wales, *The Itinerary of Archbishop Baldwin through Wales*, vol. 2, ed. by Sir Richard Colt Hoare (London: William Miller, 1806), p. 51.
46    'Often . . . beavers will tuck away their privates'; 'keeping their own treasures': quoted in Gregory McNamee, *Aelian's on the Nature of Animals* (Dublin: Trinity University Press, 2011), p. 65.
46    'We read of the beaver': Jean Paul Richter (ed.), *The Notebooks of Leonardo da Vinci: Compiled and Edited from the Original Manuscripts*, vol. 2 (Mineola, NY: Dover Publications, 1967), p. 1222.
47    'bite off their Pizzles': John Ogilby, *America: Being an Accurate Description of the New World* (London: Printed by the Author, 1671), p. 173.

48   'vulgar errors': Thomas Browne, *Pseudodoxia Epidemica* (London: Edward Dodd, 1646), p. iv.

48   'the three Determinators of Truth': ibid., p. 147.

48   'To purchase a clear and warrantable body': Reid Barbour and Claire Preston (eds), *Sir Thomas Browne: The World Proposed* (Oxford: Oxford University Press, 2008), p. 23.

48   'repugnant': Browne, quoted in *The Adventures of Thomas Browne in the Twenty-First Century*, Hugh Aldersey-Williams (London: Granta, 2015), p. 102.

48   'they will not regularly conform their breasts': *Pseudodoxia Epidemica*, p. 162.

49   'very ancient': ibid., p. 144.

49   'cods': This is Browne's term, ibid., p. 145.

49   'eunuchate'; 'not only a fruitless attempt'; 'hazardous ... if at all attempted': Browne, ibid., p. 145.

50   'hallucination'; 'electricity'; 'carnivorous'; 'misconception'; 'retromingent': quoted in Hugh Aldersey-Williams, *The Adventures of Sir Thomas Browne in the Twenty-First Century*, pp. 10–12.

50   'so named from being castrated': Stephen A. Barney, W. J. Lewis, J. A. Beach and Oliver Berghof (eds), *The Etymologies of Isidore of Seville* (Cambridge: Cambridge University Press, 2006), p. 21.

50   the Sanskrit word *kasturi*: Rachel Poliquin, *Beaver* (London: Reaktion, 2015), p. 58.

50   his death in 1566 from an overdose of figs: ibid., p. 57.

51   'Testicles are defined by their office': Browne, *Pseudodoxia Epidemica*, p. 146.

51   'the resemblance and situation of these tumours'; 'the ground of this mistake': ibid.

51   a heady cocktail of up to thirty different medicinal turds: John Redman Coxe, *The American Dispensatory* (Philadelphia: Carey & Lea, 1830), p. 172.

52   'These stones ... are of a strong and stinking savour': Edward Topsell, *The History of Four-Footed Beasts and Serpents and Insects* (London: DaCapo, 1967; f.p. 1658), p. 38.

52   Ancient and medieval pharmacopoeia positively bulged: Poliquin, *Beaver*, p. 70.

52   'a perfume made with Castoreum, Asses dung': Topsell, *History of Four-Footed Beasts*, p. 39.

52   castoreum ... as a tonic for hysteria: Poliquin, *Beaver*, p. 71.

53   'there is rarely one who is wholly free from it': Robert Gordon Latham (ed.), *The Works of Thomas Sydenham, MD*, vol. 2, trans. by Dr Greenhill (London: Sydenham Society, 1848), p. 85.

54    'delicate and irritable habits': John Eberle, *A Treatise of the Materia Medica and Therapeutics*, quoted in Poliquin, *Beaver*, p. 53.

54    the beaver's . . . anal secretions have been used to add vanilla flavour: G. A. Burdock, 'Safety Assessment of Castoreum Extract as a Food Ingredient', *International Journal of Toxicology*, 26.1 (January–February 2007), https://www.ncbi.nlm.nih.gov/pubmed/17365147, pp. 51–5.

56    'draw blood out of his nose': Topsell, *History of Four-Footed Beasts*, p. 38.

57    sequester the toxins': Poliquin, *Beaver*, p. 67.

57    Phenol from Scots pine': ibid., p. 67.

58    'a few disagreeable eructations': William Alexander, *Experimental Essays on the Following Subjects: I. On the External Application of Antiseptics in Putrid Diseases. II. On the Doses and Effects of Medicines. III. On Diuretics and Sudorifics*, 2nd ed (London: Edward and Charles Dilly, 1770), p. 84.

58    'ill deserving of a place in the current catalogue': ibid., p. 86.

59    'Let us hear no more of the half-reasoning elephant': Frances Thurtle Jamieson, *Popular Voyages and Travels Throughout the Continents and Islands of Asia, Africa and America* (London: Whittaker, 1820), p. 419.

60    'of which the industry has been most vaunted'; 'without excepting even the Ape': Nicolas Denys, *The Description and Natural History of the Coasts of North America (Acadia)*, vol. 2 (London: Champlain Society, 1908), p. 363.

60    'masons'; 'carpenters'; 'diggers'; 'hod-carriers'; 'without meddling with anything else'; 'commanders'; 'architect'; 'chastises them, beats them': ibid., pp. 363–5.

62    'beaver with a disabled tail'; 'inspector of the disabled': quoted in Poliquin, *Beaver*, p. 126.

62    'Beavers in distant solitudes build like architects': Oliver Goldsmith, *History of the Earth, and Animated Nature*, vol. 2 (1774), in *The Works of Oliver Goldsmith*, vol. 6 (London: J. Johnson, 1806), pp. 160–61.

62–3  'a kind of reasonable animal': Pierre François Xavier de Charlevoix, *Journal of a Voyage to North America*, quoted in Horace Tassie Martin, *Castorologia: Or, the History and Traditions of the Canadian Beaver* (London: E. Stanford, 1892), p. 167.

63    'Justice is everything among beavers': quoted in Poliquin, *Beaver*, p. 137.

63    'the lazy or idle kind'; 'expell'd by the other Beavers . . . just as Wasps are by Bees'; 'vagabonds': quoted in Gordon Sayre, 'The Beaver as Native and a Colonist', *Canadian Review of Comparative Literature/ Revue canadienne de littérature comparée* 22.3 4 (September and December 1995), pp. 670–71.

63    the French Romantic François-René, vicomte de Chateaubriand: Poliquin, *Beaver*, p. 137.

65    'In proportion as man rises above a state of nature', Georges-Louis Leclerc, Comte de Buffon, *Histoire Naturelle*, vol. 6, trans. by William Smellie (London: T. Cadell, 1812), p. 128.

65    'their genius, withered by fear': ibid., p. 144.

65    'perhaps, the only subsisting monument': ibid., p. 130.

66    'melancholy'; 'efforts feeble'; 'the gates of its prison': ibid., p. 134.

66    'a balcony to receive the fresh air': ibid., p. 141.

66    'tail and posterior parts'; 'changed the nature of their flesh'; 'fish': ibid., p. 142.

66    'link between quadrupeds and fishes': ibid., p. 135.

67    'In this society, however numerous, an universal peace is maintained': ibid., p. 140.

68    Cuvier held that intelligence gradually increased from rodents to ruminants: Poliquin, *Beaver*, p. 148.

72    'the beaver thinks consciously': Donald R. Griffin, *Animal Minds: Beyond Cognition to Consciousness* (Chicago: University of Chicago Press, 2001), p. 112.

73    'quick and easy': Frank Rosell, and Lixing Sun, 'Use of Anal Gland Secretion to Distinguish the Two Beaver Species *Castor canadensis* and *C. fiber*', *Wildlife Biology* 5.2 (June 1999), http://digitalcommons.cwu.edu/biology/4/, p. 119.

## 3. Sloth

75    'The degraded species of sloths': Georges-Louis Leclerc, Comte de Buffon, *Natural History, General and Particular*, vol. 9, ed. by William Wood (London: T. Cadell, 1749), p. 9.

77    'good to eat'; 'and the feet delicious': Gonzalo Fernández de Oviedo y Valdés, *The Natural History of the West Indies*, pp. 54–5.

77    'the stupidest animal': ibid.

77    'so awkward and slow in movement'; 'neither by threat, blow nor prodding': ibid.

77    'It takes them up to eight or nine minutes'; 'Neither stripes make them mend their pace': William Dampier, *Two Voyages to Campeachy*, in *A Collection of Voyages*, vol. 2 (London: James and John K. Apton, 1729), p. 61.

78    'They are quadrupeds'; 'and on each small foot'; 'But neither the claws nor the feet': Oviedo, *Natural History*, pp. 54–5.

80    'exceptional enough to be shown in a circus': Michael Goffart, *Function and Form in the Sloth* (Oxford: Pergamon Press), p. 75.

80    'I have never seen such an ugly animal': Oviedo, *Natural History*, pp. 54–5.

80    'this very deformed beast'; 'Ape Bear': Edward Topsell, *The History of Four-Footed Beasts and Serpents and Insects* (London: DaCapo, 1967; f.p. 1658), p. 15.

81    'As Nature is lively, active, and exalted'; 'One more defect': Buffon, *Natural History*, vol. 9, p. 289.

81    'All these circumstances announce their wretchedness': ibid., p. 290.

82    *Choloepus* (meaning 'crippled'): Richard Coniff, *Every Creeping Thing* (New York: Henry Holt, 1999), p. 47.

86    'are the most numerically abundant large mammal': John F. Eisenberg and Richard W. Thorington Jr, 'A Preliminary Analysis of a Neotropical Mammal Fauna', *Biotropica* 5.3 (1973), pp. 150–61.

87    'live off air': Oviedo, *Natural History*, pp. 54–5.

89    about 160 calories: Jonathan N. Pauli et al., 'Arboreal Folivores Limit their Energetic Output, All the Way to Slothfulness', *American Naturalist* 188:2 (2016), pp. 196–204.

91    'Of all animals, this poor ill-formed creature'; 'It exists long after it has received wounds': Charles Waterton, *Wanderings in South America: The North-West of the United States, and the Antilles, in the Years 1812, 1816, 1820, and 1824* (London: B. Fellowes, 1828), p. 69.

94    sloths in the wild actually sleep . . . an average of 9.6 hours: Niels C. Rattenborg, Bryson Voirin, Alexei L. Vyssotski, Roland W. Kays, Kamiel Spoelstra, Franz Kuemmeth, Wolfgang Heidrich and Martin Wikelski, 'Sleeping Outside the Box: Electroencephalographic Measures of Sleep in Sloths Inhabiting a Rainforest', *Biology Letters* 4.4 (23 August 2008), pp. 402–5, http://rsbl.royalsocietypublishing.org/content/4/4/402.

95    'Sloths have no weapons'; 'resembles withered herbs': Buffon, *Natural History*, vol. 9, p. 290.

97    'A sloth in Paris': William Beebe, 'Three-Toed Sloth', *Zoologica*, 7.1 (25 March 1926), p. 13.

97    'One of the most remarkable phases': ibid., p. 7.

97    'I have fired a gun': ibid., p. 22.

99    'They are attuned to this sound and only this sound': ibid., p. 36.

102   In 2014, American ecologists: Jonathan N. Pauli, Jorge E. Mendoza, Shawn A. Steffan, Cayelan C. Carey, Paul J. Weimar and M. Zachariah Peery, 'A Syndrome of Mutualism Reinforces the Lifestyle of a Sloth', *Proceedings of the Royal Society B* 281.1778 (7 March 2014), http://dx.doi.org/10.1098/rspb.2013.3006.

103   'little more than "flying genitals"': Veronique Greenwood, 'The Mystery of Sloth Poop: One More Reason to Love Science', *Time*, 22 January 2014, http://science.time.com/2014/01/22/the-mystery-of-sloth-poop-one-more-reason-to-love-science [accessed 9 July 2017].

103 'algae gardens': Pauli, Mendoza, Steffan, Carey, Weimar and Peery, 'A Syndrome of Mutualism'.

105 speed dating (without the speed): Henry Nicholls, *The Truth About Sloths*, BBC Earth website, www.bbc.co.uk/earth/story/20140916-the-truth-about-sloths.

## *4. Hyena*

107 'The hyena, hermaphroditic self-eating devourer': Ernest Hemingway, *Green Hills of Africa* (New York: Scribner, 2015; f.p. 1935), p. 28.

110 'rational'; 'For those Beasts which are of mixt natures'; 'seeing that they might be generated again': Sir Walter Raleigh, *The Historie of the World* (London: Thomas Basset, 1687), p. 63.

110 'It is the vulgar notion, that the hyæna possesses': John Bostock and H. T. Riley (eds), *The Natural History of Pliny*, vol. 2 (London: George Bell, 1900), p. 296.

111 'so close that sex could only be determined': Paul A. Racey and Jennifer D. Skinner, 'Endocrine Aspects of Sexual Mimicry in Spotted Hyaenas *Crocuta crocuta*', *Journal of Zoology* 187.3 (March 1979), http://onlinelibrary.wiley.com/doi/10.1111/j.1469-7998.1979. tb03372.x/full, p. 317.

114 'a large pendulous phallus'; 'normal pseudo-scrotum': Christine M. Drea et al., 'Androgens and Masculinization of Genitalia in the Spotted Hyaena (*Crocuta crocuta*) 2: Effects of Prenatal Anti-Androgens', *Journal of Reproduction and Fertility* 113.1 (May 1998), p. 121.

117 'a dirty brute': T. H. White (ed.), *The Book of Beasts: Being a Translation from a Latin Bestiary of the Twelfth Century* (Madison, WI: Parallel Press, 2002; f.p. 1954), p. 31.

117 'to live in the sepulchres of the dead': ibid.

117 'without pity for the living': Mikita Brottman, *Hyena*, (London: Reaktion, 2013) p. 40.

117 'In the Place of Tombs'; 'with bristling mane and grinning teeth': Philip Henry Gosse, *The Romance of Natural History*, ed. by Loren Coleman (New York: Cosimo Classics, 2008; f.p. 1861), p. 42.

118 'a most mysterious and awful animal'; 'rank and coarse'; 'revolting habits'; 'adapted to gorge'; 'cordially detested': Brottman, *Hyena*, p. 54.

120 'All writers agree': John Fortuné Nott, *Wild Animals Photographed and Described* (London: Sampson Low, Marston, Searle, & Rivington, 1886), p. 106.

120 'when the heart is of large size': Aristotle, *On the Parts of Animals*, trans. by W. Ogle (London: Kegan Paul, Trench, 1882), p. 70.

120 'the hare, the deer, the mouse': ibid., p. 71.

120 'all other animals that are either manifestly timorous': ibid.

NOTES

121 'are cowardly and will not fight': E. P. Walker, *Mammals of the World*, quoted in Brottman, *Hyena*, p. 57.
123 'the sobs or reachings of a man in a violent fit of vomiting': Georges-Louis Leclerc, Comte de Buffon, *Natural History* (abridged), (London: printed for C. and G. Kearsley, 1791), p. 182.

## 5. Vulture

129 'The eagle attacks his enemies': Georges-Louis Leclerc, Comte de Buffon, quoted in Stephen Jay Gould, *Leonardo's Mountain of Clams and the Diet of Worms: Essays on Natural History* (Cambridge, MA: Harvard University Press, 2011), p. 382.
130 'They are voracious, cowardly, disgusting': Buffon quoted in ibid., p. 382.
130 'an abomination': Bible, Leviticus 11:13.
131 'Vultures are accustomed to foretell the death'; 'Whenever two lines of battle are drawn': T. H. White (ed.), *The Book of Beasts: Being a Translation from a Latin Bestiary of the Twelfth Century* (Madison, WI: Parallel Press, 2002; f.p. 1954), pp. 109–110.
133 'In this bird the wit of smelling': Robert Steele (ed.), *Mediaeval Lore from Bartholomew Anglicus* (London: Chatto and Windus, 1907), p. 132.
133 'cruel, unclean and indolent'; 'sense of smelling, however, is amazingly great'; 'Nature, for this purpose, has given them two large apertures': Oliver Goldsmith, *A History of the Earth, and Animated Nature*, vol. 4 (London: Wingrave and Collingwood, 1816), p. 83.
134 'nature, although wonderfully bountiful'; 'assiduously engaged in a series of experiments': John James Audubon, 'An Account of the Habits of the Turkey Buzzard (*Vultur aura*) Particularly with the View of Exploding the Opinion Generally Entertained of Its Extraordinary Power of Smelling', *Edinburgh New Philosophical Journal* 2 (1826), p. 173.
135 'voided itself freely'; 'much fodder and hay': John James Audubon to John J. Jameson, ibid., p. 174.
137 'extraordinary formation and singular habits'; 'to admire the wonderful works': Charles Waterton, 'Why the Sloth is Slothful', quoted in *The World of Animals: A Treasury of Lore, Legend and Literature by Great Writers and Naturalists from the Fifth Century BC to the Present*, (New York: Simon & Schuster, 1961), p. 221.
137 'I grieve from my heart'; 'carefully gather up the shattered olfactory parts': Charles Waterton, *Essays on Natural History* (London: Frederick Warne, 1871), p. 244.
137 'Its grammar is bad; its composition poor': Charles Waterton, *Magazine of Natural History and Journal of Zoology, Botany, Mineralogy, Geology and Meteorology*, vol. 6 (London: Longman, Rees, Orme, Brown and Green, 1833), p. 215.

138   'Mr Audubon's story of a rattlesnake': ibid., p. 68.
138   'Nosarians' and 'Anti-Nosarians': Charles Waterton, 'Essays on Natural History, Chiefly Ornithology', *Quarterly Review* 62 (1838), p. 85.
138   'a sheep skinned and cut open': John Bachman, 'Experiments Made on the Habits of the Vultures', quoted in Gene Waddell (ed.), *John Bachman: Selected Writings on Science, Race, and Religion* (Athens: University of Georgia Press, 2011), p. 76.
138   'seemed much disappointed and surprised'; 'proved very amusing'; 'medical gentlemen': John Bachman, 'Retrospective Criticism: Remarks in Defence of [Mr Audubon] the Author of the [*Biography of the*] *Birds of America*', *Magazine of Natural History, and Journal of Zoology, Botany, Mineralogy, Geology and Meteorology*, vol. 7 (London: Longman, Rees, Orme, Brown, and Green, 1834), p. 168.
139   'the bird might not have been wholly free from the pain': Bachman, 'Retrospective Criticism', p. 169.
139   'become offensive to the neighbours': quoted in Waddell (ed.), *John Bachman*, p. 77.
139   'through their sense of sight and not of smell': ibid., p. 77.
139   'Pitiable, indeed, is the lot of the American vulture!': Waterton, *Essays on Natural History*, p. 262.
140   'stark, staring mad': Ruthven Deane and William Swainson, 'William Swainson to John James Audubon (A Hitherto Unpublished Letter)', *The Auk* 22.3 (July 1905), p. 251.
141   'food-finding sense': Herbert H. Beck, 'The Occult Senses in Birds', *The Auk* 37 (1920), p. 56.
144   'That will happen and you can't stop it'; 'But they won't remove the entire corpse': quoted in David Crossland, 'Police Train Vultures to Find Human Remains', *The National*, 8 January 2010, http://www.thenational.ae./news/world/europe/police-train-vultures-to-find-human-remains [accessed 12 June 2017].
145   Two younger vultures, named Miss Marple and Columbo: Michael Fröhlingsdorf, 'Vulture Detective Trail Hits Headwinds', *Der Spiegel*, 28 June 2011, http://www.spiegel.de/international/germany/bird-brained-idea-vulture-detective-training-hits-headwinds-a-770994.html [accessed 9 July 2017].
147   'They're disgusting': quoted in Darryl Fears, 'Birds of a Feather, Disgusting Together: Vultures are Wintering Locally', *Washington Post*, 16 January 2011, https://www.washingtonpost.com/local/birds-of-a-feather-disgusting-together-vultures-are-wintering-locally/2011/01/15/AB9oNfD_story.html?utm_term=.25c80af9dd9f [accessed 12 June 2017].
147   'They smell like ammonia'; 'They're ugly as \*\*\*\*': quoted in T. Edward Nickens, 'Vultures Take Over Suburbia', *Audubon*, November–December

2008, http://www.audubon.org/magazine/november-december-2008/
vultures-take-over-suburbia [accessed 12 June 2017].

147 'It vomited on my son'; 'It was like a half pound of ground beef':
quoted in Fears, 'Birds of a Feather, Disgusting Together'.

148 'The sloth, filth and the voraciousness': Georges-Louis Leclerc, Comte
de Buffon, *The Natural History of Birds* (Cambridge: Cambridge University Press, 2010; f.p. 1793), p. 105.

148 'a disgusting bird, with its bald scarlet head': quoted in Clifford B.
Frith, *Charles Darwin's Life with Birds: His Complete Ornithology*
(Oxford: Oxford University Press, 2016), p. 44.

151 'displaying the bitterness of unprovoked rage': Buffon, *Natural History
of Birds*, p. 105.

153 'a revolting sight of selfish greed': M. J. Nicoll, *Handlist of the Birds of
Egypt* (Cairo: Ministry of Public Works, 1919)

157 'We've had frogs, turtles, snakes': quoted in Jeff Rice, 'Bird Plus Plane
Equals Snarge', *Wired*, 23 September 2005, http://archive.wired.com/
science/discoveries/news/2005/09/68937 [accessed 12 June 2017].

159 'less interested in dead camels and goats': quoted in Matthew Kalman,
'Meet Operative PP0277: A Secret Agent – or Just a Vulture Hungry for
Dead Camel?', *Independent*, 8 December 2012, http://www.independent.
co.uk/news/world/middle-east/meet-operative-pp0277-a-secret-agent-
or-just-a-vulture-hungry-for-dead-camel-8393578.html [accessed 12
June 2017].

## 6. Bat

161 'One of the seamen declared that he had seen the Devil': Captain James
Cook, *Voyages of Discovery, 1768–1771* (Chicago: Chicago Review Press
2001), p. 83.

163 one in five perfectly sane British people: Charlotte-Anne Chivers,
'Why Isn't Everyone Batty About Bats?' *Bat News*, winter edition (10)
2015.

163 'rats with leather wings': Louis C. K., 'So I Called the Batman . . .', *Live
at the Comedy Store*, 17 August 2015, https://www.youtube.com/
watch?v=O4EyvdTTnWY [accessed 12 June 2017].

165 'blood-related to that of the devil': Divus Basilius, quoted in Glover
M. Allen, *Bats: Biology, Behavior, and Folklore* (Mineola, NY: Dover
Publications, 2004)

166 'An animal, like the bat, which is half a quadruped'; 'It is an imperfect
quadruped': Georges-Louis Leclerc, Comte de Buffon, *Barr's Buffon:
Buffon's Natural History*, vol. 6 (London: Printed for the Proprietor,
1797; f. p. 1749–1778), p. 239.

167 'The penis, which is pendulous and loose'; 'is a thing peculiar to man,
[and] the monkeys': Georges-Louis Leclerc, Comte de Buffon, *A*

*Natural History of Quadrupeds*, 3 vols, vol. 1 (Edinburgh: Thomas Nelson, 1830), p. 368.

170 'held many meetings to discuss the functions': Libiao Zhang quoted in Charles Q. Choi, *Surprising Sex Behavior Found in Bats* (Live Science, 2009), http://www.livescience.com/9754-surprising-sex-behavior-bats. html [accessed May 8, 2017].

170 'Observation . . . whether the male's tongue enters': Jayabalan Maruthu-pandian and Ganapathy Marimuthu, 'Cunnilingus Apparently Increases Duration of Copulation in the Indian Flying Fox (*Pteropus giganteus*)', *PLoS One* 8.3 (27 March 2013), p. e59743, https://doi.org/10.1371/journal. pone.0059743.

171 *Speckmaus*: Allen, *Bats*, p. 8.

173 'suck such a great amount of blood from the wound': Gonzalo Fernán-dez de Oviedo y Valdés, *General and Natural History of the Indies*, quoted in Michael P. Branch (ed.), *Reading the Roots: American Nature Writing Before Walden* (Athens: University of Georgia Press, 2004; f.p. 1535), pp. 23–4.

173 'a great plague of bats': Juan Francisco Molina Solis, *Historia del Descu-brimiento y Conquista del Yucatán*, vol. 3 (Merida de Yucatan: 1943), p. 38.

173 The word 'vampire' means 'blood drunkenness': Gary F. McCracken, 'Bats and Vampires', *Bat Conservation International* 11.3 (Fall 1993), http://www.batcon.org/resources/media-education/bats-magazine/ bat_article/603 [accessed: 12.6.2017].

174 'vampire epidemics': ibid.

174 'draws blood from the sleeping': Carl Linnaeus, *Systema Naturae*, tenth edition (Stockholm: Salvius, 1758), p. 31.

175 'a bloodsucker most cruel': Johann Baptist von Spix, *Simiarum et Vespertilionum Brasiliensium Species Novae* [*New Species of Brazilian Monkeys and Bats*] (Munich: F. S. Hübschmann, 1823). BL General Reference Collection: 1899, p. 22.

175 'long-tongued vampire': quoted in *Blood Suckers Most Cruel*, Kevin Dodd.

175 'hover like phantoms': Johann Baptist von Spix, *Travels in Brazil in the Years 1817–1820*, vol. 1 (London: Longman, Hurst, Rees, Orme, Brown and Green, 1827), p. 249.

175–6 'vulgar, false and mistaken notices': Félix de Azara, *The Natural His-tory of the Quadrupeds of Paraguay and the River la Plata* (Edinburgh: A. & C. Black, 1838), p. xxv.

176 'Vampyre'; 'the first living specimen ever seen in England': J. Timbs (ed.), *The Literary World: A Journal of Popular Information and Enter-tainment* 18 (27 July 1839), p. 274.

177 'Although this bat is the Vampyre Bat'; 'his appearance is, by no means, ferocious'; 'docile'; 'appeared fond of being noticed'; 'devour cherries': ibid.

177　'formidable species'; 'with all the art of': Mary Trimmer, *Natural History of the Most Remarkable Quadrupeds, Birds, Fishes, Serpents, Reptiles and Insects*, vol. 1 (Chiswick: Whittingham, 1825), p. 120.

181　'crowds of bats': Gary McCracken, 'Bats in Magic, Potions, and Medicinal Preparation', *Bat Conservation International* 10.3 (Fall 1992), http://www.batcon.org/resources/media-education/bats-magazine/bat_article/546 [accessed 8 May 2017].

181　'wool of bat': William Shakespeare, *Macbeth*, act 6, sc 1, l. 1560.

181　'flying ointment': Clive Harper, 'The Witches' Flying-Ointment', *Folklore* 88.1 (1977), p. 105.

182　'sixth sense': quoted in Robert Galambos, 'The Avoidance of Obstacles by Flying Bats: Spallanzani's Ideas (1794) and Later Theories', *Isis* 34.2 (1942), p. 138.

184　'We can blind a bat in two ways'; 'burning the cornea': quoted in Donald R. Griffin, *Listening in the Dark: The Acoustic Orientation of Bats and Men* (New Haven, CT: Yale University Press, 1958), p. 59.

184　'With a pair of scissors'; '[when] thrown into the air': quoted in Sven Dijkgraaf, 'Spallanzani's Unpublished Experiments on the Sensory Basis of Object Perception in Bats', *Isis* 51.1 (1960), p. 13.

185　'unharmed through the streets of a city'; 'changes through their skin': Galambos, 'The Avoidance of Obstacles', p. 133.

185　'coat the whole body of a blinded bat'; 'regained its vigour'; 'a second and third coat of varnish': ibid., p. 134.

185　'I stopped up the nostrils'; 'but the creature soon fell to the ground'; 'small fragments of sponge'; 'flew as freely as ever'; 'The removal of the tongue produced no result': quoted in Carter Beard, 'Some South American Animals', *Frank Leslie's Popular Monthly* (1892), pp. 378–9.

186　'red hot shoe nails'; 'fell down in a perpendicular direction': Lazzaro Spallanzani, 'Observations on the Organs of Vision in Bats', *Tillich's Philosophical Magazine* 1 (1798), p. 135.

186　'But how, if God love me, can we explain or even conceive in the hypothesis of hearing?': quoted in Griffin, *Listening in the Dark*, p. 61.

186　'and that they judge the distances': quoted in Dijkgraaf, 'Spallanzani's Unpublished Experiments', pp. 9–20.

187　'To us the organs of touch seem sufficient': quoted in Griffin, *Listening in the Dark*, p. 63.

187–8 'owing to extreme acuteness of hearing'; 'Since bats see with their ears': Galambos, 'Avoidance of Obstacles', p. 137.

189　'The wreck of the *Titanic*'; 'I asked myself: "Has science reached the end of its tether?"'; 'At the end of four hours': 'A Sixth Sense for Vessels', http://chroniclingamerica.loc.gov/lccn/sn88064176/1912-09-28/ed-1/seq-10.pdf [accessed 12 June 2017].

192　'This man is not a nut'; 'It sounds like a perfectly wild idea': Jack

Couffer, *Bat Bomb: World War II's Secret Weapon* (Austin: University of Texas Press, 1992), p. 5.

192 'frighten, demoralize, and excite the prejudices'; 'The lowest form of animal life': ibid.

192 'As fantastic as you may regard the idea'; 'practical, inexpensive'; 'the Japanese pest'; 'be used against us': ibid., p. 6.

195 'Think of thousands of fires breaking out'; 'Japan could have been devastated': Jared Eglan, *Beasts of War: The Militarization of Animals* (n.p.: Lulu.com, 2015), p. 14.

## 7. Frog

197 'It is a most singular thing': John Bostock and H. T. Riley (eds), *The Natural History of Pliny*, vol. 2 (London: Henry G. Bohn, 1855), pp. 462–3.

200 'thousands of millions': quoted in Pete Oxford and Renée Bish, 'In the Land of Giant Frogs: Scientists Strive to Keep the World's Largest Aquatic Frog Off a Growing Global List of Fleeting Amphibians', 1 October 2003, https://www.nwf.org/News-and-Magazines/National-Wildlife/Animals/Archives/2003/In-the-Land-of-Giant-Frogs.aspx [accessed 20 May 2017].

204 'are not produced from animals at all': Aristotle, *Historia Animalium*, quoted in Jan Bondeson, *The Feejee Mermaid: And Other Essays in Natural and Unnatural History* (Ithaca, NY: Cornell University Press, 1999), p. 194.

205 'old wax'; 'slime of vinegar'; 'damp dust'; 'books': Eugene S. McCartney, 'Spontaneous Generation and Kindred Notions in Antiquity', *Transactions and Proceedings of the American Philological Association*, 51 (1920), p. 105.

206 'fumes from the basil, acting as a leavening agent, will have transformed the vegetable matter'; 'veritable scorpions': *Les Oeuvres de Jean-Baptiste Van Helmont*, vol. 66, trans. by Jean Le Conte (Lyon: Chez Jean Antoine Huguetan, 1670), pp. 103–9.

206 'unclean woman': Bondeson, *Feejee Mermaid*, p. 199.

206 'He doubts whether mice can be procreated of putrefectation!': quoted ibid., p. 200.

207 'the toad is generated from a duck'; 'brought no result'; 'otherwise a most interesting and profound writer'; 'been too credulous': Francesco Redi, *Experiments on the Generation of Insects* (Chicago: Open Court Publishing Company, 1909), p. 64.

207 'I continued similar experiments with the raw and cooked flesh': ibid., p. 32.

208 'Having considered these things': ibid., p. 33.

208 'I put a snake, some fish, some eels': ibid.

210 'in Nature, in no case, in any living body,': quoted in John Waller, *Leaps in the Dark: The Making of Scientific Reputations* (Oxford: Oxford University Press, 2004), p. 42.

210 'an offensive putrid mass': quoted in ibid., p. 42.

211 'On March 21st we put on a pair of pants': quoted in Mary Terrall, 'Frogs on the Mantelpiece: The Practice of Observation in Daily Life', in Lorraine Daston and Elizabeth Lunbeck (eds), *Histories of Scientific Observation* (Chicago: University of Chicago Press, 2011), p. 189.

211 'too soft and floppy': quoted in ibid.

211 'the frog was adequately covered': quoted in ibid., p. 189.

211 'having made the pants and put them on': quoted in ibid.

212 'The idea of breeches': Waller, *Leaps in the Dark*, p. 43.

215 'godsend': Lancelot Thomas Hogben, *Lancelot Hogben, Scientific Humanist: An Unauthorised Autobiography* (London: Merlin Press, 1998), p. 101.

218 'the worst infectious disease ever recorded among vertebrates': Claude Gascon, James P. Collins, Robin D. Moore, Don R. Church, Jeanne E. McKay and Joseph R. Mendelson III (eds), *Amphibian Conservation Action Plan* (Cambridge: IUCN/SSC Amphibian Specialist Group, 2007), http://www.amphibianark.org/pdf/ACAP.pdf [accessed 12 June 2017].

224 'I will plague your whole country with frogs': Bible, Exodus 8:1–4.

## 8. Stork

225 'In diverse sorts of fowl': Charles Morton, 'An Essay into the Probable Solution of this Question: Whence Comes the Stork', quoted in Thomas Park (ed.), *The Harleian Miscellany: A Collection of Scarce, Curious, and Entertaining Pamphlets and Tracts*, vol. 5 (London: John White and John Murray, 1810), p. 506.

226 'the hands of an African': Ragnar K. Kinzelbach, *Das Buch Vom Pfeilstorch* (Berlin: Basilisken-Presse, 2005), p. 12.

229 'In my view, this is not a fairy tale'; 'If it were, why would Alexander tell it': quoted in Gregory McNamee, *Aelian's on the Nature of Animals* (Dublin: Trinity University Press, 2011), p. 40.

229 'hated': quoted in ibid., p. 44.

230 'Nature produces them against nature in the most extraordinary way'; 'Afterwards they hang down by their beaks': Gerald of Wales, *Topographia Hibernica*, quoted in Patrick Armstrong, *The English Parson-Naturalist: A Companionship Between Science and Religion* (Leominster: Gracewing Publishing, 2000), p. 31.

230–1 'found living things that were very naked'; 'covered with soft down': John Gerard, *Lancashire Folk-Lore: Illustrative of the Superstitious*

*Beliefs and Practices, Local Customs and Usages of the People of the County Palatine* (London: Frederick Warne, 1867), p. 118.

231 'because they are not born of flesh'; 'bishops and men of religion': Gerald of Wales, *The Historical Works of Giraldus Cambrensis* (London: Bohn, 1863), p. 36.

232 'into hiding'; 'torpor': Aristotle, *History of Animals in Ten Books*, vol. 8, trans. by Richard Cresswell (London: George Bell, 1878), p. 213.

233 'the sleeping one': 'Guide to North American Birds: Common Poor-will (*Phalaenoptilus nuttallii*)', National Audubon Society, http://www.audubon.org/field-guide/bird/common-poorwill [accessed 23 May 2017].

233 'quite denuded of their feathers': Aristotle, *History of Animals*, vol. 8, p. 213.

233 'It appears certain that swallows become torpid during winter': Georges Cuvier, *The Animal Kingdom*, ed. by H. M'Murtrie (New York: Carvill, 1831), p. 396.

234 'invaluable friend'; 'our two little prisoners'; 'showing the anxiety and convulsions of animals in a drowning state'; 'reduced, not to a state of torpidity': Charles Caldwell, *Medical & Physical Memoirs: Containing, Among Other Subjects, a Particular Enquiry Into the Origin and Nature of the Late Pestilential Epidemics of the United States* (Philadelphia: Thomas and William Bradford, 1801), p. 262–3.

235 'the swallows change their stations'; 'yet, in the northern waters', Olaus Magnus, *The History of Northern Peoples*, quoted in *Historia de Gentibus Septentrionalibus*, trans. P. Fisher and H. Higgins (London, 1998), p. 980.

236 'In the beginning of Autumn, they assemble together': ibid., p. 980.

236 'what truth there is . . . held to the fire': J. Hevelius, 'Promiscuous Inquiries, Chiefly about Cold', *Philosophical Transactions* 1 (1665), p. 345.

236 'it was most certain, that swallows sink themselves towards autumn into lakes': ibid., p. 350.

237 'lying in clay lumps': anon. ['A Person of Learning and piety'], *An Essay Towards the Probable Solution to this Question: Whence Come the Stork, and the Turtle, and the Crane, and the Swallow When They Know and Observe the Appointed Time of Their Coming* (London: E. Symon, 1739), p. 20.

237 'The stork, when it hath bred, and the young fully fledged': Charles Morton, 'An Enquiry into the Physical and Literal Sense of That Scripture', in Thomas Park (ed.), *The Harleian Miscellany*, p. 506.

238 'cheerfulness seems to intimate': ibid., p. 506.

239 'to some undiscovered satellite': Cotton Mather, *The Philosophical Transactions and Collections: Abridged and Disposed Under General Heads*, vol. 5 (London: Thomas Bennet, 1721), p. 161.

239 'will find it in the same line of direction': Morton, 'An Enquiry', p. 510.

240 'found during the time they are not in Holland': Nicholaas Witsen, Emily O'Gorman and Edward Mellilo (eds), *Beattie's Eco-Cultural Networks and the British Empire: New Views on Environmental History* (London: Bloomsbury, 2016), p. 95.

241 'They are, in fact, always so fatigued': Daines Barrington, *Miscellanies* (London: Nichols, 1781), p. 199.

241 'highly improbable': ibid., p. 219.

241 'destitute of any ocular proof': ibid., p. 176.

243 'pre-destined experimental bird': quoted in Richard Vaughan, *Wings and Rings: A History of Bird Migration Studies in Europe* (Penryn: Isabelline Books, 2009), p. 108.

243 'vain scientific humbug'; 'mass murdering of storks': quoted in Raf de Bont, *Stations in the Field: A History of Place-Based Animal Research, 1870–1930* (Chicago: University of Chicago Press, 2015), p. 159.

244 'heavenly origin'; 'our dear storks': quoted in Witsen et al. (eds), *Beattie's Eco-Cultural Networks and the British Empire*, p. 103.

246 'a ladies glove, a man's mitten, horse droppings': quoted in Vaughan, *Wings and Rings*, p. 109.

250 'these sagacious birds'; 'but never on a christian roof!' quoted in Charles MacFarlane, *Constantinople in 1828: A Residence of Sixteen Months in the Turkish Capital*, vol. 1 (London: Saunders and Otley, 1829) p. 284.

250 'a petty conceit': Thomas Browne, quoted in Aldersey-Williams, *The Adventures of Sir Thomas Browne in the Twenty-First Century*, p. 104.

## 9. Hippopotamus

257 'Some say that hee is five cubites high': Edward Topsell, *The History of Four-Footed Beasts and Serpents and Insects* (London: DaCapo, 1967; f.p. 1658), p. 61.

258 'river horse': ibid., p. 61.

258 'vomit fire': ibid., p. 61.

258 'opening its nostrils wide and snorting out a reddish smoke': quoted in David J. A. Clines, *Job 38–42: World Bible Commentary*, vol. 18B (Thomas Nelson, 2011), p. 1196.

258 'Under the lotus plants he lies'; 'What strength it has in its loins': Bible, Job 40:21.

259 'When the animal has become too bulky': John Bostock and Henry T. Riley (eds), *The Natural History of Pliny*, vol. 2 (London: Henry G. Bohn, 1855), p. 291.

260 'the first inventor of the practice of letting blood': ibid.

264 'so shocking that I am still reluctant to believe it': Richard Dawkins,

*The Ancestor's Tale: A Pilgrimage to the Dawn of Life* (London: Weiden-feld & Nicolson, 2010), p. 203.

269 'Although this animal has been celebrated': Georges-Louis Leclerc, Comte de Buffon, *Barr's Buffon: Buffon's Natural History*, vol. 6 (London: Printed for the Proprietor, 1797; f.p. 1749–1788), p. 60.

270 'the hippo swims well and eats fish': ibid., p. 62.

270 'His teeth are very strong': ibid., p. 61.

271 'Thus powerfully armed': ibid., p. 62.

271 'confined to the rivers of Africa': ibid., p. 63.

275 'My father has captured three': William Kremer, 'Pablo Escobar's Hippo's: A Growing Problem', BBC News, 26 June 2014, http://www.bbc.co.uk/news/magazine-27905743 [accessed 28 May 2017].

278 'highly mobile': Chris Walzer quoted in 'Moving testicles frustrate effort to calm hippos by castration', Michael Parker, *The Conversation*, 2 January 2014, https://theconversation.com/moving-testicles-frustrate-effort-to-calm-hippos-by-castration-21710.

## 10. Moose

281 'The Germans call this Beast Ellend': Edward Topsell, *The History of Four-Footed Beasts and Serpents and Insects* (London: DaCapo, 1967; f.p. 1658), p. 167.

282 'It is a melancholic Beast'; 'The flesh engendereth melancholy': ibid., p. 113.

283 'It is in a most miserable and wretched case': ibid., p. 167.

283 'joints in their legs to bend'; 'when they are down on the ground': ibid., p. 167.

284 'They have legs without joints': Hans-Friedrich Mueller (ed.), *Caesar: Selections from His Commentarii de Bello Gallico – Texts, Notes, Vocabu-lary* (Mundelein, IL: Bolchazy-Carducci, 2012), p. 242.

286 'Assume every moose is a serial killer': quoted in 'Caution Warned After Alaska Moose Attacks', Associated Press, 7 May 2011, http://www.cbsnews.com/news/caution-warned-after-alaska-moose-attacks/ [accessed 24 June 2017].

287 'behave in a drunken fashion': Andrew Haynes, 'The Animal World Has Its Junkies Too', *Pharmaceutical Journal*, 17 December 2010, http://www.pharmaceutical-journal.com/opinion/comment/the-animal-world-has-its-junkies-too/11052360.article [accessed 24 June 2017].

287 'were eating apples': quoted in David Landes, 'Swede Shocked by Backyard Elk "Threesome"', *The Local*, 27 October 2011, https://www.thelocal.se/20111027/36994 [accessed 24 June 2017].

288 'extremely rare'; 'Usually there are several males'; 'It's quite normal': quoted in ibid.

288 'antelope'; 'incomparable celerity'; 'can cut down very big trees': T.

H. White (ed.), *The Book of Beasts: Being a Translation from a Latin Bestiary of the Twelfth Century* (Madison, WI: Parallel Press, 2002; f.p. 1954), p. 18.

289  'all fleshly vices'; 'drunkenness and lust'; 'the shrub Booze': ibid., p. 19.

291  'become quite tipsy': William Drummond, *The Large Game and Natural History of South and South-East Africa* (Edinburgh: Edmonston and Douglas, 1875), p. 214.

293  'how to tell us what they were seeing while under the influence of LSD': quoted by Ronald K. Siegel in *Intoxication: the Universal Drive for Mind-Altering Substances* (Park Street Press, 1989), p. 13.

293  'with no history of alcohol use'; 'inappropriate behaviours': Ronald K. Siegel and Mark Brodie, 'Alcohol Self-Administration by Elephants', *Bulletin of the Psychonomic Society* 22.1 (July 1984), https://link.springer.com/article/10.3758/BF03333758, p. 50.

293  'the trained elephants' version of walking in a straight line': Siegel, *Intoxication*, p. 120.

294  'I knew a life-threatening clash'; 'I should have known better': ibid., p. 122.

294  'the environmental stress': Siegel and Brodie, 'Alcohol Self-Administration by Elephants', p. 52.

294  'These models were highly biased in favour of inebriation'; 'elephants can ordinarily become drunk': Steve Morris, David Humphreys and Dan Reynolds, 'Myth, Marula, and Elephant: An Assessment of Voluntary Ethanol Intoxication of the African Elephant (*Loxodonta africana*) Following Feeding on the Fruit of the Marula Tree (*Sclerocarya birrea*)', *Physiological and Biochemical Zoology* 79.2 (March/April 2006), https://www.ncbi.nlm.nih.gov/pubmed/16555195.

295  'People just want to believe in drunken elephants': quoted in Nicholas Bakalar, 'Elephants Drunk in the Wild? Scientists Put the Myth to the Test', *National Geographic News*, 19 December 2005, http://news.nationalgeographic.com/news/2005/12/1219_051219_drunk_elephant.html [accessed 25 June 2017].

295  dilated pupils, a struggle to stand and severe depression: Deer Industry Association of Australia, 'Fact Sheet', https://www.deerfarming.com.au/diaa-fact-sheets [accessed 24 June 2017].

296  'It prospers, runs about, dances': quoted in Adam Mosley, *Bearing the Heavens: Tycho Brahe and the Astronomical Community of the Late Sixteenth Century* (Cambridge: Cambridge University Press, 2007), p. 109.

297  'In America . . . animated Nature is weaker'; 'all the animals are much smaller': Georges-Louis Leclerc, Comte de Buffon, *The Natural History of Quadrupeds*, 3 vols, vol. 2 (Edinburgh: Thomas Nelson and Peter Brown, 1830), p. 31.

297  'degenerate': ibid., p. 51.

297  'No American animal can be compared': ibid., p. 31.

297  'moral certitude': quoted in Lee Alan Dugatkin, *Mr Jefferson and the Giant Moose: Natural History in Early America* (Chicago: University of Chicago Press, 2009), p. 35.

297  'all the animals which wallow in the mire': Buffon, *Natural History of Quadrupeds*, p. 43.

298  'absolutely dumb'; 'less juicy': quoted in Dugatkin, *Mr Jefferson and the Giant Moose*, p. 23.

298  'ardour'; 'small and feeble': Buffon, *Natural History of Quadrupeds*, p. 39.

298  'shrink and diminish under a niggardly sky': ibid.

299  'distance between the anus and the vulva': James Madison to Thomas Jefferson, 19 June 1786, in *The Writings of James Madison*, ed. by Gaillard Hunt (New York: Putnam, 1900–1910), https://cdn.loc.gov/service/mss/mjm/02/02_0677_0679.pdf [accessed 24 June 2017].

299  'certainly contradicts . . . in every instance smaller than those of the old': ibid.

300  'When Mr Jefferson shall have read this': quoted in Paul Ford (ed.), *The Works of Thomas Jefferson; Correspondence and Papers, 1816–1826*, vol. 7, (New York: Cosimo Books, 2009), p. 393.

300  'absolutely unacquainted'; 'that the reindeer could walk under': quoted in ibid., p. 393.

300  'with horns one foot long': quoted in ibid., p. 393.

300  'Do they make a rattling sound': quoted in Dugatkin, *Mr Jefferson and the Giant Moose*, p. 107.

301  'seven to ten feet tall'; 'horns of a very extraordinary size': quoted in ibid., p. 91.

301  'The readiness with which you undertook': Thomas Jefferson to John Sullivan, 7 January 1786, Founders Archive, https://founders.archives.gov/documents/Jefferson/01-09-02-0145 [accessed 24 June 2017].

301  'Leave also the bones of the head in the skin'; 'so that by sewing . . . size of the animal': ibid.

301  'a state of putrefaction': John Sullivan to Jefferson, 16 April 1787, Founders Archive, https://founders.archives.gov/documents/Jefferson/01-11-02-0285 [accessed 24 June 2017].

301  'they are not the horns of this moose': ibid.

303  'are remarkably small'; 'weighed five or six times as much': Thomas Jefferson to Georges-Louis Leclerc, Comte de Buffon, 1 October 1787, American History, http://www.let.rug.nl/usa/presidents/thomas-jefferson/letters-of-thomas-jefferson/jef163.php [accessed 24 June 2017].

303  'he promised in his next volume to set these things right': quoted in Ford (ed.), *Works of Thomas Jefferson*, p. 394.

## 11. Panda

305 'Pandas are bad at sex': 'Pandanomics', *The Economist*, 18 January 2014, http://www.economist.com/news/united-states/21594315-costly-bumbling-washington-has-perfect-mascot-pandanomics [accessed 11 May 2017].

306 'it's not a strong species': Chris Packham, 'Let Pandas Die', *Radio Times*, 22 November 2009, http://www.radiotimes.com/news/2009-09-22/chris-packham-let-pandas-die [accessed 7 July 2017].

306 There are, in fact, two pandas: Henry Nicholls, 'The Truth About Giant Pandas', BBC website, www.bbc.co.uk/earth/story/20150310-the-truth-about-giant-pandas.

307 'It is unbelievable': quoted in Richard Conniff, *The Species Seekers: Heroes, Fools, and the Mad Pursuit of Life on Earth* (New York: W. W. Norton, 2010), p. 317.

308 'that barks like a dog': quoted in ibid., p. 307.

308 'a most excellent black and white bear'; 'an interesting novelty to science': quoted in Henry Nicholls, *Way of the Panda: The Curious History of China's Political Animal* (London: Profile Books, 2011), p. 9.

308 'does not look very fierce'; 'Is full of leaves': quoted in Conniff, *Species Seekers*, p. 315.

309 'even though the giant panda is most closely related': George Schaller, *The Last Panda* (Chicago: University of Chicago Press, 1994), p. 266.

309 'The panda is a panda'; 'Just as I hope there is a yeti': ibid., p. 262.

310 'gives birth to a sort of misshapen lump': quoted in Gregory McNamee, *Aelian's on the Nature of Animals* (Dublin: Trinity University Press, 2011), p. 26.

310 'licks it into the form': ibid., p. 59.

311 'dehydrate and atrophy'; 'makes her fart'; 'eats a bunch of ants'; 'enjoys a fine defecation': ibid., p. 60.

314 Boaty McBoatface: Hannah Ellis-Petersen, 'Boaty McBoatface Wins Poll to Name Polar Research Vessel', *Guardian*, 17 April 2016, https://www.theguardian.com/environment/2016/apr/17/boaty-mcboatface-wins-poll-to-name-polar-research-vessel [accessed 8 July 2017].

314 'The external differences that the Bronx officials studied': Ramona Morris and Desmond Morris, *Men and Pandas* (London: Hutchinson and Co., 1966), p. 92.

315 'raised her tail and rear-end in sexual response'; 'intense embarrassment'; 'sexually, Chi-Chi appeared to be somewhat warped'; 'even complete strangers': Oliver Graham-Jones, *Zoo Doctor* (Fontana Books, 1973), p. 140.

315 'Chi-Chi's long isolation from other pandas': ibid., p. 141.

318 George Schaller was the first . . . that these notoriously solitary creatures are not loners: George B. Schaller, Hu Jinchu, Pan Wenshi and

Zhu Jing, *The Giant Pandas of Wolong* (Chicago: University of Chicago Press, 1985).

318 'prodigious amounts of high quality spermatozoa': Susie Ellis, Anju Zhang, Hemin Zhang, Jinguo Zhang, Zhihe Zhang, Mabel Lam, Mark Edwards, JoGayle Howard, Donald Janssen, Eric Miller and David Wildt, 'Biomedical Survey of Captive Giant Pandas: A Catalyst for Conservation Partnerships in China', in Donald Lindburg and Karen Baragona (eds), *Giant Pandas: Biology and Conservation* (Berkeley: University of California Press, 2004), p. 258, http://www.jstor.org/stable/10.1525/j.ctt1ppskn.

319 'squat', 'legcock' and 'handstand': Angela M. White, Ronald R. Swaisgood, Hemin Zhang, 'The Highs and Lows of Chemical Communication in Giant Pandas (*Ailuropoda melanoleuca*): Effect of Scent Deposition Height on Signal Discrimination', *Behavioural Ecology Sociobiology* 51.6 (May 2002), pp. 519–29, https://link.springer.com/article/10.1007/s00265-002-0473-3 [accessed 22 June 2017].

322 'George's girlfriend': Henry Nicholls, *Lonesome George: The Life and Loves of a Conservation Icon* (New York: Palgrave, 2007), p. 30.

326 'as pointless as taking off the pants': quoted in Lijia Zhang, 'Edinburgh Zoo's Pandas Are a Big Cuddly Waste of Money', *Guardian*, 7 December 2011, https://www.theguardian.com/commentisfree/2011/dec/07/edinburgh-zoo-pandas-big-waste-money [accessed 11 May 2017].

328 a suite of contracts worth an estimated £2.6 billion: Kathleen C. Buckingham, Jonathan Neil, William David and Paul R. Jepson, 'Diplomats and Refugees: Panda Diplomacy, Soft "Cuddly" Power, and the New Trajectory in Panda Conservation', *Environmental Practice* 15.3 (2013), pp. 262–70, https://www.researchgate.net/publication/255981642.

328 'The panda can be used to seal the deal'; 'soft power influence': quoted in Melissa Hogenboom, 'China's New Phase of Panda Diplomacy', BBC News, 25 September 2013, http://www.bbc.co.uk/news/science-environment-24161385 [accessed 22 June 2017].

329 'Panda-monium': Brynn Holland, 'Panda Diplomacy: The World's Cutest Ambassadors', History Channel, 16 March 2017. www.history.com/news/panda-diplomacy-the-worlds-cutest-ambassadors.

330 'One can only hope . . . "musk ox" will not be Chinese slang': quoted in Christopher Klein, 'When "Panda-Monium" Swept America', History Channel, 9 January 2014, http://www.history.com/news/when-panda-monium-swept-america [accessed 22 June 2017].

330 'in the grip of an intense giraffe-driven craze': Eric Ringmar, 'Audience for a Giraffe: European Exceptionalism and the Quest for the

Exotic', *Journal of World History* 17.4 (December 2006), http://www.jstor.org/stable/20079397, p. 385.

330 'The giant panda's exclusive natural existence'; 'While it is, of course, debatable': Falk Hartig, 'Panda Diplomacy: The Cutest Part of China's Public Diplomacy', *Hague Journal of Diplomacy* 8.1 (2013), https://eprints.qut.edu.au/59568.

332 'She made the mistake of stroking them': When Pandas Attack! (blog), https://whenpandasattack.wordpress.com [accessed 11 May 2017].

333 'I always thought they were cute': ibid.

## 12. Penguin

335 'All the world loves a penguin': Apsley Cherry-Garrard, *The Worst Journey in the World: Antarctic 1910–1913*, vol. 2 (New York: George H. Doran, 1922), p. 560.

339 'fowl which could not fly'; 'the bigness of geese': *Sir Francis Drake's Famous Voyage Round the World* (1577), quoted in Tui de Roy, Mark Jones and Julie Cornthwaite, *Penguins: The Ultimate Guide* (Princeton, NJ: Princeton University Press, 2014), p. 151.

340 'You take a kettle with you': Errol Fuller, *The Great Auk: The Extinction of the Original Penguin* (Piermont, NH: Bunker Hill, 2003), p. 34.

341 'arse-feet': quoted in Oliver Goldsmith, *A History of the Earth, and Animated Nature*, vol. 4 (Philadelphia: T. T. Ash, 1824), p. 83.

343 'eccentric to a degree': Edward A. Wilson, *Report on the Mammals and Birds, National Antarctic Expedition 1901–1904*, vol. 2 (London: Aves, 1907), p. 11.

343 'the possibility that we have in the emperor penguin': ibid., p. 38.

343 'The earliest bird, the *Archaeopteryx*'; 'One hopes to find real teeth': Edward A. Wilson and T. G. Taylor, *With Scott: The Silver Lining* (New York: Dodd, Mead and Company, 1916), p. 244.

346 'I for one had come to that point of suffering': Cherry-Garrard, *Worst Journey*, p. 237.

346 'The disturbed emperors made a tremendous row': ibid., p. 268.

346 'it spouted a blob of boiling oil'; 'unable to stifle his groans': ibid., p. 273.

347 'I always mistrusted that stove': ibid., p. 274.

347 'as though the world was having a fit'; 'whipped to little tiny strips': ibid., p. 276.

347 'face to face with real death': ibid., p. 281.

347 'Our lives had been taken away': ibid., p. 284.

347–8 'Custodian of the Sacred eggs': ibid., p. 299.

348 'Who are you? What do you want?': ibid., p. 299.

348 'I handed over the Cape Crozier embryos': Sara Wheeler, *Cherry: A Life of Apsley Cherry-Garrard* (London: Vintage, 2007), p. 186.

# NOTES

349 'add to our understanding of penguin embryology': C. W. Parsons, 'Penguin Embryos: British Antarctic Terra Nova Expedition 1910 – Natural History Reports', *Zoology* 4.7 (1934), p. 253.

349 'The Adélie penguin has a hard life': Cherry-Garrard, *Worst Journey*, vol. 1, p. 269.

349 'They are extraordinarily like children'; 'full of their own importance': ibid., p. 50.

349 'at first sight, the look of a child': William Clayton, 'An Account of Falkland Islands', *Philosophical Transactions of the Royal Society of London* 66 (1 January 1776), p. 103.

349 'stand upright like little Children': John Narborough, Abel Tasman, John Wood and Friderich Martens, *An Account of Several Late Voyages and Discoveries to the South and North* (Cambridge: Cambridge University Press, 2014; f.p. 1711), p. 59.

350 'ridiculous air of gravity': 'The Zoological Gardens Regents Park', *The Times*, 18 April 1865, p. 10.

350 'This is the incredible true story': Luc Jacquet and Bonne Pioche (dirs), *March of the Penguins* (National Geographic Films, 2005).

351 'the motion picture that most passionately affirms'; 'Some of the circumstances': quoted in Jonathan Miller, 'March of the Conservatives: Penguin Film as Political Fodder', *New York Times*, 13 September 2005, http://www.nytimes.com/2005/09/13/science/march-of-the-conservatives-penguin-film-as-political-fodder.html [accessed 26 June 2017].

352 'nutritively rather than sexually motivated': Bruce Bagemihl, *Biological Exuberance: Animal Homosexuality and Natural Diversity* (New York: St Martin's Press, 1999), p. 115.

354 'rocked the gay scene': Andrew Sullivan quoted in Miller, 'New Love Breaks Up Six-Year Relationship at Zoo', *New York Times*, 24 September 2005.

358 'gangs of hooligan cocks'; 'passions seem to have passed beyond their control': Douglas G. D. Russell, William J. L. Sladen and David G. Ainley, 'Dr George Murray Levick (1876–1956): Unpublished Notes on the Sexual Habits of the Adélie Penguin', *Polar Record* 48.4 (October 2012), https://doi.org/10.1017/S0032247412000216, p. 388.

358 'constant acts of depravity': ibid., p. 392.

358 'sexually misused by these hooligans': ibid.

358 'misused it before the very eyes of its parent': ibid.

358 'very often suffer indignity': ibid.

359 'We will have this cut out': ibid.

360 'astonishing acts of depravity': ibid., p. 389.

360 'actually engaged in sodomy': ibid.

360 'there seems to be no crime too low': ibid.

361 'irresistible': ibid., p. 390.

361   'a frozen head, with self-adhesive white O's': ibid.
361   'sufficient stimulus for males to copulate': ibid., p. 389.
361   'feral pigeon'; 'a dead house martin'; 'a much smaller bird': username
      Zheljko, 'Avian Necrophilia' discussion board, *Birdforum*, 6 May 2014
      18:43  http://www.birdforum.net/showthread.php?t=282175 [accessed
      on 23 May 2017].
361   'as if presenting to a male'; 'was duly squashed, its turn': username
      Farnboro John, 'Avian Necrophilia' discussion board, *Birdforum*, 6
      May 2014 17:20, http://www.birdforum.net/showthread.php?t=282175
      [accessed on 23 May 2017].
362   'Grim stuff, but I have photos': username Capercaillie71, 'Avian Necro-
      philia' discussion board, *Birdforum*, 6 May 2014 21:34, http://www.
      birdforum.net/showthread.php?t=282175 [accessed on 23 May 2017].

## 13. Chimpanzee

363   'A brute, but a brute of a kind': Georges-Louis Leclerc, Comte de
      Buffon, *History of Quadrupeds*, vol. 3 (Edinburgh: Thomas Nelson,
      1830), p. 248.
367   'The constitution of the ape is hot': Hildegard of Bingen, quoted in
      H. W. Janson, *Apes and Ape Lore in the Middle Ages and the Renaissance*
      (London: Warburg Institute, 1952), p. 77.
367   'He also shares the habits of beasts': ibid.
368   'two kinds of Monsters': Andrew Battel, *Purchas, His Pilgrimage*, quoted
      in Robert Yerkes and Ada Yerkes, *The Great Apes: A Study of Authropoid
      Life* (New Haven, CT: Yale University Press, 1929), pp. 42–3.
368   'pongos' and 'engecos': ibid., pp. 42–3.
368   'which they do not very well love': Willem Bosman, *A New and Accurate
      Description of the Coast of Guinea* (London: Alfred Jones, 1705), p. 254.
368   'terribly pernicious sort of brutes': ibid., p. 254.
369   'an animal of remarkably and terribly hideous countenance': Jonathan
      Marks, *What It Means to Be 98% Chimpanzee: Apes, People, and Their
      Genes* (Berkeley: University of California Press, 2002), p. 19.
369   'It seeks food from its own excrement': ibid., p. 19.
369   'illicit sexual intercourse': Marks, ibid., p. 19.
369   'one would be apt to think': Edward Tyson, quoted in John M. Batch-
      erlder, 'Letters to the Editor: Dr. Edward Tyson and the Doctrine of
      Descent', *Science* 11.270 (1888), pp. 169–70.
370   'cave-dwelling man': quoted by Marks, *What It Means to Be 98% Chim-
      panzee*, p. 21.
370   'in the human species have we not similar variety?': Georges-Louis
      Leclerc, Comte de Buffon, *Barr's Buffon: Buffon's Natural History*,
      vol. 9 (London: Symonds, 1797), p. 157.
370   'fleshy posteriors': ibid., p.175.

370 'power of thought and speech': ibid., p. 138.
370 'animated by a superior principle': ibid., p. 167.
372 'destiny as the supreme master': Richard Owen, 'On the Characters, Principles of Division, and Primary Groups of the Class Mammalia', *Journal of the Proceedings of the Linnean Society I: Zoology* (London: Longman, 1857), p. 34.
372 'ruling brain': Richard Owen, quoted in Carl Zimmer, 'Searching for Your Inner Chimp', *Natural History*, Dec. 2002–Jan. 2003.
372 'what a Chimpanzee [would] say': Charles Darwin to J. D. Hooker, 5 July 1857, Darwin Correspondence Project, http://www.darwinproject.ac.uk/DCP-LETT-2117 [accessed 5 May 2017].
372 'he was not ashamed to have a monkey': J. R. Lucas, 'Wilberforce and Huxley: A Legendary Encounter', *Historical Journal* 22.2 (1979), pp. 313–30.
373 'nail . . . that mendacious humbug': Thomas Henry Huxley, quoted in Stephen Jay Gould, *Leonardo's Mountain of Clams and the Diet of Worms* (Cambridge, MA: Harvard University Press, 2011), p. 129.
373 'a Corinthian portico in cow dung': Thomas Henry Huxley to Joseph Dalton Hooker, 5 September 1858, in G. W. Beccaloni (ed.), Wallace Letters Online, http://www.nhm.ac.uk/research-curation/scientific-resources/collections/library-collections/wallace-letters-online/3758/3670/T/details.html [accessed 25 June 2017].
374 'extraordinarily interesting evidence': Kirill Rossiianov, 'Beyond Species: Il'ya Ivanov and His Experiments on Cross-Breeding Humans with Anthropoid Apes', *Science in Context* 15.2 (2002), p. 279.
375 'a decisive blow to the religious teachings'; 'possible and desirable': ibid.
375 'rejuvenation therapy' and 'monkey gland': Serge Voronoff, *The Conquest of Life* (New York: Brentano, 1928), p. 130.
376 'grafting is in no way an aphrodisiac': ibid., p. 150.
377 'the sperm was not completely fresh': Rossiianov, 'Beyond Species', p. 289.
377 'a bolt from the blue': ibid., p. 289.
381 'I am a psychotherapist. My daughter, Lucy': Maurice K. Temerlin, *Lucy: Growing up Human – a Chimpanzee Daughter in a Psychotherapist's Family* (Palo Alto, CA: Science & Behavior Books, 1975), p. 1.
381 'symbolic equivalent of the act of giving birth': ibid., p. 8.
381 'Jewish mommas boy': ibid., p. 130.
382 'fix her a cocktail or two': ibid., p. 49.
382 'Now we must redefine tool': Louis Leakey, quoted in David Quammen, 'Fifty Years at Gombe', *National Geographic*, October 2010, http://ngm.nationalgeographic.com/print/2010/10/jane-goodall/quammen-text [accessed 27 May 2017].

383   'to see what would happen': Temerlin, *Lucy: Growing Up Human*, p. 109.
383   'Lucy was into everything': ibid., p. 19.
393   'building shrines' at a 'sacred tree': Simon Barnes, 'Is This Proof Chimps
      Believe in God?', *Daily Mail*, 4 March 2006, http://www.dailymail.co.uk/
      sciencetech/article-3475816/Is-proof-chimps-believe-God-Scientists-
      baffled-footage-primates-throwing-rocks-building-shrines-sacred-tree-
      no-reason.html [accessed 27 May 2017].
395   'perhaps triggered by feelings of awe and wonder': Jane Goodall, 'Waterfall
      Displays', Vimeo, 3 January 2011, https://vimeo.com/18404370 [accessed
      27 June 2017].
396   'They are not men': Edward Topsell, *The History of Four-Footed Beasts
      and Serpents and Insects*, vol. 1 (London: DaCapo, 1967; f.p. 1658), p. 3.

# BIBLIOGRAPHY

## Introduction

Aldersey-Williams, Hugh, *The Adventures of Sir Thomas Browne in the Twenty-First Century* (London: Granta, 2015)

Clark, Anne, *Beasts and Bawdy* (London: Dent, 1975)

Curley, Michael J. (trans.), *Physiologus: A Medieval Book of Natural Lore* (Chicago: University of Chicago Press, 1979)

Raven, Charles E., *English Naturalists from Neckam to Ray: A Study of the Making of the Modern World* (Cambridge: Cambridge University Press, 2010)

White, T. H., *The Book of Beasts: Being a Translation from a Latin Bestiary of the Twelfth Century* (Madison, WI: Parallel Press, 2002; f.p. 1954)


## 1. Eel

Amilhat, Elsa, Kim Aarestrup, Elisabeth Faliex, Gaël Simon, Håkan Westerberg and David Righton, 'First Evidence of European Eels Exiting the Mediterranean Sea During Their Spawning Migration', *Nature Scientific Reports* 6.21817 (24 February 2016), https://www.nature.com/articles/srep21817

Aristotle, 'Historia Animalium', *The Works of Aristotle*, vol. 4, trans. by D'Arcy Wentworth Thompson (Oxford: Clarendon Press, 1910)

Cairncross, David, *The Origin of the Silver Eel: With Remarks on Bait and Fly Fishing* (London: G. Shield, 1862)

Fort, Tom, *The Book of Eels* (London: HarperCollins, 2002)

Goode, G. Brown, 'The Eel Question', *Transactions of the American Fisheries Society*, vol. 10 (New York: Johnson Reprint Corp., 1881), pp. 81–124

Grassi, G. B., 'The Reproduction and Metamorphosis of the Common Eel (*Anguilla vulgaris*)', *Reproduction and Metamorphosis of Fish* (1896), p. 371

Jacoby, Leopold, 'The Eel Question', in US Commission of Fish and Fisheries, *Report of the Commissioner for 1879* (Washington: US Government Printing Office, 1882), http://penbay.org/cof/COF_1879_IV.pdf

Magnus, Albert, *On Animals: A Medieval Summa Zoologica*, vol. 2, trans. by Kenneth F. Kitchell Jr and Irven Michael Resnick (Baltimore: John Hopkins University Press, 1999)

Marsh, M. C., 'Eels and the Eel Questions', *Popular Science Monthly* 61.25 (September 1902), pp. 426–33

Poulsen, Bo, *Global Marine Science and Carlsberg: The Golden Connections of Johannes Schmidt (1877–1933)* (Leiden: Brill, 2016)

Prosek, James, *Eels: An Exploration, from New Zealand to the Sargasso, of the World's Most Amazing and Mysterious Fish* (London: HarperCollins, 2010)

Righton, David, Kim Aarestrup, Don Jellyman, Phillipe Sébert, Guido van den Thillart and Katsumi Tsukamato, 'The *Anguilla* spp. Migration Problem: 40 Million Years of Evolution and Two Millennia of Speculation', *Journal of Fish Biology* 81.2 (July 2012), pp. 365–86, https://www.ncbi.nlm.nih.gov/pubmed/22803715

Schmidt, Johannes, 'The Breeding Places of the Eel', *Philosophical Transactions of the Royal Society of London, Series B* 211.385 (1922), pp. 179–208

Schmidt, Johannes, 'Breeding Places and Migrations of the Eel', *Nature* 111.2776 (13 January 1923), pp. 51–4

Schweid, Richard, *Consider the Eel: A Natural and Gastronomic History* (Chapel Hill: University of North Carolina Press, 2002)

Schweid, Richard, *Eel* (London: Reaktion, 2009)

Schweid, Richard, 'Slippery Business: Scientists Race to Understand the Reproductive Biology of Freshwater Eels', *Natural History* 118.9 (November 2009), pp. 28–33, http://www.naturalhistorymag.com/features/291856/slippery-business

Walton, Izaak, and Charles Cotton, *The Complete Angler: Or the Contemplative Man's Recreation*, ed. by John Major (London: D. Bogue, 1844)

## 2. Beaver

Browne, Thomas, *Pseudodoxia Epidemica* (London: Edward Dodd, 1646)

Buffon, Georges-Louis Leclerc, Comte de, *History of Quadrupeds*, vol. 6, trans. by William Smellie (London: T. Cadell, 1812)

Campbell-Palmer, Róisín, Derek Gow and Robert Needham, *The Eurasian Beaver* (Exeter: Pelagic Publishing, 2015)

# BIBLIOGRAPHY

Clark, W. B., *A Medieval Book of Beasts: The Second-Family Bestiary: Commentary, Art, Text and Translation* (Suffolk: Boydell and Brewer, 2006)

Dolin, Eric Jay, *Fur, Fortune, and Empire: The Epic History of the Fur Trade in America* (New York: W. W. Norton, 2011)

Gerald of Wales, *The Itinerary of Archbishop Baldwin Through Wales*, vol. 2, ed. by Sir Richard Colt Hoare (London: William Miller, 1806)

Gould, James L., and Carol Grant Gould, *Animal Architects: Building and the Evolution of Intelligence* (New York: Basic Books, 2012)

Gould, Stephen Jay, *The Mismeasure of Man* (New York: W. W. Norton, 1996)

Griffin, Donald R., *Animal Minds: Beyond Cognition to Consciousness* (Chicago: University of Chicago Press, 2001)

McNamee, Gregory, *Aelian's on the Nature of Animals* (Dublin: Trinity University Press, 2011)

Martin, Horace Tassie, *Castorologia: Or, the History and Traditions of the Canadian Beaver* (London: E. Stanford, 1892)

Mortimer, C., 'The Anatomy of a Female Beaver, and an Account of Castor Found in Her', *Philosophical Transactions* 38 (1733), pp. 172–83, http://rstl.royalsocietypublishing.org/content/38/427-435/172

Müller-Schwarze, Dietland, *The Beaver: Its Life and Impact*, 2nd ed. (Ithaca, NY: Cornell University Press, 2011)

Müller-Schwarze, Dietland and Lixing Sun, *The Beaver: History of a Wetlands Engineer* (Ithaca, NY: Cornell University Press, 2003)

Nolet, Bart A., and Frank Rosell, 'Comeback of the Beaver *Castor fiber*: An Overview of Old and New Conservation Problems', *Biological Conservation* 83.2 (1998), pp. 165–73, http://hdl.handle.net/20.500.11755/6cc63738-2516-44f4-b31a-f4d686b4e249

Platt, Carolyn V., *Creatures of Change: An Album of Ohio Animals* (Kent, OH: Kent State University Press, 1998)

Poliquin, Rachel, *Beaver* (London: Reaktion, 2015)

Sax, Boria, *The Mythical Zoo: An Encyclopedia of Animals in World Myth, Legend, and Literature* (Santa Barbara, CA: ABC-Clio, 2001)

Sayre, Gordon, 'The Beaver as Native and a Colonist', *Canadian Review of Comparative Literature/Revue canadienne de littérature comparée* 22.3–4 (September and December 1995), pp. 659–82

Simon, Matt, 'Fantastically Wrong: Why People Used to Think Beavers Bit Off Their Own Testicles', wired.com, 2014.

Tasca, Cecilia, Mariangela Rapetti, Mauro Giovanni Carta and Bianca Fadda, 'Women and Hysteria in the History of Mental Health', *Clinical Practice and Epidemiology in Mental Health* 8 (October 2012), pp. 110–19, https://www.ncbi.nlm.nih.gov/pmc/articles/PMC3480686

# BIBLIOGRAPHY

Wilsson, Lars, *Observations and Experiments on the Ethology of the European Beaver (*Castor Fiber L.*): A Study in the Development of Phylogenetically Adapted Behaviour in a Highly Specialized Mammal* (Uppsala: Almqvist & Wiksell, 1971)

## 3. Sloth

Beebe, William, 'Three-Toed Sloth', *Zoologica*, 7.1 (25 March 1926)

Buffon, Georges-Louis Leclerc, Comte de, *Natural History, General and Particular*, vol. 9, ed. by William Wood, (London: T. Cadell, 1749)

Choi, Charles Q., 'Freak of Nature: Sloth Has Rib-Cage Bones in Its Neck', *LiveScience*, 21 October 2010, https://www.livescience.com/10178-freak-nature-sloth-rib-cage-bones-neck.html

Cliffe, Rebecca N., Judy A. Avey-Arroyo, Francisco J. Arroyo, Mark D. Holton and Rory P. Wilson, 'Mitigating the Squash Effect: Sloths Breathe Easily Upside Down', *Biology Letters* 10.4 (April 2014), http://rsbl.royalsocietypublishing.org/content/10/4/20140172

Cliffe, Rebecca N., Ryan J. Haupt, Judy A. Avey-Arroyo and Rory P. Wilson, 'Sloths Like It Hot: Ambient Temperature Modulates Food Intake in Brown-Throated Sloth (*Bradypus variegatus*)', *PeerJ* 3 (2 April 2015), p. e875, https://www.ncbi.nlm.nih.gov/pubmed/25861559

Conniff, Richard, *Every Creeping Thing: True Tales of Faintly Repulsive Wildlife* (New York: Henry Holt, 1999)

Eisenberg, John F., and Richard W. Thorington Jr, 'A Preliminary Analysis of a Neotropical Mammal Fauna', *Biotropica* 5.3 (1973), pp. 150–61

Goffart, Michael, *Function and Form in the Sloth* (Oxford: Pergamon Press, 1971)

Gould, Carol Grant, *The Remarkable Life of William Beebe: Naturalist and Explorer* (Washington, DC: Island Press: 2004)

Gould, Stephen Jay, *Leonardo's Mountain of Clams and the Diet of Worms* (Belknap Press, 2011)

Horne, Genevieve, 'Sloth Fur Has a Symbiotic Relationship with Green Algae', *Biomed Central* blog, 14 April 2010, https://blogs.biomedcentral.com/on-biology/2010/04/14/sloth-fur-has-symbiotic-relationship-with-green-algae [accessed 28 May 2017]

Montgomery, G. Gene, and M. E. Sunquist, 'Habitat Selection and Use by Two-Toed and Three-Toed Sloths', in *The Ecology of Arboreal Folivores* (Washington, DC: Smithsonian Institute, 1978), pp. 329–59

Oviedo y Valdés, Gonzalo Fernández de, *The Natural History of the West Indies* ed. by Sterling A. Stoudemire (Chapel Hill: University of North Carolina Press, 1959), pp. 54–5

# BIBLIOGRAPHY

Pauli, Jonathan N., Jorge E. Mendoza, Shawn A. Steffan, Cayelan C. Carey, Paul J. Weimar and M. Zachariah Peery, 'A Syndrome of Mutualism Reinforces the Lifestyle of a Sloth', *Proceedings of the Royal Society B* 281.1778 (7 March 2014), http://dx.doi.org/10.1098/rspb.2013.3006

Rattenborg, Niels C., Bryson Voirin, Alexei L. Vyssotski, Roland W. Kays, Kamiel Spoelstra, Franz Kuemmeth, Wolfgang Heidrich and Martin Wikelski, 'Sleeping Outside the Box: Electroencephalographic Measures of Sleep in Sloths Inhabiting a Rainforest', *Biology Letters* 4.4 (23 August 2008), pp. 402–5, http://rsbl.royalsocietypublishing.org/content/4/4/402

Voirin, Bryson, Roland Kays, Martin Wikelski and Margaret Lowman, 'Why Do Sloths Poop on the Ground?', in Margaret Lowman, T. Levy and Soubadra Ganesh (eds), *Treetops at Risk* (New York: Springer, 2013), pp. 195–9


## 4. Hyena

Aristotle, *On the Parts of Animals*, trans. by W. Ogle (London: Kegan Paul, Trench, 1882)

Baynes-Rock, Markus, *Among the Bone Eaters: Encounters with Hyenas in Harar* (State College: Pennsylvania State University Press, 2015)

Benson-Amram, Sarah, and Kay E. Holekamp, 'Innovative Problem Solving by Wild Spotted Hyenas', *Proceedings of the Royal Society B* 279.1744 (October 2012), pp. 4087–95, https://www.ncbi.nlm.nih.gov/pmc/articles/PMC3427591

Benson-Amram, Sarah, Virginia K. Heinen, Sean L. Dryer and Kay E. Holekamp, 'Numerical Assessment and Individual Call Discrimination by Wild Spotted Hyaenas, *Crocuta crocuta*', *Animal Behaviour* 82.4 (October 2011), pp. 743–52, https://doi.org/10.1016/j.anbehav.2011.07.004

Brottman, Mikita, *Hyena* (London: Reaktion, 2013)

Cunha, Gerald R., Yuzhuo Wang, Ned J. Place, Wenhui Liu, Larry Baskin and Stephen E. Glickman, 'Urogenital System of the Spotted Hyena (*Crocuta crocuta Erxleben*): A Functional Histological Study', *Journal of Morphology* 256.2 (May 2003), pp. 205–18, http://onlinelibrary.wiley.com/doi/10.1002/jmor.10085/full

Drea, Christine M., Mary L. Weldele, Nancy G. Forger, Elizabeth M. Coscia, Laurence G. Frank, Paul Licht and Stephen E. Glickman, 'Androgens and Masculinization of Genitalia in the Spotted Hyaena (*Crocuta crocuta*) 2: Effects of Prenatal Anti-Androgens', *Journal of Reproduction and Fertility* 113.1 (May 1998), pp. 117–27, https://www.ncbi.nlm.nih.gov/pubmed/9713384

# BIBLIOGRAPHY

Drea, Christine M., and Allisa N. Carter, 'Cooperative Problem Solving in a Social Carnivore', *Animal Behaviour* 78.4 (October 2009), pp. 967–77, http://dx.doi.org/10.1016/j.anbehav.2009.06.030

Frank, Laurence G., Stephen E. Glickman and Irene Powch, 'Sexual Dimorphism in the Spotted Hyaena (*Crocuta crocuta*)', *Journal of Zoology* 221.2 (1990), pp. 308–13, http://onlinelibrary.wiley.com/doi/10.1111/j.1469-7998.1990.tb04001.x/full

Frank, Laurence G., 'Evolution of Genital Masculinization: Why do Female Hyaenas have such a Large "Penis"?', *Trends in Ecology & Evolution* 12.2 (February 1997), pp. 58–62, https://www.ncbi.nlm.nih.gov/pubmed/21237973

Glickman, Stephen E., 'The Spotted Hyena from Aristotle to *The Lion King*: Reputation Is Everything', *Social Research* 62.3 (Fall 1995), pp. 501–37

Glickman, Stephen E., Gerald R. Cunha, Christine M. Drea, Al J. Conley and Ned J. Place, 'Mammalian Sexual Differentiation: Lessons from the Spotted Hyena', *Trends in Endocrinology & Metabolism* 17.9 (November 2006), pp. 349–56, https://www.ncbi.nlm.nih.gov/pubmed/17010637

Gould, Stephen Jay, *Hen's Teeth and Horse's Toes: Further Reflections in Natural History* (New York: W. W. Norton, 1984)

Holekamp, Kay E., Sharleem Sakai and Barbara Lundrigan, 'Social Intelligence in the Spotted Hyena (*Crocuta crocuta*)', *Philosophical Transactions of the Royal Society of London B* 362.1480 (29 April 2007), pp. 523–38, https://www.ncbi.nlm.nih.gov/pmc/articles/PMC2346515

Hyena Specialist Group, www.hyaenas.org

Kemper, Steve, 'Who's Laughing Now?', *Smithsonian Magazine*, May 2008.

Kruuk, Hans, *The Spotted Hyena: A Study of Predation and Social Behaviour* (Chicago: University of Chicago Press, 1972)

Nicholls, Henry, 'The Truth About Spotted Hyenas', BBC Earth, 28 October 2014, http://www.bbc.co.uk/earth/story/20141028-the-truth-about-spotted-hyenas

Racey, Paul A., and Jennifer D. Skinner, 'Endocrine Aspects of Sexual Mimicry in Spotted Hyaenas *Crocuta crocuta*', *Journal of Zoology* 187.3 (March 1979), pp. 315–26, http://onlinelibrary.wiley.com/doi/10.1111/j.1469-7998.1979.tb03372.x/full

Sakai, Sharon, Bradley M. Arsznov, Barbara Lundrigan and Kay E. Holekamp, 'Brain Size and Social Complexity: A Computed Tomography Study in Hyaenidae', *Brain, Behavior and Evolution* 77.2 (2011), pp. 91–104, https://www.ncbi.nlm.nih.gov/pubmed/21335942

Sax, Boria, *The Mythical Zoo: Animals in Life, Legend and Literature* (The Overlook Press, 2013)

Smith, Jennifer E., Joseph M. Kolowski, Katharine E. Graham, Stephanie E. Dawes and Kay E. Holekamp, 'Social and Ecological Determinants of Fission–Fusion Dynamics in the Spotted Hyaena', *Animal Behaviour* 76.3 (September 2008), pp. 619–36, https://doi.org/10.1016/j.anbehav.2008.05.001

Szykman, Micaela, Russell C. Van Horn, Anne L. Engh, Erin E. Boydston and Kay E. Holekamp, 'Courtship and Mating in Free-Living Spotted Hyenas', *Behaviour* 144.7 (July 2007), pp. 815–46, http://www.jstor.org/stable/4536481

Watson, Morrison, 'On the Female Generative Organs of Hyaena *Crocuta*', *Proceedings of the Zoological Society of London* 24 (1877), pp. 369–79

Zimmer, Carl, 'Sociable and Smart', *New York Times*, 4 March 2008

## 5. Vulture

Audubon, John James, 'An Account of the Habits of the Turkey Buzzard (*Vultur aura*) Particularly with the View of Exploding the Opinion Generally Entertained of Its Extraordinary Power of Smelling', *Edinburgh New Philosophical Journal* 2 (Edinburgh: Adam Black, 1826)

Beck, Herbert H., 'The Occult Senses in Birds', *The Auk* 37 (1920), pp. 55–9

Birkhead, Tim, *Bird Sense: What It's Like to Be a Bird* (London: Bloomsbury, 2012)

Blackburn, Julia, *Charles Waterton, 1782–1865: Traveller and Conservationist* (London: Vintage, 1989)

Buffon, Georges-Louis Leclerc, Comte de, *The Natural History of Quadrupeds by the Count of Buffon; Translated from the French. With an Account of the Life of the Author* (Edinburgh: Thomas Nelson and Peter Brown, 1830).

Darlington, P. J., 'Notes on the Senses of Vultures', *The Auk* 47.2 (1930), pp. 251–2

Dooren, Thom van, *Vulture* (London: Reaktion, 2011)

Dooren, Thom van, 'Vultures and Their People in India: Equity and Entanglement in a Time of Extinctions', *Australian Humanities Review* 50 (May 2011), pp. 130–46, http://www.australianhumanitiesreview.org/archive/Issue-May-2011/vandooren.html

Gurney, J. H., 'On the Sense of Smell Possessed by Birds', *Ibis* 4.2 (April 1922)

Henderson, Carrol L., *Birds in Flight: The Art and Science of How Birds Fly* (Minneapolis: Voyageur Press, 2008)

Houston, David C., 'Scavenging Efficiency of Turkey Vultures in Tropical Forest', *Condor* 88.3 (1986), pp. 318–23, https://sora.unm.edu/sites/default/files/journals/condor/v088n03/p0318-p0323.pdf

Jackson, Andrew L., Graeme D. Ruxton and David C. Houston, 'The Effect of Social Facilitation on Foraging Success in Vultures: A Modelling', *Biology Letters* 4.3 (23 June 2008), p. 311, http://rsbl.royalsocietypublishing.org/content/4/3/311

Kendall, Corinne J., Munir Z. Virani, J. Grant C. Hopcraft, Keith L. Bildstein and Daniel I. Rubenstein, 'African Vultures Don't Follow Migratory Herds: Scavenger Habitat Use Is Not Mediated by Prey Abundance', *PLoS One* 9.1 (8 January 2014), https://doi.org/10.1371/journal.pone.0083470

Markandya, Anil, Tim Taylor, Alberto Longo, M. N. Murty, Sucheta Murty and Kishore Kumar Dhavala, 'Counting the Cost of Vulture Decline: An Appraisal of the Human Health and Other Benefits of Vultures in India', *Ecological Economics* 67.2 (September 2008), pp. 194–204, http://dx.doi.org/10.1016/j.ecolecon.2008.04.020

Martin, Graham R., Steven J. Portugal and Campbell P. Murn, 'Visual Fields, Foraging and Collision Vulnerability in *Gyps* Vultures', *Ibis* 154.3 (July 2012), pp. 626–31, http://onlinelibrary.wiley.com/doi/10.1111/j.1474-919X.2012.01227.x/abstract

Rabenold, Patricia Parker, 'Recruitment to Food in Black Vultures: Evidence for Following from Communal Roosts', *Animal Behaviour* 35.6 (December 1987), pp. 1775–85, http://www.sciencedirect.com/science/article/pii/S0003347287800702

Smith, Steven A., and Richard A. Paselk, 'Olfactory Sensitivity of the Turkey Vulture (*Cathartes aura*) to Three Carrion-Associated Odorants', *The Auk* 103.3 (July 1986), pp. 586–92, http://mambobob-raptorsnest.blogspot.co.uk/2008/02/olfactory-capabilities-in-t-rex-and.html

Stager, Kenneth E., 'The Role of Olfaction in Food Location by the Turkey Vulture (*Cathartes aura*)', PhD thesis, University of Southern California (2014), https://nhm.org/site/sites/default/files/pdf/contrib_science/CS81.pdf

'Vultures', Vulture Conservation Foundation website, http://www.4vultures.org/vultures

Waddell, Gene (ed.), *John Bachman: Selected Writings on Science, Race, and Religion* (Athens: University of Georgia Press, 2011)

Ward, Jennifer, Dominic J. McCafferty, David C. Houston and Graeme D. Ruxton, 'Why Do Vultures have Bald Heads? The Role of

Postural Adjustment and Bare Skin Areas in Thermoregulation', *Journal of Thermal Biology* 33.3 (April 2008), pp. 168–73, https://www.researchgate.net/publication/223457788

Waterton, Charles, *Essays on Natural History* (London: Frederick Warne, 1871)

Wilkinson, Benjamin Joel (dir.), *Carrion Dreams 2.0: A Chronicle of the Human–Vulture Relationship* (Abominationalist Productions, 2012)

## 6. Bat

Allen, Glover M., *Bats: Biology, Behavior, and Folklore* (Mineola, NY: Dover Publications, 2004)

Boyles, Justin G., Paul M. Cryan, Gary F. McCracken and Thomas H. Kunz, 'Economic Importance of Bats in Agriculture', *Science* 332.6025 (1 April 2011), pp. 41–2, http://science.sciencemag.org/content/332/6025/41

Carter, Gerald G., and Gerald S. Wilkinson, 'Food Sharing in Vampire Bats: Reciprocal Help Predicts Donations More than Relatedness or Harassment', *Proceedings of the Royal Society B* 280.1753 (22 February 2013), pp. 1–6, https://www.ncbi.nlm.nih.gov/pmc/articles/PMC3574350

Chivers, Charlotte, 'Why Isn't Everyone "Batty" About Bats?', One Poll, 19 May 2015, http://www.onepoll.com/why-isnt-everyone-batty-about-bats

Dijkgraaf, Sven, 'Spallanzani's Unpublished Experiments on the Sensory Basis of Object Perception in Bats', *Isis* 51.1 (1960), pp. 9–20

Ditmars, Raymond, 'The Vampire Bat: A Presentation of Undescribed Habits and Review of its History', *Zoologica*, vol. XIX, no.2, 1935

Dodd, Kevin, *Blood Suckers Most Cruel: The Vampire and the Bat in and before Dracula* (Kevin Dodd, Visiting Scholar, Vanderbilt University)

Galambos, Robert, 'The Avoidance of Obstacles by Flying Bats: Spallanzani's Ideas (1794) and Later Theories', *Isis* 34.2 (1942), pp. 132–40

Greenhall, Arthur, *Natural History of Vampire Bats* (CRC Press, 1988)

Griffin, Donald R., *Listening in the Dark: The Acoustic Orientation of Bats and Men* (New Haven, CT: Yale University Press, 1958)

Gröger, Udo, and Lutz Wiegrebe, 'Classification of Human Breathing Sounds by the Common Vampire Bat, *Desmodus rotundus*', *BMC Biology* 4.1 (16 June 2006), https://bmcbiol.biomedcentral.com/articles/10.1186/1741-7007-4-18

McCracken, Gary F., 'Bats and Vampires', *Bat Conservation International* 11.3 (Fall 1993), http://www.batcon.org/resources/media-education/bats-magazine/bat_article/603

# BIBLIOGRAPHY

McCracken, Gary F., 'Bats in Belfries and Other Places', *Bat Conservation International* 10.4 (Winter 1992), http://www.batcon.org/resources/media-education/bats-magazine

McCracken, Gary F. 'Bats in Magic, Potions, and Medicinal Preparation', *Bat Conservation International* 10.3 (Fall 1992), http://www.batcon.org/resources/media-education/bats-magazine/bat_article/546

Müller, Briggite, Martin Glösmann, Leo Peichl, Gabriel C. Knop, Cornelia Hagemann and Josef Ammermüller, 'Bat Eyes Have Ultraviolet-Sensitive Cone Photoreceptors', *PLoS One* 4.7 (28 July 2009), p. e6390, https://doi.org/10.1371/journal.pone.0006390

Pitnick, Scott, Kate E. Jones and Gerald S. Wilkinson, 'Mating System and Brain Size in Bats', *Proceedings of the Royal Society of London B* 273.1587 (22 March 2006), pp. 719–24

Riskin, Daniel K., and John W. Hermanson, 'Biomechanics: Independent Evolution of Running in Vampire Bats', *Nature* 434 (17 March 2005), p. 292, https://www.nature.com/nature/journal/v434/n7031/full/434292a.html

Schutt, Bill, *Dark Banquet: Blood and the Curious Lives of Blood-Feeding Creatures* (Broadway Books, 2009)

Schutt, William A., J. Scott Altenbach, Young Hui Chang, Dennis M. Cullinane, John W. Hermanson, Farouk Muradali and John E. A. Bertram, 'The Dynamics of Flight-Initiating Jumps in the Common Vampire Bat *Desmodus rotundus*', *Journal of Experimental Biology* 200.23 (1997), pp. 3003–12, http://jeb.biologists.org/content/200/23/3003

Surlykke, Annemarie, and Elisabeth K. V. Kalko, 'Echolocating Bats Cry Out Loud to Detect Their Prey', *PLoS One* 3.4 (30 April 2008), https://doi.org/10.1371/journal.pone.0002036

Tan, Min, Gareth Jones, Guangjian Zhu, Jianping Ye, Tiyu Hong, Shanyi Zhou, Shuyi Zhang and Libiao Zhang, 'Fellatio by Fruit Bats Prolongs Copulation Time', *PLoS One*, 4.10 (28 October 2009), https://doi.org/10.1371/journal.pone.0007595

Wilkinson, Gerald S., 'Social Grooming in the Common Vampire Bat, *Desmodus rotundus*', *Animal Behaviour* 34.6 (1986), pp. 1880–89

Wilson, E. O., and Stephen R. Kellert (eds), *The Biophilia Hypothesis* (Washington, DC: Island Press, 1993)

## 7. Frog

Berger, Lee, Richard Speare, Peter Daszak, D. Earl Green, Andrew A. Cunningham, C. Louise Goggin, Ron Slocombe, Mark A. Ragan, Alex D. Hyatt, Keith R. McDonald, Harry B. Hines, Karen R. Lips,

# BIBLIOGRAPHY

Gerry Marantelli and Helen Parkes, 'Chytridiomycosis Causes Amphibian Mortality Associated with Population Declines in the Rain Forests of Australia and Central America', *Proceedings of the National Academy of Sciences USA* 95.15 (21 July 1998), pp. 9031–6, http://www. pnas.org/content/95/15/9031.full

Bondeson, Jan, *The Feejee Mermaid: And Other Essays in Natural and Unnatural History* (Ithaca, NY: Cornell University Press, 1999)

Cobb, Matthew, *The Egg and Sperm Race: the Seventeenth-Century Scientists Who Unravelled the Secrets of Sex, Life, and Growth* (London: Simon & Schuster, 2007)

Collins, James P., Martha L. Crump and Thomas E. Lovejoy III, *Extinction in Our Times: Global Amphibian Decline* (Oxford: Oxford University Press, 2009)

Cousteau, Jacques (dir.), 'Legend of Lake Titicaca', *The Undersea World of Jacques Cousteau* (Metromedia Productions, 1969)

Daston, Lorraine, and Elizabeth Lunbeck, *Histories of Scientific Observation* (Chicago: University of Chicago Press, 2011)

Gurdon, John B., and Nick Hopwood, 'The Introduction of *Xenopus Laevis* into Developmental Biology: of Empire, Pregnancy Testing and Ribosomal Genes', *International Journal of Developmental Biology* 44.1 (2003), pp. 43–50, http://www.ijdb.ehu.es/web/paper.php?doi=10761846

Hogben, Lancelot Thomas, *Lancelot Hogben, Scientific Humanist: An Unauthorised Autobiography* (London: Merlin Press, 1998)

Lips, Karen R., Forrest Brem, Roberto Brenes, John D. Reeve, Ross A. Alford, Jamie Voyles, Cynthia Carey, Lauren Livo, Allan P. Pessier and James P. Collins, 'Emerging Infectious Disease and the Loss of Biodiversity in a Neotropical Amphibian Community', *Proceedings of the National Academy of Sciences USA* 103.9 (28 February 2006), pp. 3165–70, http://www.pnas.org/content/103/9/3165

McCartney, Eugene S., 'Spontaneous Generation and Kindred Notions in Antiquity', *Transactions and Proceedings of the American Philological Association* 51 (1920), pp. 101–15, http://www.jstor.org/stable/282874

Olszynko-Gryn, Jesse, 'Pregnancy Testing in Britain, c. 1900–67: Laboratories, Animals and Demand from Doctors, Patients and Consumers', PhD thesis, University of Cambridge (2015)

Oxford, Pete, and Renée Bish, 'In the Land of Giant Frogs: Scientists Strive to Keep the World's Largest Aquatic Frog Off a Growing Global List of Fleeting Amphibians', 1 October 2003, https://www. nwf.org/News-and-Magazines/National-Wildlife/Animals/ Archives/2003/In-the-Land-of-Giant-Frogs.aspx

# BIBLIOGRAPHY

Piper, Ross and Mike Shanahan, *Extraordinary Animals: An Encyclopedia of Curious and Unusual Animals* (Westport, CT: Greenwood, 2007)

Redi, Francesco, *Experiments on the Generation of Insects* (Chicago: Open Court Publishing Company, 1909)

Skerratt, Lee Francis, Lee Berger, Richard Speare, Scott Cashins, Keith R. McDonald, Andrea D. Phillott, Harry B. Hines and Nicole Kenyon, 'Spread of Chytridiomycosis Has Caused the Rapid Global Decline and Extinction of Frogs', *EcoHealth* 4 (2007), pp. 125–34, https://link.springer.com/article/10.1007%2Fs10393-007-0093-5

Sleigh, Charlotte, *Frog* (London: Reaktion, 2012)

Soto-Azat, Claudio, Barry T. Clarke, John C. Poynton, Matthew Charles Fisher, S. F. Walker and Andrew A. Cunningham, 'Non-Invasive Sampling Methods for the Detection of *Batrachochytrium dendrobatidis* in Archived Amphibians', *Diseases of Aquatic Organisms* 84.2 (6 April 2009), pp. 163–6, https://www.ncbi.nlm.nih.gov/pubmed/19476287

Soto-Azat, Claudio, Andés Valenzuela Sánchez, Ben Collen, J. Marcus Rowcliffe, Alberto Veloso and Andrew A. Cunningham, 'The Population Decline and Extinction of Darwin's Frogs', *PLoS One* 8.6 (12 June 2013), p. e66957, https://www.ncbi.nlm.nih.gov/pmc/articles/PMC3680453

Soto-Azat, Claudio, Alexandra Peñafiel-Ricaurte, Stephen J. Price, Nicole Sallaberry-Pincheira, María Pía García, Mario Alvarado-Rybak and Andrew A. Cunningham, '*Xenopus laevis* and Emerging Ampibian Pathogens in Chile', *EcoHealth* 13.4 (December 2016), pp. 775–83, https://link.springer.com/article/10.1007/s10393-016-1186-9

Terrall, Mary, 'Frogs on the Mantelpiece: The Practice of Observation in Daily Life', in Lorraine Daston and Elizabeth Lunbeck (eds), *Histories of Scientific Observation* (Chicago: University of Chicago Press, 2011)

van Sittert, Lance, and G. John Measey, 'Historical Perspectives on Global Exports and Research of African Clawed Frogs (*Xenopus laevis*)', *Transactions of the Royal Society of South Africa* 71.2 (2016), pp. 157–66, http://www.tandfonline.com/doi/abs/10.1080/0035919X.2016.1158747.

Waller, John, *Leaps in the Dark: The Making of Scientific Reputations* (Oxford: Oxford University Press, 2004)

## 8. Stork

Aldersey-Williams, Hugh, *The Adventures of Sir Thomas Browne in the Twenty-First Century* (London: Granta, 2015)

# BIBLIOGRAPHY

Aristotle, *History of Animals in Ten Books*, vols. 8–9, trans. by Richard Cresswell (London: George Bell, 1878)

Arnott, Geoffrey, *Birds in the Ancient World from A to Z* (Routledge, 2012)

Barrington, Daines, *Miscellanies* (London: Nichols, 1781)

Beattie, James, et al., *Eco-Cultural Networks of the British Empire* (Bloomsbury, 2014)

Birkhead, Tim, *Bird Sense: What It's Like to Be a Bird* (London: Bloomsbury, 2011)

Birkhead, Tim, Jo Wimpenny and Bob Montgomerie, *Ten Thousand Birds: Ornithology Since Darwin* (Princeton, NJ: Princeton University Press, 2014)

Birkhead, Tim, *The Wisdom of Birds: An Illustrated History of Ornithology* (London: Bloomsbury, 2008)

Bont, Raf de, *Stations in the Field: A History of Place-Based Animal Research, 1870–1930* (Chicago: University of Chicago Press, 2015)

Buffon, Georges-Louis Leclerc, Comte de, *The Book of Birds: Edited and Abridged from the Text of Buffon* (London: R. Tyas, 1841)

Cocker, Mark, and David Tipling, *Birds and People* (London: Jonathan Cape, 2013)

Cuvier, Georges, *The Animal Kingdom*, ed. by H. M'Murtrie (New York: Carvill, 1831)

Gerald of Wales, *Topographia Hibernica*, quoted in Patrick Armstrong, *The English Parson-Naturalist: A Companionship Between Science and Religion* (Leominster: Gracewing Publishing, 2000)

'Guide to North American Birds: Common Poorwill (*Phalaenoptilus nuttallii*)', National Audubon Society, http://www.audubon.org/field-guide/bird/common-poorwill

Harrison, C. J. O., 'Pleistocene and Prehistoric Birds of South-west Britain', *Proceedings of the University of Bristol Spelaeological Society* 18.1 (1987), pp. 81–104, http://www.ubss.org.uk/resources/proceedings/vol18/UBSS_Proc_18_1_81-104.pdf

Haverschmidt, F., *The Life of the White Stork* (Leiden: Brill Archive, 1949)

Kinzelbach, Ragnar K., *Das Buch Vom Pfeilstorch* (Berlin: Basilisken-Presse, 2005)

Lewis, Andrew J., *A Democracy of Facts: Natural History in the Early Republic* (Philadelphia: University of Pennsylvania Press, 2011)

McCarthy, Michael J., *Say Goodbye to the Cuckoo* (London: John Murray, 2010)

McNamee, Gregory, *Aelian's on the Nature of Animals* (Dublin: Trinity University Press, 2011)

Park, Thomas (ed.), *The Harleian Miscellany: A Collection of Scarce, Curious, and Entertaining Pamphlets and Tracts*, vol. 5 (London: White and Murray, 1810)

Rennie, James, *Natural History of Birds: Their Architecture, Habits, and Faculties* (London: Harper, 1859)

Rickard, Bob, and John Michell, *The Rough Guide to Unexplained Phenomena* (London: Penguin, 2010)

Simon, Matt, 'Fantastically Wrong: The Scientist Who Thought That Birds Migrate to the Moon', *Wired*, 22 October 2014, https://www.wired.com/2014/10/fantastically-wrong-scientist-thought-birds-migrate-moon

Tate, Peter, *Flights of Fancy: Birds in Myth, Legend and Superstition* (London: Random House, 2007)

Turner, Angela, *Swallow* (London: Reaktion, 1994)

Vaughan, Richard, *Wings and Rings: A History of Bird Migration Studies in Europe* (Penryn: Isabelline Books, 2009)

Wilcove, David S., and Martin Wikelski, 'Going, Going, Gone: Is Animal Migration Disappearing', *PLoS Biology* 6.7 (29 July 2008), http://journals.plos.org/plosbiology/article?id=10.1371/journal.pbio.0060188

Wilkins, John, *The Discovery of a World in the Moone* (London: Sparke and Forrest, 1638)

Witsen, Nicholaas, Emily O'Gorman and Edward Mellilo (eds), *Beattie's Eco-Cultural Networks and the British Empire: New Views on Environmental History* (London: Bloomsbury, 2016)

## 9. Hippopotamus

Barklow, William E., 'Amphibious Communication with Sound in Hippos, *Hippopotamus amphibius*', *Animal Behaviour* 68.5 (2004), pp. 1125–32, doi:10.1016/j.anbehav.2003.10.034

Bostock, John, and Henry T. Riley (eds), *The Natural History of Pliny* (London: Henry G. Bohn, 1855)

Dawkins, Richard, *The Ancestor's Tale: A Pilgrimage to the Dawn of Life* (London: Weidenfeld & Nicolson, 2010)

Gatesy, John, 'More DNA Support for a Cetacea/Hippopotamidae Clade: The Blood-Clotting Protein Gene Gamma-Fibrinogen', *Molecular Biology and Evolution* 14.5 (May 1997), pp. 537–43, https://www.ncbi.nlm.nih.gov/pubmed/9159931

Grice, Gordon, *Book of Deadly Animals* (London: Penguin, 2012)

Kremer, William, 'Pablo Escobar's Hippos: A Growing Problem', *BBC News*, 26 June 2014, http://www.bbc.com/news/magazine-27905743

Lihoreau, Fabrice, Jean-Renaud Boisserie, Frederick Kyalo Manthi and Stéphane Ducrocq, 'Hippos Stem from the Longest Sequence of Terrestrial Cetartiodactyl Evolution in Africa', *Nature Communications* 6.6264 (24 February 2015), https://www.nature.com/articles/ncomms7264

Saikawa, Yoko, Kimiko Hashimoto, Masaya Nakata, Masato Yoshihara, Kiyoshi Nagai, Motoyasu Ida and Teruyuki Komiya, 'Pigment Chemistry: The Red Sweat of the Hippopotamus', *Nature* 429 (27 May 2004), p. 363, https://www.nature.com/nature/journal/v429/n6990/full/429363a.html

Sax, Boria, *The Mythical Zoo: An Encyclopedia of Animals in World Myth, Legend, and Literature* (Santa Barbara, CA: ABC-Clio, 2001)

Thewissen, J. G. M. 'Hans', *The Walking Whales: From Land to Water in Eight Million Years* (Berkeley: University of California Press, 2014)

Thompson, Ken, *Where Do Camels Belong?: The Story and Science of Invasive Species* (London: Profile, 2014)

## 10. Moose

Ceaser, James W., *Reconstructing America: The Symbol of America in Modern Thought* (London: Yale University Press, 2000)

Dudley, Theodore Robert, *The Drunken Monkey: Why We Drink and Abuse Alcohol* (Berkeley: University of California Press, 2014)

Dugatkin, Lee Alan, *Mr Jefferson and the Giant Moose: Natural History in Early America* (Chicago: University of Chicago Press, 2009)

Ford, Paul (ed.), *The Works of Thomas Jefferson; Correspondence and Papers, 1816–1826*, vol. 7 (New York: Cosimo Books, 2009)

Griggs, Walter S., and Frances P. Griggs, *A Moose's History of North America* (Richmond, VA: Brandylane Publishers, 2009)

Jackson, Kevin, *Moose* (London: Reaktion, 2008)

Jefferson, Thomas, *Notes on the State of Virginia* (Boston, MA: H. Sprague, 1802)

Merrill, Samuel, *The Moose Book: Facts and Stories from Northern Forests* (New York: Dutton, 1920)

Mooallem, Jon, *Wild Ones: A Sometimes Dismaying, Weirdly Reassuring Story About Looking at People Looking at Animals in America* (London: Penguin Books, 2014)

Morris, Steve, David Humphreys and Dan Reynolds, 'Myth, Marula, and Elephant: An Assessment of Voluntary Ethanol Intoxication of the African Elephant (*Loxodonta africana*) Following Feeding on the Fruit of the Marula Tree (*Sclerocarya birrea*)', *Physiological and Biochemical Zoology* 79.2 (March/April 2006), pp. 363–9, http://www.journals.uchicago.edu/doi/abs/10.1086/499983

Mosley, Adam, *Bearing the Heavens: Tycho Brahe and the Astronomical Community of the Late Sixteenth Century* (Cambridge: Cambridge University Press, 2007)

Siegel, Ronald K., and Mark Brodie, 'Alcohol Self-Administration by Elephants', *Bulletin of the Psychonomic Society* 22.1 (July 1984), https://link.springer.com/article/10.3758/BF03333758

Siegel, Ronald K., *Intoxication: the Universal Drive for Mind-Altering Substances* (Park Street Press, 1989).

## 11. Panda

Becker, Elizabeth, *Overbooked: The Exploding Business of Travel and Tourism* (New York: Simon & Schuster, 2016)

Buckingham, Kathleen C., Jonathan Neil, William David and Paul R. Jepson, 'Diplomats and Refugees: Panda Diplomacy, Soft "Cuddly" Power, and the New Trajectory in Panda Conservation', *Environmental Practice* 15.3 (2013), pp. 262–70, https://www.researchgate.net/publication/255981642.

Christiansen, Per, and Stephen Wroe, 'Bite Forces and Evolutionary Adaptations to Feeding Ecology in Carnivores', *Ecology* 88.2 (February 2007), pp. 347–58, https://www.jstor.org/stable/27651108

Conniff, Richard, *The Species Seekers: Heroes, Fools, and the Mad Pursuit of Life on Earth* (New York: W. W. Norton, 2010)

Cooke, Lucy, 'The Power of Cute', BBC Radio4, http://www.bbc.co.uk/programmes/p03w3sxn

Croke, Vicky, *The Lady and the Panda: The True Adventures of the First American Explorer to Bring Back China's Most Exotic Animal* (New York: Random House, 2006)

Davis, D. Dwight, *The Giant Panda: A Morphological Study of Evolutionary Mechanisms* (Chicago: Natural History Museum, 1964)

Ellis, Susie, Anju Zhang, Hemin Zhang, Jinguo Zhang, Zhihe Zhang, Mabel Lam, Mark Edwards, JoGayle Howard, Donald Janssen, Eric Miller and David Wildt, 'Biomedical Survey of Captive Giant Pandas: A Catalyst for Conservation Partnerships in China', in Donald Lindburg and Karen Baragona (eds), *Giant Pandas: Biology and Conservation* (Berkeley: University of California Press, 2004), pp. 250–63, http://www.jstor.org/stable/10.1525/j.ctt1ppskn

'Giant Panda Feeding on Carrion', BBC Natural History Unit, http://www.arkive.org/giant-panda/ailuropoda-melanoleuca/video-08b.html [accessed 7 July 2017]

Graham-Jones, Oliver, *Zoo Doctor* (Fontana Books, 1973)

# BIBLIOGRAPHY

Hagey, Lee R. and Edith A. MacDonald, 'Chemical Composition of Giant Panda Scent and Its Use in Communication', in Donald Lindburg and Karen Baragona (eds), *Giant Pandas: Biology and Conservation* (Berkeley: University of California Press, 2004), pp. 121–4.

Hartig, Falk, 'Panda Diplomacy: The Cutest Part of China's Public Diplomacy', *Hague Journal of Diplomacy* 8.1 (2013), pp. 49–78, https://eprints.qut.edu.au/59568

Hull, Vanessa, Jindong Zhang, Shiqiang Zhou, Jinuyan Huang, Rengui Li, Dian Liu, Weihua Xu, Yan Huang, Zhiyun Ouyang, Hemin Zhang and Jianguo Liu, 'Space Use by Endangered Giant Pandas', *Journal of Mammalogy* 96.1 (2015), pp. 230–36, https://doi.org/10.1093/jmammal/gyu031

Lindburg, Donald, and K. Baragona (eds), *Giant Pandas: Biology and Conservation* (Berkeley: University of California Press, 2004)

Morris, Ramona, and Desmond Morris, *Men and Pandas* (London: Hutchinson, 1966)

Nicholls, Henry, *Lonesome George: The Life and Loves of a Conservation Icon* (New York: Palgrave, 2007)

Nicholls, Henry, *Way of the Panda: The Curious History of China's Political Animal* (London: Profile, 2011)

Ringmar, Erik, 'Audience for a Giraffe: European Exceptionalism and the Quest for the Exotic', *Journal of World History* 17.4 (December 2006), pp. 375–97

Schaller, George, *The Last Panda* (Chicago: University of Chicago Press, 1994)

Schaller, George, Hu Jinchu, Pan Wenshi and Zhu Jing, *The Giant Pandas of Wolong* (Chicago: University of Chicago Press, 1985)

White, Angela M., Ronald R. Swaisgood, Hemin Zhang, 'The Highs and Lows of Chemical Communication in Giant Pandas (*Ailuropoda melanoleuca*): Effect of Scent Deposition Height on Signal Discrimination', *Behavioural Ecology Sociobiology* 51.6 (May 2002), pp. 519–29

Zhang, Peixun, Tianbing Wang, Jian Xiong, Feng Xue, Hailin Xu, Jianhai Chen, Dianying Zhang, Zhongguo Fu and Baoguo Jiang, 'Three Cases of Giant Panda Attaching on Human at Beijing Zoo', *International Journal of Clinical and Experimental Medicine* 7.11 (2014), pp. 4515–18, https://www.ncbi.nlm.nih.gov/pmc/articles/PMC4276236

Zhao, Shancen, Pingping Zheng, Shanshan Dong, Xiangjiang Zhan, Qi Wu, Xiaosen Guo, Yibo Hu, Weiming He, Shanning Zhang, Wei Fan, Lifeng Zhu, Dong Li, Xuemei Zhang, Quan Chen, Hemin Zhang, Zhihe Zhang, Xuelin Jin, Jinguo Zhang, Huanming Yang, Jian Wang, Jun Wang and Fuwen Wei, 'Whole-Genome Sequencing of Giant Pandas Provides Insights into Demographic History and Local Adaptation', *Nature Genetics* 45.1 (January 2013), pp. 67–71, http://www.nature.com/ng/journal/v45/n1/full/ng.2494.html

## 12. Penguin

Bagemihl, Bruce, *Biological Exuberance: Animal Homosexuality and Natural Diversity* (New York: St Martin's Press, 1999)

Bried, Joël, Frédéric Jiguet and Pierre Jouventin, 'Why Do *Aptenodytes* Penguins Have High Divorce Rates?', *The Auk* 116.2 (1999), pp. 504–12, https://sora.unm.edu/sites/default/files/journals/auk/v116n02/p0504-p0512.pdf

Cherry-Garrard, Apsley, *The Worst Journey in the World: Antarctic, 1910–1913*, vol. 2 (New York: George H. Doran, 1922)

Clayton, William, 'An Account of Falkland Islands', *Philosophical Transactions of the Royal Society of London* 66 (1 January 1776), pp. 99–108, http://rstl.royalsocietypublishing.org/content/66/99.full.pdf+html

Davis, Lloyd S., and Martin Renner, *The Penguins* (London: Bloomsbury, 2010)

Davis, Lloyd S., Fiona M. Hunter, Robert G. Harcourt and Sue Michelsen Heath, 'Short Communication: Reciprocal Homosexual Mounting, Adélie Penguins *Pygoscelis adeliae*', *Emu* 98.2 (2001), pp. 136–7, http://www.publish.csiro.au/mu/MU98015

Fuller, Errol, *The Great Auk: The Extinction of the Original Penguin* (Piermont, NH: Bunker Hill Publishing, 2003)

Gurney, Alan, *Below the Convergence: Voyages Toward Antarctica, 1699–1839* (New York: W. W. Norton, 2007)

Haeckel, Ernst, *The Riddle of the Universe at the Close of the Nineteenth Century* (New York: Harper, 1905)

Hunter, Fiona M., and Lloyd S. Davis, 'Female Adélie Penguins Acquire Nest Material from Extrapair Males After Engaging, Extrapair Copulations', *The Auk* 115.2 (April 1998), pp. 526–8, http://www.jstor.org/stable/4089218

Jacquet, Luc, and Bonne Pioche (dirs), *March of the Penguins* (National Geographic Films, 2005)

Larson, E. J., *An Empire of Ice: Scott, Shackleton, and the Heroic Age of Antarctic Science* (London: Yale University Press, 2011)

Martin, Stephen, *Penguin* (London: Reaktion, 2009)

Narborough, John, Abel Tasman, John Wood and Friderich Martens, *An Account of Several Late Voyages and Discoveries to the South and North* (Cambridge: Cambridge University Press, 2014; f.p. 1711)

Roy, Tui de, Mark Jones and Julie Cornthwaite, *Penguins: The Ultimate Guide* (Princeton, NJ: Princeton University Press, 2014)

Russell, Douglas G. D., William J. L. Sladen and David G. Ainley, 'Dr George Murray Levick (1876–1956): Unpublished Notes on the Sexual Habits of the Adélie Penguin', *Polar Record* 48.4 (October 2012), pp. 387–93, https://doi.org/10.1017/S0032247412000216

Wheeler, Sara, *Cherry: A Life of Apsley Cherry-Garrard* (London: Vintage, 2007)

Williams, T. D., 'Mate Fidelity, Penguins', *Oxford Ornithology Series* 6.1, pp. 268–85

Wilson, Edward A., and T. G. Taylor, *With Scott: The Silver Lining* (New York: Dodd, Mead and Company, 1916)

Wilson, Edward A., *Report on the Mammals and Birds, National Antarctic Expedition 1901–1904*, vol. 2 (London: Aves, 1907)

## 13. Chimpanzee

Bedford, J. M., 'Sperm/Egg Interaction: The Specificity of Human Spermatozoa', *Anatomical Record*, 188 (1977), pp. 477–87. doi:10.1002/ar.1091880407

Buffon, Georges-Louis Leclerc, Comte de, *History of Quadrupeds*, vol. 3 (Edinburgh: Thomas Nelson, 1830)

Cohen, Jon, 'Almost Chimpanzee: Redrawing the Lines that Separate Us from Them' (London: St Martin's Press, 2002)

Crockford, Catherine, Roman M. Wittig, Roger Mundry and Klaus Zuberbühler, 'Wild Chimpanzees Inform Ignorant Group Members of Danger', *Current Biology* 22.2 (24 January 2012), pp. 142–6, https://www.ncbi.nlm.nih.gov/pubmed/22209531

Cuperschmid, E. M. and T. P. R. D. Campos, 'Dr. Voronoff's Curious Glandular Xeno-Implants', *História, Ciências, Saúde-Manguinhos* 14.3 (2007), pp. 737–60

de Waal, Frans, and Jennifer J. Pokorny, 'Faces and Behinds: Chimpanzee Sex Perception', *Advanced Science Letters* 1.1 (June 2008), pp. 99–103, https://doi.org/10.1166/asl.2008.006

Gould, Stephen Jay, *Leonardo's Mountain of Clams and the Diet of Worms* (Cambridge, MA: Harvard University Press, 2011)

Gross, Charles, 'Hippocampus Minor and Man's Place in Nature: A Case Study in the Social Construction of Neuroanatomy', *Hippocampus* 3.4 (1993), pp. 403–16

Hawks, John, 'How Strong Is a Chimpanzee, Really?', *Slate*, http://www.slate.com/articles/health_and_science/science/2009/02/how_strong_is_a_chimpanzee.html

# BIBLIOGRAPHY

Hobaiter, Cat, and Richard W. Byrne, 'The Meanings of Chimpanzee Gestures', *Current Biology* 24.14 (21 July 2014), pp. 1596–600, https://www.ncbi.nlm.nih.gov/pubmed/24998524

Hockings, Kimberley J., Nicola Bryson-Morrison, Susana Carvalho, Michiko Fujisawa, Tatyana Humle, William C. McGrew, Miho Nakamura, Gaku Ohashi, Yumi Yamanashi, Gen Yamakoshi and Tetsuro Matsuzawa, 'Tools to Tipple: Ethanol Ingestion by Wild Chimpanzees Using Leaf-Sponges', *Royal Society: Open Science* 2.6 (9 June 2015), http://rsos.royalsocietypublishing.org/content/2/6/150150

IUCN, 'Four Out of Six Great Apes One Step Away from Extinction – IUCN Red List', 2016, https://www.iucn.org/news/species/201609/four-out-six-great-apes-one-step-away-extinction-%E2%80%93-iucn-red-list [accessed 6 May 2017]

Janson, H. W., *Apes and Ape Lore in the Middle Ages and the Renaissance* (London: Warburg Institute, 1952)

Kahlenberg, Sonya M., and Richard W. Wrangham, 'Sex Differences in Chimpanzees' Use of Sticks as Play Objects Resemble Those of Children', *Current Biology* 20.24 (21 December 2010), pp. R1067–8, http://dx.doi.org/10.1016/j.cub.2010.11.024

Kühl, Hjalmar S., Ammie S. Kalan, Mimi Arandjelovic, Floris Aubert, et al., 'Chimpanzee Accumulative Stone Throwing', *Scientific Reports* 6 (29 February 2016), https://www.nature.com/articles/srep22219

Lucas, J. R., 'Wilberforce and Huxley: A Legendary Encounter', *Historical Journal* 22.2 (1979)

Marks, Jonathan, *What It Means to Be 98% Chimpanzee: Apes, People, and Their Genes* (Berkeley: University of California Press, 2002)

Owen, Richard, 'On the Characters, Principles of Division, and Primary Groups of the Class Mammalia', *Journal of the Proceedings of the Linnean Society I: Zoology* (London: Longman, 1857)

Pain, Stephanie, 'Blasts from the Past: The Soviet Ape-Man Scandal', *New Scientist*, 2008, https://www.newscientist.com/article/mg19926701-000-blasts-from-the-past-the-soviet-ape-man-scandal [accessed 5 May 2017]

Patterson, Nick, Daniel J. Richter, Sante Gnerre, Eric S. Lander and David Reich, 'Genetic Evidence for Complex Speciation of Humans and Chimpanzees', *Nature* 441 (29 June 2006), pp. 1103–8, https://www.nature.com/nature/journal/v441/n7097/full/nature04789.html

Pliny the Elder, *The Natural History*, trans. by H. Rackham (London: William Heinemann, 1940)

Pruetz, Jill D., Paco Bertolani, Kelly Boyer Ontl, Stacy Lindshield, Mack Shelley and Erin G. Wessling, 'New Evidence on the

# BIBLIOGRAPHY

Tool-Assisted Hunting Exhibited by Chimpanzees (*Pan troglodytes verus*) in a Savannah Habitat at Fongoli, Sénégal', *Royal Society: Open Science* 2.4 (15 April 2015), http://rsos.royalsocietypublishing.org/content/2/4/140507

Rossiianov, Kirill, 'Beyond Species: Il'ya Ivanov and His Experiments on Cross-Breeding Humans with Anthropoid Apes', *Science in Context* 15.2 (2002), pp. 277–316, https://www.cambridge.org/core/journals/science-in-context/article/div-classtitlebeyond-species-ilya-ivanov-and-his-experiments-on-cross-breeding-humans-with-anthropoid-apesdiv/D3E0E117E953A0038D63984AD92F4B80

Sax, Boria, *The Mythical Zoo: An Encyclopedia of Animals in World Myth, Legend, and Literature* (Santa Barbara, CA: ABC-Clio, 2001)

Schwartz, Jeffrey H., *Orang-utan Biology* (Oxford: Oxford University Press, 1988)

Sorenson, John, *Ape* (Reaktion, 2009)

Temerlin, Maurice K., *Lucy: Growing Up Human – A Chimpanzee Daughter in a Psychotherapist's Family* (Palo Alto, CA: Science & Behavior Books, 1975)

Topsell, Edward, *The History of Four-Footed Beasts and Serpents and Insects,* vol. 1 (New York: DaCapo, 1967; f.p. 1658)

Yerkes, Robert, and Ada Yerkes, *The Great Apes: A Study of Anthropoid Life* (New Haven, CT: Yale University Press, 1929)

Zimmer, Carl, 'Searching for Your Inner Chimp', *Natural History*, December 2002–January 2003, http://www.carlzimmer.com/articles/PDF/02.ChimpDNA.pdf

## Conclusion

de Waal, Frans, http://www.npr.org/2014/08/15/338936897/do-animals-have-morals

Mills, Brett, 'The Animals Went in Two by Two: Heteronormativity in Television Wildlife Documentaries', *European Journal of Cultural Studies* 16(1), pp. 100–114. © The Author(s) 2012, reprints and permission: sagepub.co.uk/journalsPermissions.nav DOI: 10.1177/1367549412457477

# INDEX

Page numbers in **bold** refer to illustrations.

459

# INDEX

# INDEX

# INDEX

# INDEX

# INDEX

# INDEX